Absolute Beginner's Guide

to

eBay®

Michael Miller

201 West 103rd Street,
Indianapolis, Indiana 46290

D0564503

Absolute Beginner's Guide to eBay®

International Standard Book Number: 0-7897-2928-8

Library of Congress Catalog Card Number: 2002115888

Printed in the United States of America

First Printing: February 2003

06   05   04   03   4   3   2   1

Trademarks

Warning and Disclaimer

Associate Publisher
Greg Wiegand

Acquisitions Editor
Angelina Ward

Development Editor
Christy Miller Kuziensky

Managing Editor
Charlotte Clapp

Project Editor
Tonya R. Simpson

Copy Editor
Margaret Berson

Indexer
Ken Johnson

Proofreader
Kay Hoskin

Technical Editor
Steve Schwartz

Team Coordinator
Sharry Lee Gregory

Interior Designer
Anne Jones

Cover Designer
Dan Armstrong

Page Layout
Cheryl Lynch

Contents at a Glance

Table of Contents

About the Author

Michael Miller is a top eBay seller and a successful and prolific author. He has a reputation for practical, real-world advice and an unerring empathy for the needs of his readers.

Mr. Miller has written more than four dozen how-to and reference books since 1989, for Que and other major publishers. His books for Que include *Absolute Beginner's Guide to Computer Basics, Special Edition Using the Internet and Web, The Complete Idiot's Guide to Online Auctions*, and, with Jim Louderback, *TechTV's Guide to Microsoft Windows XP for Home Users*. He is known for his casual, easy-to-read writing style and his ability to explain a wide variety of complex topics to an everyday audience.

Mr. Miller is also president of The Molehill Group, a strategic consulting and authoring firm based in Carmel, Indiana. As a consultant, he specializes in providing strategic advice to and writing business plans for Internet- and technology-based businesses.

You can e-mail Mr. Miller directly at abg-ebay@molehillgroup.com. His Web site is located at www.molehillgroup.com.

Dedication

To my mother and father—who spend too much time and money on eBay auctions!

Acknowledgments

Thanks to the usual suspects at Que, including but not limited to Greg Wiegand, Angelina Ward, Christy Miller Kuziensky, Tonya Simpson, Margaret Berson, Kay Hoskin, Ken Johnson, and Steven Schwartz.

We Want to Hear from You!

As the reader of this book, *you* are our most important critic and commentator. We value your opinion and want to know what we're doing right, what we could do better, what areas you'd like to see us publish in, and any other words of wisdom you're willing to pass our way.

As an associate publisher for Que, I welcome your comments. You can email or write me directly to let me know what you did or didn't like about this book—as well as what we can do to make our books better.

Please note that I cannot help you with technical problems related to the *topic* of this book. We do have a User Services group, however, where I will forward specific technical questions related to the book.

When you write, please be sure to include this book's title and author as well as your name, email address, and phone number. I will carefully review your comments and share them with the author and editors who worked on the book.

Email: feedback@quepublishing.com

Mail: Greg Wiegand
          Que Publishing
          201 West 103rd Street
          Indianapolis, IN 46290 USA

For more information about this book or another Que title, visit our Web site at www.quepublishing.com. Type the ISBN (excluding hyphens) or the title of a book in the Search field to find the page you're looking for.

INTRODUCTION

eBay is a true phenomenon.

In 2002, eBay transactions defined a new economy worth more than $14 billion. Read that number again; it's not a misprint. *Fourteen billion dollars.* That's $14 billion in sales that didn't exist before eBay. Fourteen billion dollars of transactions that appeared seemingly out of thin air. Fourteen billion dollars in merchandise that wouldn't have been sold otherwise.

Where did that $14 billion come from? It came from you and from me and from 50 million other people around the world who log on to the eBay site to buy and to sell all manner of merchandise. Before eBay, there was no global marketplace for the 50 million of us; there was no way to buy and to sell that $14 billion of merchandise, except for small local garage sales and flea markets.

eBay made that $14 billion happen. eBay brought 50 million of us together.

And in doing so, eBay became one of the first—and maybe the only—online business to make a profit from day one of its existence. eBay kept its costs low by not actually handling any of the merchandise traded on its site, and generated revenue by charging listing fees and sales commissions on every transaction.

Smart people, with a smart concept.

And here's somebody else who's smart about eBay:

You.

You're smart because you bought this book to help you learn how to buy and sell merchandise on the eBay site. You know that you need to learn how eBay works before you can start buying and selling, and you also know that a little extra knowledge can give you the edge you need to be a real auction winner.

Absolute Beginner's Guide to eBay will help you get started with eBay auctions—even if you've never bought anything online in your life. Read this book and you'll learn how to bid and how to sell, and what to do when the auction ends.

More important, you'll learn how to maximize your chances of winning important eBay auctions—without paying through the nose. And if you're a seller, you'll learn how to stand out from the crowd and generate more bids—and higher selling prices.

You'll also learn that buying and selling on eBay isn't that hard, and that it can be a lot of fun. You'll even discover that you can actually make a living from your eBay activities, if you don't mind a little hard work.

Really!

How This Book Is Organized

This book is organized into five main parts, as follows:

- **Part 1, Essential eBay**, shows you how online auctions work, as well as how to find your way around the eBay site. You'll also learn how to sign up and become an eBay member.

- **Part 2, eBay for Bidders**, tells you everything you need to know about bidding for items in eBay auctions. You'll take the Bidding 101 tutorial, learn how to search for specific types of items, discover the best ways to pay for those auctions you win, and find out how to avoid getting ripped off by unscrupulous sellers.

- **Part 3, eBay for Sellers**, is the flip side of the coin. This section tells you everything you need to know about selling on eBay; you'll take the Selling 101 tutorial, figure out what to sell and for how much, determine what payment methods to accept, learn how to create more effective item listings, find out how to pack and ship your merchandise, and discover how to best manage your current auctions.

- **Part 4, Using eBay's Advanced Features**, is all about the little extras you can find on the eBay site. You'll learn about your My eBay page, discover how to create a personal About me page, find out how to use post-auction feedback, and learn how to buy and sell in eBay Stores, Half.com, eBay Motors, and eBay Real Estate.

- **Part 5, Becoming a Power Seller**, is for the really ambitious eBay user. You'll learn how to manage your auctions with third-party software and services, use bulk loading software, use PayPal and other payment services, and sell and ship internationally. You'll even learn how to turn your hobby into a full-time profession—and make a real living from your eBay auctions.

Taken together, the 32 chapters in this book will help you get the most from your eBay experience. By the time you get to the end of the final chapter, you'll be buying and selling online just like a pro!

Conventions Used in This Book

I hope that this book is easy enough to figure out on its own, without requiring its own instruction manual. As you read through the pages, however, it helps to know precisely how I've presented specific types of information.

Web Page Addresses

There are a lot of Web page addresses in this book—including addresses for specific pages on the eBay site. They're noted as such:

www.molehillgroup.com

Technically, a Web page address is supposed to start with http:// (as in http://www.molehillgroup.com). Because Internet Explorer and other Web browsers automatically insert this piece of the address, however, you don't have to type it— and I haven't included it in any of the addresses in this book.

Special Elements

This book also includes a few special elements that provide additional information not included in the basic text. These elements are designed to supplement the text to make your learning faster, easier, and more efficient.

note

A *note* is designed to provide information that is generally useful but not specifically necessary for what you're doing at the moment. Some are like extended tips—interesting, but not essential.

caution

A *caution* will tell you to beware of a potentially dangerous act or situation. In some cases, ignoring a caution could cause you significant problems—so pay attention to them!

"Mike Sez"

This element is my personal opinion or recommendation regarding the topic at hand. Remember—I might not always be right, but I'll always have an opinion!

tip

A *tip* is a piece of advice—a little trick, actually—that helps you use your computer more effectively or maneuver around problems or limitations

Finally, in various parts of this book you'll find big *checklists*. Use these checklists to prepare for the upcoming task—just check off the items on the list, and you'll be ready to go.

Let Me Know What You Think

I always love to hear from readers. If you want to contact me, feel free to email me at abg-ebay@molehillgroup.com. I can't promise that I'll answer every message, but I will promise that I'll read each one!

If you want to learn more about me and any new books I have cooking, check out my Molehill Group Web site at www.molehillgroup.com. Who knows—you might find some other books there that you'd like to read.

PART I

ESSENTIAL EBAY

1

ALL ABOUT ONLINE AUCTIONS

Looking for an imported Japanese-language Dragon Ball Z DVD? How about a copy of *Detective Comics #27*, from 1939—the one with the first appearance of the Batman? Or, perhaps, a vintage Barbie doll? Or a good used flute? Or maybe even a brand-new hard disk drive for your computer—but at a bargain price? Or, perhaps, you have one of these items that you would like to sell?

Whatever you're buying or selling, there's a new way to trade merchandise—over the Internet.

It's called an *online auction*.

And the biggest online auction is *eBay*.

How Popular Are Online Auctions?

Online auctions have created an entirely new market for many types of merchandise, allowing both individuals and small businesses to sell items to and buy items from other Internet users worldwide. Every day millions of items are listed at online auctions, and millions of users—people like you and me—place bids on these items.

Just how big is the market for online auctions? Just look at these statistics from eBay, the world's largest online auction site:

- On any given day eBay has more than **7 million items** listed for auction.
- At mid-year 2002, eBay had **49.7 million registered users**—more than double the number of users just two years previously.
- During the entire year of 2001, it is estimated that **$9.3 billion worth of merchandise**, in more than **423 million individual auctions**, was traded over eBay.

All this activity makes eBay not only the biggest shopping site on the Internet, but also the largest online community of any type—bigger even than America Online. And that's not small potatoes.

What Is an Online Auction, Exactly?

An online auction is an Internet-based version of a traditional auction—you know, the type where a fast-talking auctioneer stands in the front of the room, trying to coax potential buyers into bidding *just a little bit more* for the piece of merchandise up for bid. The only difference is, there's no fast-talking auctioneer online (the bidding process is executed by special auction software on the auction site), and your fellow bidders aren't in the same room with you—in fact, they might be located anywhere in the world, as long as they have Internet access.

At today's online auctions, you're likely to find a wide variety of items up for bid—everything from the hottest action figures to vintage sports memorabilia, from rare antiques to the latest computer equipment. If you're a bidder, you can choose from literally millions of individual items available for sale on any given day; if you're a seller, your potential customer base is tens of millions of users strong.

What Makes Online Auctions So Popular?

The already immense and rapidly growing popularity of online auctions is due in part to the mania with which some people collect things. Hardcore collectors—whether they collect PEZ dispensers, vintage Barbie dolls, Faberge eggs, or antique chairs—often exhibit obsessive-compulsive behavior (you know you do—admit it!), expending huge amounts of time and effort to track down the most obscure items for their collections. Even if you're not that hardcore, there are still precious things that you collect, and it's relatively easy to get caught up in the thrill of bidding on a one-of-a-kind item that you find online.

Of course, another factor in the surge of online auction popularity is the all-too-human love of a bargain. In many ways, an online auction is just a high-tech version of a garage sale—and people *love* to scrounge through others' leftovers, hunting for that one item at a rock-bottom price.

On the selling front, online auctions are popular because there is no better or cheaper way to guarantee such wide exposure to the stuff you want to sell. The more people you have looking at an item, the more likely it is that someone will buy it—and, thanks to the auction format, more bidders equals a higher selling price.

In addition, many merchants are using online auctions to move overstocked, refurbished, and discontinued merchandise. Goods that used to sit unsold in moldy old warehouses are now being dusted off and auctioned off at discounted prices to users looking for bargains.

In fact, online auctions are really helping to create a new buyer-and-seller economy. Whether you're talking about buyers devoted to their hobbies or sellers running small retail businesses out of their homes, online auctions are providing unique new opportunities for millions of people to buy and sell things that they simply couldn't buy or sell before.

Why Should *You* Use an Online Auction?

If you have something to sell, why would you choose to auction it instead of just selling it outright, through a classified ad or some similar means? Conversely, if you want to buy something, why would you want to bid on it in an auction, as opposed to just buying it normally?

In other words, *what's in it for you?*

Why Sellers Like Online Auctions

For a seller, the value of an auction is readily apparent.

You have something to sell, and you want to get the highest possible dollar for it. If you list it in a classified ad for a fixed amount, that amount is the most you'll receive for it—and you could get less, if a buyer tries to haggle you down on the price. But in an online auction, the price you set is the *minimum* you'll receive—and if several potential buyers are interested in your item, it's possible that they'll bid up the price over and beyond what you would have gotten if you sold the item in a more traditional fashion.

The bottom line for sellers is that online auctions provide the possibility of *upside* that you don't get when you sell something outright—plus, thanks to the Internet, you can reach a potential audience much bigger than just the folks in your neighborhood or town.

Why Buyers Like Online Auctions

For a buyer, the value of an auction isn't as obvious. After all, if you buy something outright, you know how much you're going to pay, and you know you can get it right now, just as soon as you pay for it.

With an online auction, the price you pay is less certain. Yes, the seller wants a certain amount for the item, but another buyer might come along and offer a higher amount. Even if you hold out to be the high bidder, you still have to wait until the end of the auction—which could be a week from now!—to receive the item. Truth be told, online auctions may not be as easily predictable or immediately gratifying as just buying something outright.

On the other hand, the sheer number of items available at online auction sites benefits you as a potential buyer. If you want something relatively common, you'll probably have your choice of several different items to buy. If you're looking for something a bit more rare, chances are you'll actually find it when you look at an online auction.

And as for price—well, with the huge number of items up for auction on any given day, the reality is that prices, driven by supply and demand, adjust to market levels. If an item is rare and has a lot of interested bidders, the price will go up accordingly; if it's a common item with few bidders, the price stays low (or it doesn't sell!). Say what you like, that's *fair*.

More About eBay—And Other Online Auction Sites

In the online auction world, there's one big dog—and a handful of much smaller dogs.

eBay (www.ebay.com) is the big dog, logging close to *one billion* items sold since its launch in 1995. No other auction comes close to eBay's volume of users and numbers of items for sale; if you want to play in the online auction game, eBay is the place to play.

This book focuses on eBay, although there are some other online auction sites you might want to check out. Chief among eBay's competitors are Amazon.com Auctions (auctions.amazon.com) and Yahoo! Auctions (auctions.yahoo.com), although neither is nearly as big as eBay. There used to be a lot of smaller, more specialized online auctions, but most of these sites went out of business during the dot-com implosion—and as eBay consolidated its user base.

How Does an eBay Online Auction Work?

If you've never used eBay before, you might be a little anxious about what might be involved. Never fear; participating in an online auction is a piece of cake, something tens of millions of other users have done before you. That means you don't have to reinvent any wheels; the procedures you have to follow are well established and well documented.

Before you can list an item for sale or place a bid on an item, you first have to register with eBay. There's no fee to register, although eBay does charge the seller a small *listing fee* to list an item for sale, and another small *transaction fee* when the item is sold. eBay doesn't charge any fees to buyers.

We'll get into the detailed steps involved with buying and selling later in this book; for now, let's walk through the general operation of a typical eBay auction:

1. You begin (either as a buyer or seller) by registering with eBay.

2. The seller creates an ad for an item and lists the item on the auction site. (eBay charges anywhere from $0.30 to $3.30 to list an item.) In the item listing, the seller specifies the length of the auction (3, 5, 7, or 10 days), and the minimum bid he or she will accept for that item.

3. A potential buyer searching for a particular type of item (or just browsing through all the merchandise listed in a specific category) reads the item listing and decides to make a bid. The bidder specifies the *maximum* amount he or she will pay; this amount has to be above the seller's *minimum* bid.

4. eBay's built-in bidding software automatically places a bid for the bidder that bests the current bid by a specified amount—but doesn't reveal the bidder's maximum bid. For example, the current bid on an item might be $25. A bidder is willing to pay up to $40 for the item, and enters a maximum bid of $40. eBay's "proxy" software places a bid for the new bidder in the amount of $26—higher than the current bid, but less than the specified maximum bid. If there are no other bids, this bidder will win the auction with a $26 bid. Other potential buyers, however, can place additional bids;

note

eBay is kind of like a newspaper that runs classified ads—eBay isn't the actual seller, and isn't even really a "middleman." All eBay does is facilitate the transaction, and therefore can't be held responsible for anything that goes wrong with any particular auction or sale. When you buy an item, you buy it from the individual who put it up for sale—you don't pay anything to eBay.

unless their maximum bids are more than the current bidder's $40 maximum, they are informed (by e-mail) that they have been outbid—and the first bidder's current bid is automatically raised to match the new bids (up to the specified maximum bid price).

5. At the conclusion of an auction, eBay informs the high bidder of his or her winning bid. The seller is responsible for contacting the high bidder and arranging payment. When the seller receives the buyer's payment (generally by check or money order), the seller then ships the merchandise directly to the buyer.

6. Concurrent with the close of the auction, eBay bills the seller for a small percentage (starting at 5.25%) of the final bid price. This selling fee is directly billed to the seller's credit card.

That's how it works, in general. For more detailed instructions on how to bid in an eBay auction, see Chapter 4, "Bidding 101: A Tutorial for Beginning Bidders." For more detailed instructions on how to place an item for sale on eBay, see Chapter 10, "Selling 101: A Tutorial for Beginning Sellers."

THE ABSOLUTE MINIMUM

Here are the key points to remember from this chapter:

■ Online auctions facilitate one-to-one trading of all types of merchandise between buyers and sellers around the world.

■ Online auctions are big business; more than $9.3 billion worth of merchandise was handled by eBay in 2001.

■ An online auction is similar to a traditional auction, except that automated bidding software replaces the role of the human auctioneer.

■ The biggest online auction site is eBay; other popular online auctions include Amazon.com Auctions and Yahoo! Auctions.

2

INTRODUCING EBAY, THE WORLD'S LARGEST ONLINE AUCTION

What is it you need?

A new modem for your computer? A vintage German military helmet? An authentic prop from your favorite movie? A specific trading card or comic book or Barbie doll? How about some jewelry, or an antique desk, or an answering machine for your office?

You can find all these items—and more—at eBay, the largest online auction site on the Web. eBay is a huge site, with more than 7 million items listed every day; no matter what you're looking to buy (or sell), eBay has something for you.

What Is eBay—And How Did It Come to Be?

What is eBay? I think the site's official mission statement does a good job of summing up what eBay is all about:

"eBay's mission is to help practically anyone trade practically anything on earth."

What eBay does is simple—it facilitates the trading of merchandise from one user to another, over the Internet. This makes eBay a person-to-person auction. eBay itself doesn't buy or sell anything; it carries no inventory and collects no payments. eBay is just the middleman in the auction process, hooking up buyers and sellers around the world—and collecting fees for doing so.

eBay was one of the first auction sites on the Internet, launched way back on Labor Day of 1995. It almost single-handedly pioneered the concept of online auctions, and in doing so, carved out a dominant market share. (It also made a lot of money for those who invested in the firm—especially in the early years.)

As the official story goes, founder Pierre Omidyar launched eBay as the result of a conversation with his then-girlfriend, an avid collector of PEZ™ dispensers. She supposedly commented to Pierre about how great it would be if she were able to collect PEZ dispensers using the Internet. Pierre did her a favor and developed a small PEZ-dispenser trading site, originally called Auction Web.

This small site quickly became a big site. Pierre started charging users a small fee to list items, to help pay his expenses. The day that Pierre opened his mail box and saw $10,000 worth of fees was the day he quit his day job and made eBay a full-time proposition.

Because of its fee-based model, eBay is that rare Web site that made money from day one. That made eBay an attractive candidate for venture capital investment and eventual IPO; the company did, in fact, go public in 1998, and made a lot of people (including Pierre) a lot of money.

Today eBay is one of the most successful Internet businesses in the world, having weathered the storms of the dot-com implosion quite nicely, thank you. It also survived (and thrived) as dozens of smaller online auction sites closed their doors. The result is that eBay, under the leadership of current CEO Meg Whitman, is the dominant online auction site, with no real competition. It truly is the number-one place to buy and sell any type of item online.

note

The word *eBay* comes from a combination of two other words—*electronic* and *bay* (for the San Francisco Bay Area).

What You Can—And What You Can't—Trade on eBay

As you can tell from eBay's mission statement, you should be able to trade practically anything you can think of on the eBay site. You can't trade *literally* everything, of course; there are some types of items that eBay refuses to deal with. Read on to learn more.

Major Categories

To give you an idea of what you'll find up for auction, here's a list of eBay's major item categories:

- Airline tickets
- Antiques
- Art
- Baby items
- Books
- Business and industrial
- Cars, trucks, and parts
- Charity
- Clothing and accessories
- Coins
- Crafts
- Dolls and bears
- DVDs and movies
- Electronics and computers (including Computers, Consumer Electronics, Networking and Telecom, PDAs, Photo, and Video Games)
- Event tickets
- Food and wine
- Gifts and occasions
- Health and beauty
- Home and living
- Home improvement
- Jewelry, gems, and watches
- Live auctions
- Motorcycles

- Music
- Musical instruments
- Pet supplies
- Pottery and glass
- Professional services
- Real estate and timeshares
- Sports (including Fan Shop, Memorabilia, Sporting Goods, and Tickets)
- Stamps
- Toys and hobbies
- Travel
- TV
- Wholesale
- Everything else...

note

eBay management is constantly reevaluating its category listings—introducing new categories, subdividing crowded existing categories, or eliminating little-used categories.

Most of these major categories include dozens—or hundreds—of subcategories for specific types of items. For example, the Collectibles category has more than three dozen different subcategories (from Advertising to Vintage Sewing), and most of these subcategories have subcategories of their own. The result is that eBay is divided into literally thousands of separate categories and subcategories—with more being added every day.

What You *Can't* Trade on eBay

The list of what you *can't* buy or sell on eBay makes a lot of sense. Most of these items are illegal, controversial, or could expose eBay to various legal actions. This list includes:

- Alcohol
- Animal parts from endangered species
- Child pornography
- Counterfeit CDs, videos, computer software, or other items that infringe on someone else's copyright or trademark
- Counterfeit currency and stamps
- Credit cards
- Current vehicle license plates—or plates that resemble current ones
- Drugs or drug paraphernalia
- Embargoed goods and goods from prohibited countries

- Firearms, military weapons, and accessories
- Forged autographs and other items
- Human body parts and remains
- Locksmithing devices
- Mailing lists and personal information
- Pets and wildlife
- Plants and seeds
- Police and other law-enforcement badges and IDs
- Postage meters
- Prescription drugs and devices
- Recalled items
- Replicas of official government identification documents or licenses
- Satellite and cable TV descramblers
- Stocks, bonds, or negotiable securities
- Stolen items
- Surveillance equipment
- Tobacco

note

For an up-to-date list of prohibited items, check eBay's Questionable Items page at `pages.ebay.com/help/community/png-items.html`.

eBay's Specialty Services

eBay's main business is conducting online auctions. But there are several other features of the eBay site that you might want to check out, depending on your personal interests.

- **PayPal**. eBay recently acquired the PayPal electronic payment service. You can use PayPal to accept credit card payments in your auctions, to pay a seller via credit card, or to "wire" money to just about anyone anywhere in the world. (Learn more about PayPal in Chapter 30, "Using PayPal and Other Payment Services.")
- **Half.com**. Half.com is eBay's fixed-price (non-auction) marketplace. You can use Half.com to buy and sell previously owned or closeout items, with a particular emphasis on books, CDs, DVDs, videotapes, and video games. (Learn more about Half.com in Chapter 26, "Buying and Selling Right Now: eBay Stores and Half.com.")

- **Local Auctions**. Local auctions make it easier to buy and sell large or regional items; eBay now has local sites for 60 U.S. cities.

- **eBay International**. eBay doesn't limit you to buying and selling only within U.S. borders. You can use eBay International to offer your items to users all around the world. And if you live in a foreign country, there's probably a local version of eBay just for you. eBay has country-specific sites in Argentina, Australia, Austria, Belgium, Brazil, Canada, France, Germany, Ireland, Italy, Korea, Mexico, Netherlands, New Zealand, Singapore, Spain, Switzerland, Taiwan, and the U.K. See Chapter 31, "Going International," for more information.

- **eBay Motors**. Have a car or a boat or a motorcycle to sell? Then use eBay Motors, the Internet's largest auction-style marketplace for all things automotive—including auto parts. (Learn more about eBay Motors in Chapter 27, "Buying and Selling Wheels and Walls: eBay Motors and Real Estate.")

- **Buy It Now**. The Buy It Now option, which can be applied to any auction item, lets you end the auction when a seller agrees to pay a specified fixed price. (Learn more about Buy It Now in Chapter 13, "Choosing the Right Listing Options.")

- **eBay Stores**. eBay enables large sellers to create their own online retail presence for the items they have up for auction. With an eBay Store, you can let buyers make immediate and multiple-item purchases for both fixed-price and auction items. (Learn more about eBay Stores in Chapter 26.)

- **eBay Professional Services**. This innovative part of the eBay site lets small businesses find freelancers for all sorts of business needs, including accounting, Web design, and so on.

- **eBay Live Auctions and Sothebys.com**. If you're looking for a more traditional real-time auction, check out eBay Live Auctions; this service lets you bid on items up for live auction on the sales floors of the world's leading auction houses. Along the same line is Sothebys.com (www.sothebys.ebay.com), a separate site for the live-auction firm recently purchased by eBay.

- **eBay Charity Fundraising**. This is a separate site on the eBay site devoted to charity and fundraising auctions. You can bid in various charity auctions, and even set up your own fundraisers on the eBay site.

What's What (and What's Where) on eBay

Not even counting the millions of individual auction listings, eBay has a ton of content and community on its site—if you know where to find it. (And the home page isn't always the best place to find what you're looking for!)

eBay's Home Page

When you're getting to know eBay, the place to start is the home page, shown in Figure 2.1. From here, you can access eBay's most important features and services.

FIGURE 2.1

Access the most important parts of eBay from the home page (www.ebay.com).

The big chunk of space in the middle of the page is probably best ignored; it's nothing more than a big advertisement for the category or items *du jour*. Better to focus on the links along the top and left side of the page.

Across the top of the home page—across virtually every eBay page, as a matter of fact—is the Navigation Bar. This bar includes links to the major sections of the eBay site: Browse, Sell, Services, Search, Help, and Community. When you click one of these links, you not only go to the main page for that section, you also display a list of subsections underneath the Navigation Bar. For example, Figure 2.2 shows the additional sections listed when you click the Services link.

note

There are also four links *above* the Navigation Bar— Home, My eBay, Site Map, and Sign Out. Like the Navigation Bar, these links appear at the top of most eBay pages.

FIGURE 2.2

The Services section of the Navigation Bar, expanded.

Browse	Sell	Services	Search	Help	Community
overview	registration	buying & selling	my eBay	about me	feedback forum	rules & safety

Along the left side of the home page is a collection of links to specific eBay item categories and specialty sites. When you want to find an item to bid on, it's easy to click through the categories listed on the left of the home page—or to search for items using the Search box (labeled "What are you looking for?"), located underneath the Navigation Bar.

For other key activities, refer to the information in Table 2.1, which shows you which links to click.

TABLE 2.1 Key Home Page Operations

To Do This	Click This Link
Sign up for eBay membership	Register Now
Search for an item or user	Search
Browse items for sale	Browse
Sell an item	Sell
Access your My eBay page	My eBay

To Do This	Click This Link
Access other parts of eBay via the Site Map	Site Map
Access message boards	Community
Get help	Help

Where to Find Everything Else: eBay's Site Map

Unfortunately, there's just so much stuff on the eBay site—and it's so haphazardly organized—that most users never find some of eBay's most interesting and useful features. In fact, you simply can't access many features from the home page. To really dig down into the eBay site, you need a little help—which you can get from eBay's Site Map page.

You can access the Site Map page by clicking the Site Map link on the eBay home page. This page, shown in Figure 2.3, serves as the true access point to eBay's numerous and diverse features.

If you've never visited the Site Map page, I guarantee you'll be surprised at everything you'll find there. The Site Map offers direct links to a bunch of features and services that you probably didn't even know existed!

The Site Map is organized into the following categories:

- **Browse**. Links to eBay's major item categories, as well as to Featured, Big Ticket, Gallery, New Today, Ending First, and Completed auctions.
- **Sell**. Links to the Sell Your Item page, as well as to "how to sell" tutorials and various selling services.
- **Search.** Links to eBay's three advanced search pages—Search for Items, Search for Members, and Favorite Searches.
- **Services**. Links to all of eBay's various buyer and seller services, as well as the Feedback Forum, SafeHarbor, and My eBay.
- **Community.** Links to message boards where you can chat with other users (and eBay staff), as well as links to the latest eBay news and announcements.
- **Help.** Links to general help information and FAQs.

You can also use the links on the Site Map page to keep up with all the new features of the site—and keep up on the daily events and happenings. For example, if you're new to eBay, you might want to check out the Discussion, Help, and Chat links in the Community section. If you want to learn how to use various site features, try the Buyer Guide and Seller Guide links in the Help section. To find out about any technical system updates (or planned outages), click the News & Announcements link.

FIGURE 2.3

Use the Site Map to discover parts of eBay you didn't even know existed.

home | my eBay | site map | sign out

Browse | Sell | Services | Search | Help | Community

All Sports Play Here!
Free Shipping on thousands of Sports items! **Click Here!**

Search   Advanced Search

☐ Search titles and descriptions

Browse

Categories
Antiques
Art
Automotive (eBay Motors)
Books | Movies | Music
Business, Office & Industrial
Clothing & Accessories
Coins | Stamps
Collectibles
Computers | Network, IT
Dolls & Bears
eBay Live Auctions
Home & Garden
Jewelry, Gemstones
Photo | Electronics
Pottery & Glass
Real Estate
Sothebys.com
Sports (Memorabilia | Goods)
Tickets | Travel
Toys | Hobbies & Crafts
Everything Else

Featured *don't miss!*

Big Ticket

Gallery

Category Overview

New Today

Ending First

Completed Auctions

eBay Official Time

Sell

Sell Your Item Form

Learn how to sell

Search

Search for Items

Search for Members

Favorite Searches

Help

Basics

Buyer Guide

Seller Guide

eBay Education

My Info

Billing

Rules & Safety

User to User eBay Q&A Board

Images/HTML Board

Is my item allowed on eBay?
Prohibited, Questionable & Infringing Items

eBay Toolbar NEW!

Services

Services Overview

eBay Education: Learn all about eBay

Registration
Register now
Confirm registration
I forgot my password
I forgot my Billpoint security key

Buying and Selling
Manage My Items for Sale
Where is an item
Revise my item
Add to my item description
Change my item's category
Manage/Edit my Andale.com counters
Add an Andale.com counter to my listing
Feature my item
Fix my gallery image
Promote your listings with link buttons
Cancel bids on my item
End my listing early
Relist my item
Blocked Bidder/Buyer List
Pre-approved Bidder/Buyer List
PowerSellers
Services
Seller Accounts
Check my seller account status
Make payments toward my account
Select or choose a payment option for my eBay seller fees
Sign up/update eBay Direct Pay for seller fees
Place or update my credit card on file with my eBay
Request final value fee credit
Cash out your credit balance
Change your billing currency
View My Payments (Billpoint) account
Selling Tools
Category overview with numbers
Mister Lister bulk upload
eBay Seller's Assistant
Seller Services
Shipping Education Center
eBay Live Auctions
Buyer Tools
eBay Payments
eBay Toolbar NEW!
Retract my bid
Fraud Protection
Escrow
Send a Gift Alert message
eBay Anywhere - Wireless

My eBay
Change my User ID
Change my password
Change my registration information
Change my email address
Change of E-mail Address Confirmation
Add/Change my wireless email address
Change my notification preferences
Create my Secret Question and Answer

Community

Community Overview

News & Announcements
Latest buzz on new features
Calendar

Discussion, Help and Chat
eBay User to User Discussion Boards
eBay Live Conference
Talk to others about 2002, and plan for 2003.
The Front Porch NEW!
The Homestead NEW!
New to eBay Board
The Park
eBay Town Square
The Soapbox
Night Owl's Nest NEW!
eBay Category-Specific Discussion Boards
Animals | Antiques
Art & Artists | Bears
Book Readers | Book Sellers
Clothing & Accessories | Coins & Paper Money
Collectibles | Comics
Computers, Networking & I.T.
Cooks Nook | Dolls
Decorative & Holiday NEW!
eBay Motors
Health & Beauty NEW!
Historical Memorabilia
Hobbies & Crafts | Home & Garden
Jewelry & Gemstones
Motorcycle Boulevard | Movies & Memorabilia
Music & Musicians | Needle Arts & Vintage Textiles NEW! | Outdoor Sports
Photography | Pottery, Glass & Porcelain
Science & Mystery
Sports Memorabilia & Trading Cards
Toys, Games & Trading Cards
Travel, Vacation & Adventure
Vintage Clothing & Accessories
eBay Workshops
Workshops board
Community Help
Auction Listings
Bidding
PayPal / Billpoint
Checkout
eBay Stores
Escrow/Insurance
Feedback
International Trading
Miscellaneous
My eBay
Packaging & Shipping
Photos/HTML
Policies/User Agreement
Registration
Search
Technical Issues
Tools - Mister Lister / Turbo Lister
Tools - SA Basic

How to Go Directly to the Most Important Stuff

Tired of clicking to eBay's site map and then clicking to another link (and maybe another after that) to access a specific eBay feature? Don't despair; just about every part of eBay's site has its own unique Web address. Just reference Table 2.2 to find the direct URLs for eBay's most important features.

TABLE 2.2   Direct Access Addresses for Key eBay Services

Feature/Area	URL
Home page	www.ebay.com
About Me personal pages	members.ebay.com/aw-cgi/eBayISAPI.dll?AboutMeLogin
Auctions ending today	listings.ebay.com/aw/listings/endtoday/index.html
Auctions new today	listings.ebay.com/aw/listings/newtoday/all/category0/
Big ticket items	pages.ebay.com/buy/bigticket/index.html
Cancel a bid (seller)	cgi.ebay.com/aw-cgi/eBayISAPI.dll?CancelBidShow
Category overview	listings.ebay.com/pool1/listings/list/overview.html
Community Overview	pages.ebay.com/community/
Community standards: questionable items	pages.ebay.com/help/community/png-items.html
Completed auctions	listings.ebay.com/pool1/listings/list/completed.html
Customer support	pages.ebay.com/help/basics/select-support.html
Discussion, help, and chat	pages.ebay.com/community/chat/
eBay Education	pages.ebay.com/education/
eBay Motors	pages.ebay.com/ebaymotors/
eBay official time	cgi3.ebay.com/aw-cgi/eBayISAPI.dll?TimeShow
eBay Real Estate	pages.ebay.com/realestate/
eBay Seller's Assistant software	pages.ebay.com/sellers_assistant/
eBay Stores	www.stores.ebay.com
eBay system status	calculus.ebay.com/aw/announce.shtml
End an auction early	cgi3.ebay.com/aw-cgi/eBayISAPI.dll?EndingMyAuction
Escrow	pages.ebay.com/help/buy/buytrust-escrow.html
Featured listings	listings.ebay.com/aw/listings/list/featured/index.html
Fee list	pages.ebay.com/help/sell/fees.html
Feedback Forum	pages.ebay.com/services/forum/feedback.html
Fraud protection program	pages.ebay.com/help/community/fpp.html

TABLE 2.2 Continued

Feature/Area	URL
Gallery	pages.ebay.com/buy/gallery.html
Half.com	half.ebay.com
Help	pages.ebay.com/help/index_popup.html
Library	pages.ebay.com/community/library/
List an item	cgi5.ebay.com/aw-cgi/eBayISAPI.dll?SellYourItem
My eBay	cgi1.ebay.com/aw-cgi/eBayISAPI.dll?MyEbayLogin
News and announcements	pages.ebay.com/community/news/
Password (forgotten)	pages.ebay.com/services/registration/reqpass.html
PayPal	www.paypal.com
Relist an item	pages.ebay.com/help/sell/relist.html
Search	pages.ebay.com/search/items/basicsearch.html
SquareTrade	www.squaretrade.com
Turbo Lister software	pages.ebay.com/turbo_lister/

Contacting eBay—*Directly!*

Although you *could* use eBay's various discussion boards to try to contact eBay, you'll quickly discover that this method of communication often leaves something to be desired—like a fast response! Instead, try contacting eBay staff *directly* via the following e-mail addresses— addresses, by the way, that eBay does a good job of hiding from its user base.

Table 2.3 lists some of eBay's most important direct e-mail addresses you can contact for specific problems and issues.

> **tip**
>
> To avoid repeatedly entering these long URLs, you might want to bookmark any of these pages you go to frequently.

TABLE 2.3 "Secret" eBay Contact Addresses

Issue	Contact
Questions of an urgent nature	timesensitive@ebay.com
Questions of a general and non-urgent nature	support@ebay.com
Questions about user agreement	agree-questions@ebay.com

Questions about why an auction ended early	whyended@ebay.com
Questions about buying and selling outside the U.S.	goglobal@ebay.com
Questions about finding a job working for eBay	jobs@ebay.com
Questions about eBay's privacy policy	privacy@ebay.com
Questions about account status and credit cards	billing@ebay.com
Request merging of two accounts into a single account	e-merge@ebay.com
Remove your credit card from your account	ccard@ebay.com
Report bidding offenses, selling offenses, and other potential abuses	safeharbor@ebay.com
Report suspected pirated items	buddyitems@ebay.com
Report suspected illegal items	ctywatch@ebay.com
Report problems with the Gallery	gallery@ebay.com
Make a suggestion to eBay	suggest@ebay.com

note

If all else fails, you can always contact eBay by phone (800.322.9266 or 408.369.4830) or by snail mail, at

eBay Inc.
2145 Hamilton Avenue
San Jose, CA 95125

THE ABSOLUTE MINIMUM

Here are the key points to remember from this chapter:

- eBay was founded in 1995 as a site for trading PEZ dispensers.

- Today eBay is the world's largest online auction community, facilitating the trading of all sorts of items.

- You can trade practically anything on eBay—except illegal or regulated items.

- eBay's home page (www.ebay.com) lets you access the most important operations—although the Site Map page is better for finding all of eBay's features and services.

- You can go directly to many key eBay pages—and save yourself a few mouse clicks.

3

JOINING UP AND GETTING STARTED

You can browse through eBay's millions of listings anonymously (and without registering), but if you want to buy or sell items, you have to register with the eBay site. Registration involves telling eBay who you are, where you live, and how to contact you. If you're interested in selling on eBay, you'll also need to give eBay a valid credit card number—which won't be charged. (At least, not yet!)

Although eBay registration is free, selling an item isn't. You have to pay eBay a fee for every item you list for sale, and for every item you actually sell. You *don't* have to pay eBay when you buy an item; fees are charged exclusively to sellers.

Read on to learn more about eBay's registration process—and its fee structure!

Everybody Does It: Filling Out eBay's Registration Form

Registration is free, easy, and relatively quick. But before you register, you need to prepare some key information, as detailed in the following checklist:

Checklist: Before You Register

- ☐ Your name
- ☐ Your street address
- ☐ Your e-mail address
- ☐ Your phone number
- ☐ Your date of birth
- ☐ Your credit card number (optional if you're only going to be bidding on items; mandatory if you're going to be selling items on auction)

With this information at hand, you register as an eBay user by following these steps:

1. From eBay's home page, click the Register Now button.

2. When the eBay Registration page appears (as shown in Figure 3.1), enter the following information:
   - ▪ First name and last name
   - ▪ Street address (including city, state, Zip code, and country)
   - ▪ Telephone number
   - ▪ E-mail address

3. Still on the same page, create and enter a user ID into the Create Your eBay User ID box.

4. Create and enter a password (at least six characters long, with no spaces) into the Create Password box.

note

eBay asks all members to supply a valid physical address and telephone number. They don't disclose this info to any third parties outside the eBay site, although they will supply personal data to other eBay users on their request. (It's how they try to contact deadbeat bidders and sellers.) You can get more details from eBay's Privacy Policy, found at `pages.ebay.com/help/community/png-priv.html`.

Your eBay user ID must be at least two characters long, and can contain letters, numbers, and/or certain symbols. It cannot contain spaces, Web page URLs, or the following symbols: $, &, <, or >—which means you can't use your e-mail address as your user ID.

If you ever move, you'll need to change the address and phone number information eBay has on file. Just go to the Site Map page, scroll to the My eBay section, and click the item you want to change: User ID, Password, Registration Information, E-Mail Address, and so on.

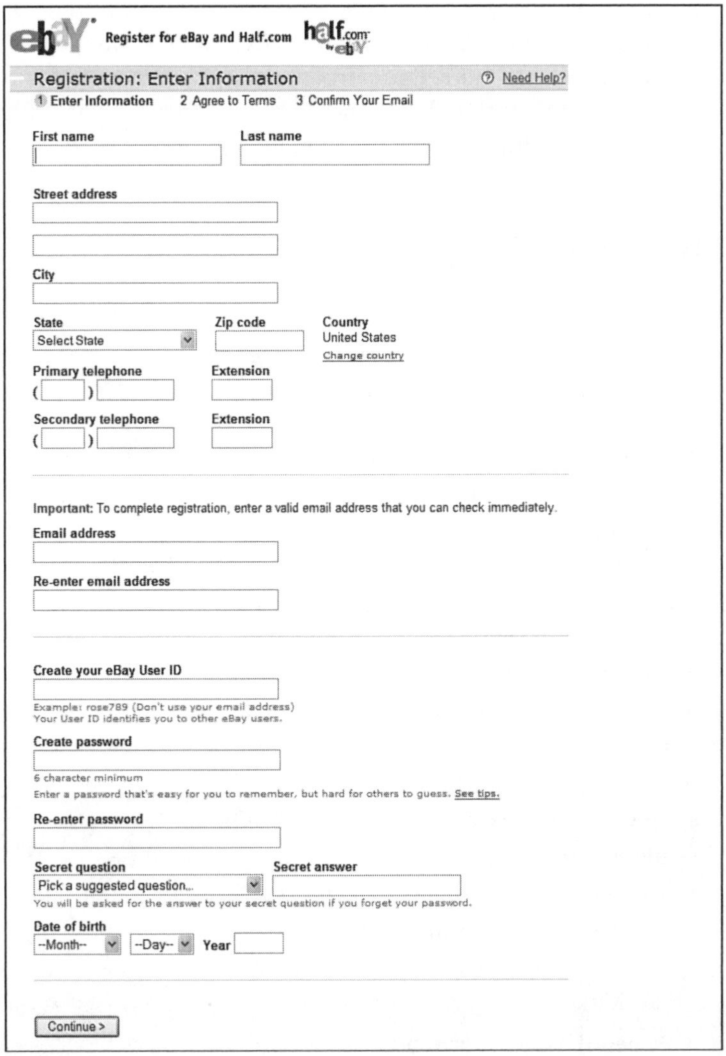

FIGURE 3.1

Enter the first page of your registration info.

5. Select a question from the Secret Question list, and then enter your answer in the Secret Answer box. (This is used if you ever forget your password.)

6. Enter your date of birth, and then click the Continue button.

7. eBay now displays its user agreements. Read these agreements (if you want), check each of the I Agree boxes, and then click the I Agree to These Terms button.

8. eBay now verifies your e-mail address, and sends you a confirmation message. Click the Web page link in the confirmation e-mail message to continue.

9. eBay now displays a congratulations page, along with a pop-up window that asks you to enter more (optional) information about yourself. This information is used for marketing purposes; you can choose to fill in the blanks, or close the window and click the Home link to go directly to eBay's home page—and start buying and selling!

Setting Up Your Payment Options

If you intend to sell items on eBay, you'll need to give eBay either your credit card number or your checking account number. (You *can* pay eBay fees by check or money order, at least theoretically; it's a hassle to do, and not encouraged.)

When you set up your eBay account for credit card billing, eBay bills your credit card once a month for all the fees you incur in the previous 30 days. When you set up eBay to debit your checking account (called eBay Direct Pay), you authorize eBay to automatically remove funds from your account on a specified day each month.

To set up your eBay account for credit card billing, follow these steps:

1. Go to the Site Map page and click Place or Update my Credit Card on File with eBay (in the Seller Accounts section of the Services section).

2. When the credit card submission form appears (see Figure 3.2), enter your user ID or e-mail address, password, and credit card billing information, and then check the I Would Like to Use This Credit Card to Pay Seller Fees option.

3. Click the Submit button.

tip

If you're a buyer, you might also want to register your credit card—not that eBay requires it, or will charge anything against it. Registering your card allows you to access eBay's adult areas and sets everything in place in case you do want to list items for sale in the future.

" Mike Sez "

I recommend you go with credit card billing. I don't like the idea of eBay (or any other company) having automatic access to my checking account; who knows if I'll have enough funds on tap the day they decide to make the automatic withdrawal? Credit card payment is easy and just as automatic, with few (if any) hassles.

FIGURE 3.2
Entering credit card informa-tion for your eBay seller's account.

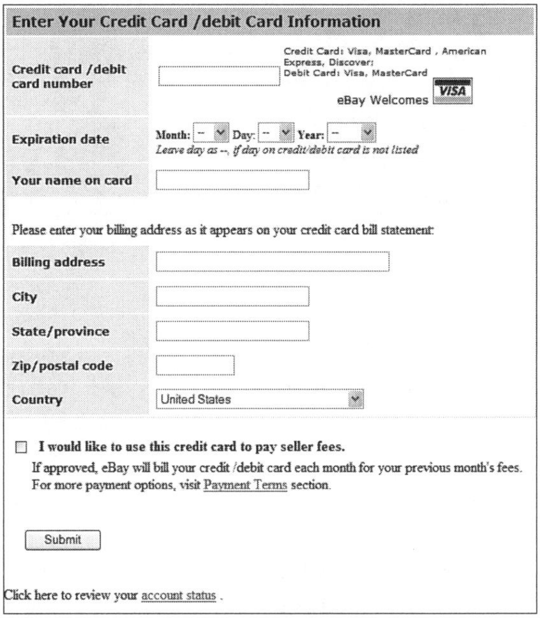

Your credit card information will be applied to your eBay account within 12–24 hours—at which time you'll be able to participate fully in everything eBay has to offer.

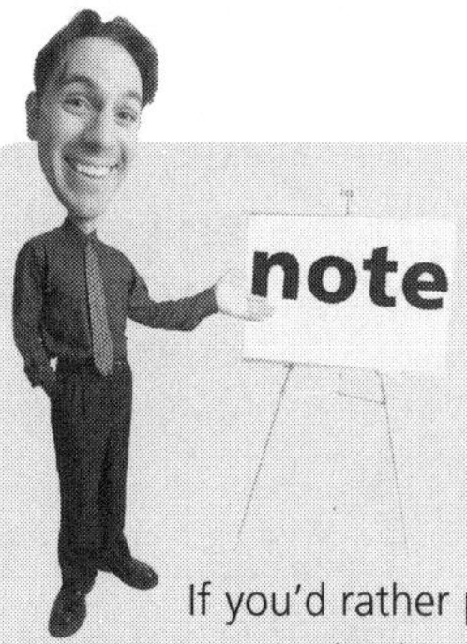

The Costs of Using eBay

You don't have to pay eBay anything to browse through items on their site. You don't have to pay eBay anything to bid on an item. You don't even have to pay eBay anything if you actually buy an item (although you will be paying the seller directly, of course). But if you're listing an item for sale, you gotta pay.

eBay charges two main types of fees:

▦ **Insertion fees** (I prefer to call them *listing* fees) are what you pay every time you list an item for sale on eBay. These fees are based on the minimum bid or reserve price of the item listed. These fees are nonrefundable.

note

If you'd rather pay via automatic checking account withdrawal, go to the Site Map page and (in the Seller Accounts section of the Services section) select Sign Up/Update eBay Direct Pay for Seller Fees.

eBay automatically assigns all new users a $10 "credit line." That means that you can immediately start listing items for sale, as long as the listing fees total less than your $10 limit. If you want to list more items, you definitely need to set up your account for credit card billing or eBay Direct Pay.

■ **Final value fees** (I prefer to call them *selling* fees, or *commissions*) are what you pay when an item is actually sold to a buyer. These fees are based on the item's final selling price (the highest bid). If your item doesn't sell, you aren't charged a final value fee.

eBay also charges a variety of fees for different types of listing enhancements. Table 3.1 lists all the fees eBay charges, current as of Fall 2002. (Fees for items listed in the Real Estate/Timeshare and eBay Motors categories are typically higher.)

note

View eBay's current fee structure at `pages.ebay.com/help/sell/fees.html`.

TABLE 3.1   eBay Fees

Type of Fee	Explanation	Fee
Insertion fee	In a regular auction, based on the opening value or minimum bid. In a fixed price auction, based on the Buy It Now price. In a reserve price auction, based on the reserve price of the item. In a Dutch auction, based on the opening value or minimum bid—multiplied by the number of items offered, up to a maximum of $3.30.	Items priced $0–$9.99: $0.30 Items priced $10.00–$24.99: $0.55 Items priced $25.00–$49.99: $1.10 Items priced $50.00–$199.99: $2.20 Items priced $200.00+: $3.30
Final value fee	In regular and successful reserve price auctions, based on the closing (high) bid. In Dutch auctions, based on the lowest successful bid—multiplied by the number of items sold.	5.25% of the amount of the high bid to $25.00, *plus* 2.75% of that part of the high bid from $25.01 up to $1,000, *plus* 1.5% of the remaining amount of the high bid that is greater than $1,000. For example, if the item sold for $1,500, you'd pay 5.25% of the first $25 ($1.31) plus 2.75% of the next $975 ($26.81) plus 1.5% of the remaining $500 ($7.50), for a total fee of $35.62.
Scheduled listings	Schedules your item to be listed at a specific date and time, up to three weeks in advance.	$0.10
List in two categories	Enables you to list your item in two separate categories.	Double listing and upgrade fees

Type of Fee	Explanation	Fee
Reserve price auction	Additional fee for holding a reserve price auction.	Items priced $0–$24.99: $0.50 Items priced $25.00–$199.99: $1.00 Items priced $200+: $2.00
Buy It Now	Fee to use the Buy It Now option.	$0.05
10-day auction	Additional fee for extending your auction from the normal 7-day to the longer 10-day format.	$0.10
Bold	Boldfaces the title of your item on the listing pages.	$2.00
Highlight	Puts a color shading behind your item on the listing pages.	$5.00
Gallery	Displays a thumbnail picture of your item in the Gallery section.	$0.25
Gallery Featured	Randomly displays your Gallery listing at the top of the category, at a larger size.	$19.95
Featured Plus!	Puts your listing at the top of the listing pages for that category, and also displays your listing (randomly) in the Featured Items section of the related category home page.	$19.95
Home Page Featured	Puts your listing at the top of the main Listings page and also displays your listing (randomly) in the Featured area on eBay's home page and on the Featured Items section of the related category home page.	$99.95

There's all manner of fine print associated with these fees. Here are some of the more important points to keep in mind:

- Insertion fees are nonrefundable.

- You will not be charged a final value fee if there were no bids on your item or (in a reserve price auction) if there were no bids that met the reserve price—that is, if your item didn't sell.

- It doesn't matter whether the buyer actually pays you (or how much he or she actually pays); you still owe eBay the full final value fee.

Invoicing on your account occurs once a month for the previous month's activity. You'll get an invoice by e-mail detailing your charges for the month; if you've set up your account for automatic credit card billing (see the next section), your credit card will be charged at that time. (If you prefer to pay by check, now's the time to get out the old checkbook.)

Getting Started

Now that you're all signed up (and aware of eBay's fee structure), you're ready to start bidding—and selling. The bidding process is fee-free; all you have to do is find something you want to buy, and start bidding. (This process is detailed in Chapter 4, "Bidding 101: A Tutorial for Beginning Bidders.") The selling process is a little more involved, and costs a little money. (This process is detailed in Chapter 10, "Selling 101: A Tutorial for Beginning Sellers.")

So, turn the page to get started with bidding, or flip forward to Chapter 10 to get started selling. Whichever you choose, get ready for lots of action—and fun!

THE ABSOLUTE MINIMUM

Here are the key points to remember from this chapter:

- Before you can bid or sell on eBay, you need to create an eBay user account.
- Registration is free.
- If you want to sell items on eBay, you'll either have to leave a credit card number on file, or sign up for eBay Direct Pay (automatic deductions from your checking account).
- Buyers are never charged any fees by eBay.
- eBay charges sellers a variety of fees, including listing fees (non-refundable) and final value fees (if your item actually sells).

PART II

EBAY FOR BIDDERS

4

BIDDING 101: A TUTORIAL FOR BEGINNING BIDDERS

After you've browsed through or searched the item listings and actually found something you're interested in, it's time to pony up and make a bid.

How does bidding work? In a nutshell, it's as simple as telling eBay how much you'd be willing to pay for an item—and then finding out whether anyone else is willing to pay more than you. If you've made the highest bid, you win the auction—and you have to buy the item.

It's important to remember that it doesn't cost you anything to bid. You only have to pay if you win—and even then, you don't have to pay any fees to eBay. (All eBay fees are charged to the seller.) You'll have to pay the seller the amount of your winning bid, plus any reasonable shipping and handling costs to get the item to you.

Sounds easy enough, doesn't it?

Understanding the Bidding Process

It's important that you know all about the item that you want to buy before you place your bid. It's also important that you know how eBay's bidding process works—or you could end up paying too much, or (even worse) not enough to win the auction!

Deciding How Much to Bid

Determining how much to bid on an item on eBay is no more complex than determining how much you'd pay for an item at a flea market or garage sale. You should bid an amount no higher and no lower than what the item is worth for you—and what you can afford. It doesn't matter what the current bid level is; you should make your bid in the amount of what you're willing to pay.

That doesn't mean you'll actually have to pay that amount, of course. Thanks to eBay's automated bidding software (discussed in the next section, "Understanding Proxy Bidding"), your registered bid will only be as high as necessary to beat out the next-highest bidder. If you bid $40 but the next highest bidder only bid $20, you'll win the auction with a $21 bid.

And you should make that $40 bid even if, at the time, the current bid is only $1.00. Now, you might think that if the bidding is at the $1.00 level, you should bid no more than $2.00 or so. This isn't the case, again thanks to eBay's automated bidding software. If the item is worth $40 to you, bid the $40—and let eBay's proxy software handle the mechanics of it.

How, then, do you determine that an item is worth $40—or $4 or $400? The key thing is to never bid blind; always make sure you know the true value of an item before you offer a bid.

This means that you need to do a little research before you make a bid. If you're bidding on a piece of new merchandise, check the price in a catalog, at your local retailer, or with an online retailer.

note

Learn more about browsing and searching the item listings in Chapter 5, "Searching for Items (and People)."

"Mike Sez"

If you remember nothing else from this book, remember this: Always enter the highest amount that you're willing to pay for an item, no matter what the current bid level. If you think an item is worth $40, enter $40 as your maximum bid—and don't worry if the current bid is half that amount. You also shouldn't get upset if the bidding goes higher than your specified maximum; have the discipline to bid only as high as you initially thought the item was worth.

If you're bidding on a collectible, invest in an up-to-date price guide (or reference one online). Whatever you're bidding on, search eBay for completed auctions on similar items, and determine a reasonable price range. Make it a point to shop around, and make your bid accordingly.

Understanding Proxy Bidding

The automated bidding software used by eBay is called *proxy* (or "robot") software. If you're a bidder, eBay's proxy software can save you time and help ensure that you get the items you want. (If you're a seller, it doesn't really matter, because all you're interested in is the highest price at the end of the auction—no matter how it got there!)

On eBay, proxy software operates automatically as an *agent* that is authorized to act in your place—but with some predefined bidding parameters. You define the maximum amount you are willing to bid, and then the proxy software takes over and does your bidding for you.

The proxy software bids as little as possible to outbid new competition, up to the maximum bid you specified. If it needs to up your bid $1, it does. If it needs to up your bid $5, it does—until it hits your bid ceiling, when it stops and bows out of the bidding.

The proxy software bids in the official bid increments used by eBay. If the next bid is $.50 higher than the current bid, the software ups your bid $.50. In no instance does the software place a bid *over* the next bid increment. (It's pretty smart software!)

Of course, because all bidders are using eBay's proxy software, what happens when you have two users bidding against each other? Simple—you get a proxy bidding war! In this instance, each proxy automatically ups its bid in response to the last bid by the other proxy, which rapidly (seemingly instantaneously!) increases the bid price until one of the proxies reaches its maximum bid level.

Let's say one proxy has been programmed with a maximum bid of $25, and another with a maximum bid of $26. Even though the initial bid might be $10, the bids rapidly increase from $10 to $11 to $12 and on to $26, at which point the first proxy drops out and the second proxy holds the high bid.

note

The bid increment is automatically calculated by eBay based on the current price of the item—the higher the price, the higher the bid increment.

Proxy Bidding, by Example

Let's walk through a detailed example of proxy bidding. The process is totally auto-mated, and goes like this:

1. You see an item that has a current bid of $100, and you tell eBay that you're willing to pay $115 for it. The $115 becomes your maximum bid.

2. The bid increment on this item is $2.50, so eBay's bidding software—your proxy—bids $102.50 in your name. This becomes the current high bid.

3. Another bidder sees this item, and bids the next bid increment (as specified on the item listing page), $105.00.

4. Your proxy sees the new bid, and ups its bid automatically to $107.50.

5. A third bidder sees the item, and enters a maximum bid of $150. In accor-dance with the current bid increment, his proxy enters a bid of 110.00.

6. Your proxy responds with a bid of $112.50.

7. The third bidder's proxy responds with a bid of $115.00.

8. Your proxy drops out of the bidding, and eBay notifies you (by e-mail) that your bid has been surpassed. (If the auction were to end right then, the third bidder would win the auction with a bid of $115. Even though he specified a $150 maximum bid, the bidding never got that high.)

9. At this point, you can place a new maximum bid for the item, or you can throw in the towel and let the new bidder have the item.

Proxy Bidding Advice

The nice thing about proxy bidding is that you can engage in a fierce bidding war— and never get your hands dirty! The proxy software does all the dirty work for you, and just notifies you of the results.

When you're placing your bid, realize that just because you set a maximum bid price doesn't mean you'll have to actually pay that price. The proxy software works in your favor to keep your final price as low as possible; don't assume that just because you specified a price, the bidding will always rise to that level.

Also feel comfortable that the proxy software will never exceed your maximum bid price. It just won't happen; the software is smart enough to know your limits. And, by bidding your maximum right away, you guarantee that you won't get carried away and pay too much at the end of a heated competition. Remember, if you lose an auction because the bidding goes higher than your maximum, you didn't want to pay that much for the merchandise, anyway. Get comfortable with that—and be glad the proxy software helped you stay within your limits.

Of course, some bidders don't like proxy bidding. It is true that if two or more people are bidding for the same item, the bids can automatically (and quickly) rocket up until they max out. For this reason, some bidders prefer to bid the bare minimum on every single one of their bids—effectively defeating the purpose of the proxy software. Of course, if you choose to operate this way, you have to be a lot more hands-on with your bidding, essentially checking back on all your bids as frequently as necessary to ensure that you always end up on top.

How to Read an Item Listing

Before we do any bidding, let's take a look at a typical eBay item listing to see what you can find out about the item and its seller.

Each listing page includes five major sections:

- Auction details
- Description
- Payment details
- Payment instructions
- Bidding

Each of these sections is equally important. The auction details section tells you all the mechanical details of the auction: who's doing the selling, how many bids there are, what the current bid price is, and so on. The Description section tells you all about the item for sale—and contains pictures of the item, if provided by the seller. The Payment Details and Payment Instructions sections tell you how much shipping/handling you have to pay, and what kinds of payment are accepted. And the Bidding area is where you place your bid.

All of which means, of course, that you need to take your time and read through the *entire* item listing before you place your bid. Don't skim; read carefully, and pay attention to the details. If the seller mentions a known fault with the merchandise (in the Description section) but you gloss over it, don't even think about complaining when you receive the item after the auction, fault and all. It's your responsibility to read—and agree to—all the information in the listing.

Auction Details

The auction details section is the section (untitled, actually) at the very top of the item listing page, as shown in Figure 4.1. It starts with a listing title, followed by the item number.

> **tip**
>
> The item number is important; you use this number to reference the auction in all correspondence, and when paying by PayPal or other payment services.

Directly underneath the item number is the category that the item is listed in; click the category link to view other auctions in this category.

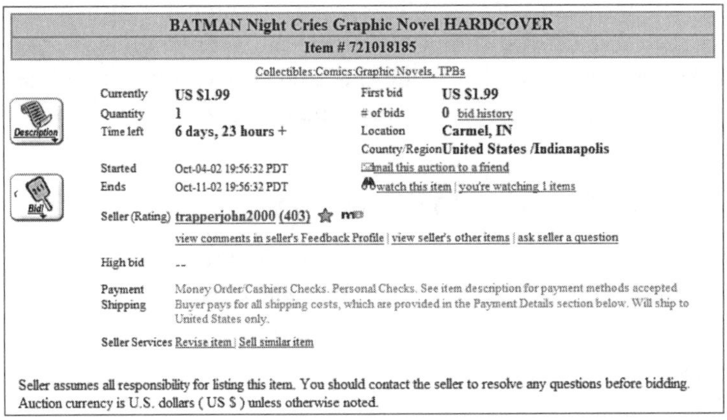

FIGURE 4.1

The auction details section at the top of the item listing.

The next part of the auction details section tells you about the status of the current auction, as detailed in Table 4.1.

TABLE 4.1 Elements in the Auction Details Section of the Item Listing Page

Field	Information
Currently	Current bid price
First Bid	Starting bid price
Quantity	Number of items for auction (quantity is always 1, except in a Dutch auction)
Location, Country/Region	Where the item will be shipped from
Time Left	Number of days, hours, and minutes until the end of the auction
Started	Date and time the auction started
Ends	Date and time the auction is scheduled to end
Seller (Rating)	The user ID of the seller, along with the seller's feedback rating
High Bid	The user ID of the current high bidder, along with the bidder's feedback rating
Payment	Payment methods the seller will accept for this auction
Shipping	Shipping details, such as who pays shipping (typically the buyer) and where the seller will ship

There are also a handful of useful links within the auction details section:

- If you want to see who else has bid on this item, click the Bid History link. This displays all the past bidders—but doesn't list the amounts they bid. The details of each bid are kept hidden until the auction is over; after the auction has ended, click the Bid History link again to see how much each person bid.

- If you want to let someone else know about this auction, click the Mail This Auction to a Friend link. You'll be asked to provide your friend's e-mail address, as well as an optional personal message. eBay will then mail this auction page's URL to the person you specified.

- If you want to keep tabs on this auction without actually placing a bid, click the Watch This Item link. This adds this auction to the Items I'm Watching section of your My eBay page; you can then use your My eBay page to track the high bids in this auction. (Learn more about My eBay in Chapter 22, "Creating a Home Base with My eBay.")

- If you want to see other items this seller has for auction, click the View Seller's Other Items link.

- If you have any questions about the item, click the Ask Seller a Question link to send an e-mail message to the seller.

> **"Mike Sez"**
>
> If I find an item I'm interested in, I like to take a look at that seller's other items. I've often found other items worth buying from a particular seller. (And some sellers will combine items for lower shipping costs if you buy more than one item.)

Description

This section offers a description of the item for sale, as written by the seller. As you can see in Figure 4.2, this section is typically plain text but sometimes includes one or more pictures of the item.

FIGURE 4.2

The Description section of an item listing.

Description
Near-mint condition hardcover graphic novel **BATMAN: NIGHT CRIES**. Written by Archie Goodwin, beautiful painted art by Scott Hampton. One of the best Batman graphic novels ever, period.
DC Comics, 1992, hardcover, near-mint. No dust jacket, sorry.

00001
Free Counters powered by Andale!

Because this section is written completely by the seller, the amount of detail varies from seller to seller (and from auction to auction). Some sellers provide a wealth of detail; some write terse one-line descriptions. If the seller doesn't include enough detail in the description, you can always e-mail for more information—or decide that if this wasn't important enough for the seller to spend more time on, it's not important enough for you to bid on, either.

Some accompanying pictures might appear a tad small. If you see a Supersize Picture link under a thumbnail picture, click the picture to view it at a larger size.

> **" Mike Sez "**
>
> Some item listings include a counter at the bottom of the Description section. Watch the counter over a several-day period to judge the interest in this item. A large counter number (in the hundreds) indicates a lot of interest, and a lot of potential last-minute bidders. A small counter number (in the single digits or the teens) indicates less interest—which means you may be able to win this item without bidding too high.

Payment Details and Payment Instructions

These two sections offer information about how you can pay for your auction—although, as you can see in Figure 4.3, they somewhat duplicate the Payment field in the auction details section.

Payment Details		Payment Instructions
United States Shipping and handling	US $2.00	Shipping/handling $2.00 via USPS Media Mail. U.S.
Shipping insurance per item (not available)	--	bidder only, please.

Sellers can use the Payment Details section to list the payment methods they accept—although that's probably the same information listed in the Payment field. They can use the Payment Instructions section to provide detailed instructions on how to proceed when the auction is over.

In any case, these short sections are probably worth examining, just in case the seller has any special payment requirements.

Bidding

eBay makes you scroll through all the other stuff before you can bid. As you can see in Figure 4.4, the Bidding section is at the very bottom of the page, and includes the following information:

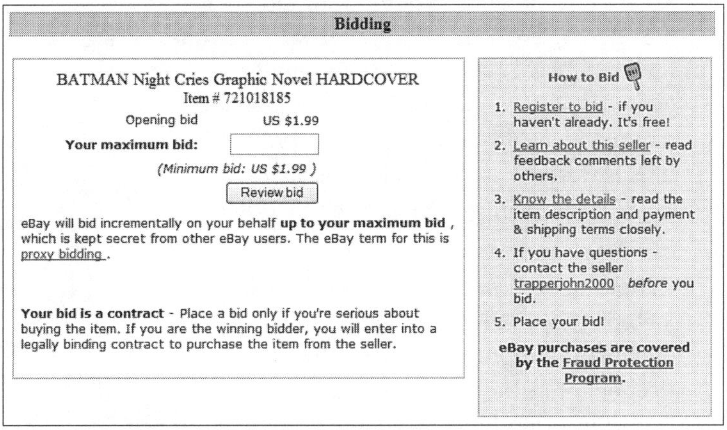

FIGURE 4.4
Use the Bidding section to place your bid.

Bidding

BATMAN Night Cries Graphic Novel HARDCOVER
Item # 721018185

Opening bid   US $1.99

Your maximum bid:

(Minimum bid: US $1.99)

Review bid

eBay will bid incrementally on your behalf **up to your maximum bid** , which is kept secret from other eBay users. The eBay term for this is proxy bidding .

Your bid is a contract - Place a bid only if you're serious about buying the item. If you are the winning bidder, you will enter into a legally binding contract to purchase the item from the seller.

How to Bid

1. Register to bid - if you haven't already. It's free!
2. Learn about this seller - read feedback comments left by others.
3. Know the details - read the item description and payment & shipping terms closely.
4. If you have questions - contact the seller trapperjohn2000 *before* you bid.
5. Place your bid!

eBay purchases are covered by the Fraud Protection Program.

- Item title
- Item number
- Current bid price
- Bid increment (how much higher each new bid is from the last)
- Your maximum bid

Okay. This last field is the important one—it's where you enter your bid amount.

Before You Bid

Although anyone is free to browse on eBay, to place a bid you have to be a registered user. If you haven't registered yet, now's the time. (For information on registering, see Chapter 3, "Joining Up and Getting Started.")

Before you place your bid, make sure you read all the details of the item you're interested in. In particular, look at the following:

- Is the item you're bidding on new or used? If it's new, what kind of warranty does it come with? If it's used, what's your recourse if you're dissatisfied with the item?

- What condition is the item in? Is it an original, or a reproduction? Is there any way to verify that condition—through photos of the item, perhaps?

Mike Sez

If you have any questions about a particular item, ask 'em! Click the Ask Seller a Question link on the item listing page (under the seller's user ID) to send the seller an e-mail, and ask whatever questions you want. If the seller doesn't respond, pass this auction by. And if something about the listing sounds too good to be true—it probably is!

- Check out the seller's feedback rating—is it positive? (*Never* deal with a user with a negative total feedback number.) You might even want to click the number next to the seller's name to view his or her feedback profile; this is where you can read the individual comments about this person left by other users.

- What methods of payment will the seller accept? (These are typically listed in the Payment paragraph in the auction details section, or in the Payment Detail section.) Are you comfortable using one of these payment options?

- How much shipping and handling is the seller charging? Are these fees in line with what you think actual shipping will cost? If you (or the seller) live outside the U.S., will the seller ship internationally?

In other words, take your time and become knowledgeable about and comfortable with both the item an the seller before you place your bid. If you find anything—anything at all—that makes you uncomfortable, don't bid.

That said, let's look at a final checklist for buyers; check off each item before you make your bid.

note

The seller's feedback rating reflects the number of successful auctions the seller has conducted. The higher the rating, the more reliable the seller. (Learn more about feedback in Chapter 24, "Understanding and Using Feedback.")

" Mike Sez "

It's okay for shipping/handling to be a little higher than actual shipping; the seller has to pay for packing materials and so forth. But if the charge runs more than 10–15% (up to a buck or so) higher, the seller is viewing shipping/handling as a profit center, at your expense.

Checklist: Before You Bid

- ☐ Make sure you're an official registered eBay member.
- ☐ Read the item description—thoroughly.
- ☐ Note the payment methods that the seller will accept.
- ☐ Note how the seller intends to ship the item, and the shipping/handling price being charged.
- ☐ Check the seller's feedback rating—and click the feedback rating to browse through comments from other eBay users.

Continues…

☐ Note the current bid level, and the next bid price.

☐ Research the value of the item. (That means searching eBay for pricing on completed auctions of similar items, as well as doing your own online and offline research.)

☐ Determine the maximum amount you're willing to pay for the item.

☐ Subtract the estimated shipping/handling price from the price you're willing to pay; this becomes your maximum bid price.

☐ E-mail the seller if you have any questions about anything.

☐ Decide whether you really want to bid or not; every bid you make should be a serious, binding bid.

Just Do It—Placing a Bid

You've waited long enough. Now it's time to finally place your bid!

Here's what you do:

1. Scroll down to the Bidding section of the listing page, and enter your maximum bid amount.

2. If you're bidding in a Dutch auction (where the quantity is more than one), enter the number of items you want to bid on.

3. Click the Review Bid button.

4. If you're not currently signed in to eBay, you'll be prompted for your user ID and password. Enter them now.

5. Check the information on the Confirm and Place Your Bid page (shown in Figure 4.5)—especially your bid amount. If everything is correct, click the Place Bid button.

6. Your bid is officially entered and the Bid Confirmation screen appears. It's here that eBay indicates whether you're the current high bidder or you've already been outbid.

Remember, eBay's proxy bidding system will automatically place your bids for you, up to but not exceeding your specified maximum bid amount. If the minimum bid is currently $10, and you entered a maximum bid of $20, eBay enters your bid as $10. Your bid will get raised automatically if and when other bidders enter their (higher) bids.

note

Learn specific techniques for bidding in—and winning—eBay auctions in Chapter 9, "Secrets of Successful Bidders."

FIGURE 4.5

One last chance to confirm your bid...

eɒY®

Confirm and Place Your Bid   ⑦ Need Help?

Confirm that your bid is correct and then place your bid.

1971 LUDWIG PERCUSSION CATALOG...NICE!
Item # 910433555

Your current bid: $15.49
Your maximum bid: $15.50

eBay User ID
ebay@molehillgroup.com (Not ebay@molehillgroup.com? Change User ID)

☑ Remember my User ID and password for bidding.

[Place Bid >]   Back to item

Copyright © 1995-2002 eBay Inc. All Rights Reserved.
Designated trademarks and brands are the property of their respective owners.
Use of this Web site constitutes acceptance of the eBay User Agreement and Privacy Policy.   TRUSTⓔ site privacy statement

Bidding in Other Types of Auctions

The previous section covered the typical eBay auction, one without a lot of bells and whistles. eBay offers a lot of different auction options, however (as you'll learn in Chapter 13, "Choosing the Right Listing Options"), and the bidding procedure is slightly different depending on the type of auction being held.

Dutch Auctions

A Dutch auction is an auction where the seller has more than one of an item for sale. An example might be a seller with a half-dozen T-shirts (all identical), or a gross of inkjet cartridges, or something similar. Although most sellers on Dutch auctions are small businesses that want to unload multiple quantities of an item, you'll also find some individuals with several like items to sell.

In a Dutch auction, the seller specifies both the minimum bid and the number of items available in the auction, as shown in Figure 4.6. As in a normal auction, bidders bid at or above that minimum for the item—although, in a Dutch auction, bidders can specify a specific *quantity* that they're interested in purchasing.

Current lowest qualifying bid

FIGURE 4.6

An example of a Dutch auction—note the quantity available in the left column.

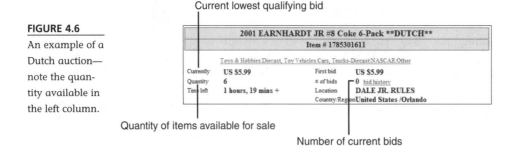

2001 EARNHARDT JR #8 Coke 6-Pack **DUTCH**		
Item # 1785301611		

Toys & Hobbies:Diecast, Toy Vehicles:Cars, Trucks-Diecast:NASCAR:Other

Currently	US $5.99	First bid	US $5.99
Quantity	6	# of bids	0 bid history
Time left	1 hours, 19 mins +	Location	DALE JR. RULES
		Country/Region	United States /Orlando

Quantity of items available for sale

Number of current bids

When you're bidding in a Dutch auction, you not only have to place your bid, but you also have to indicate how many of the item you'd like to buy. You enter the desired amount in the Quantity of Items Desired box in the Bidding section of the listing page. (This box—shown in Figure 4.7—appears only in Dutch auctions, not in regular auctions.)

FIGURE 4.7

Enter the quantity you want for a Dutch auction item.

Determining who "wins" a Dutch auction is a little different from determining who wins a normal auction. In a Dutch auction, the highest bidders purchase the items, but all buyers pay only the amount that matches the lowest successful bid.

Dutch Auctions, by Example

Let's work through an example. Say a seller has 10 identical copies of a particular *Lord of the Rings* T-shirt. The seller indicates the number of items available (10), and the minimum bid (let's say $5). Potential buyers enter their bids, which must be equal to or higher than the minimum bid of $5; each buyer also indicates the quantity (from 1 to 10) that he or she is interested in purchasing.

If 11 people bid $5 each (for one shirt apiece), the first 10 bidders will win the auction, each paying $5 for their items, and the last bidder will be out of luck. But if the 11th person had placed a higher bid—$6, let's say—then that 11th bidder would be listed as the #1 bidder, and the last $5 bidder (chronologically) would be knocked from the list. All ten winning bidders, however—including the person who bid $6— would only have to pay $5 for the item. (Highest bidders, lowest bids—get it?)

In a Dutch auction, the minimum price ends up being raised only if enough bidders place bids above the minimum bid. In our example, if 9 bidders bid over the minimum, but the 10th bidder bid $5, all bidders would still pay $5. But if the lowest bid was $6 (and the other bidders bid from $6 to $10), all 10 bidders would pay $6 (the lowest current bid). So posting a higher bid increases a buyer's chances of winning an item at a Dutch auction, but it also increases the risk of raising the price for everybody.

When a potential buyer bids on multiple copies of the item, those toward the end of the list may not get the quantity they desire. Still using our T-shirt example, if the top bidder wants three shirts, the remaining shirts are distributed among the next seven bidders—leaving the last or lowest two bidders out in the cold.

Tips on Bidding in Dutch Auctions

Dutch auctions actually benefit the buyer more than any other type of auction by letting higher bidders pay the lowest bid price. Should you bid on a Dutch auction? Why not? If someone is selling something you want, by all means, bid!

How much should you bid? Ah, there's the issue! I actually like bidding on Dutch auctions later in the game, so that I can get a handle on how many other bidders I'm competing with. The number of bidders versus the quantity of items available determines my strategy:

> **note**
>
> Remember, the higher bidders get first dibs on multiple quantities. So, if the lowest bidder wants multiple quantities of the item on the block, he or she may find that there aren't enough to go around. If only a partial quantity is available, the bidder can officially walk away from his/her bid.

- If the seller has a large quantity of items and a small number of bidders, bid the minimum. In this scenario, everybody wins because there's more than enough merchandise to go around.

- If the seller has a small quantity of items and a large number of bidders, you probably should bid higher than the minimum. In fact, in this scenario, treat it like a normal auction and bid the highest amount you're willing to pay. The worst thing that could happen is you lose the auction; the second worst is that you're a winning bidder and you have to pay your maximum bid; the best scenario is that you're a winning bidder but get to pay a lower amount (because of a lower bid entered by another winning bidder).

Reserve Price Auctions

In a *reserve price* auction, the seller has reserved the option to set a second price (the *reserve price*) that is higher than the opening bid. At the end of an auction, if the high bid does not meet or exceed the seller's reserve price, the auction is unsuccessful and the seller does *not* sell the item to the high bidder. Sellers sometimes use a reserve price on high-end items if they want to make sure the market does not undervalue what they are selling.

In other words, the reserve price is the lowest price at which a seller is willing to sell an item (unrelated to the opening bid price). The seller specifies the reserve price when the item is initially listed (naturally, the reserve price should be above the minimum bid price). The reserve price is known only to the seller (and to eBay), and is never disclosed to bidders—even though reserve price auctions are typically identified as such in the item's description.

A reserve price auction begins just like any other auction, at the minimum bid price. The only difference is the reserve price indication in the listing's auction details, as shown in Figure 4.8. You place your bid as you would in a normal auction, and the auction proceeds pretty much as normal.

note

Reserve price auctions are not available for Dutch auctions. In a Dutch auction, the minimum price is the minimum price.

FIGURE 4.8

Example of a Reserve auction where the reserve price hasn't yet been met.

CUSTOM 1960's LUDWIG SUPRA-400 SNARE DRUM			
Item # 910162007			
Music:Musical Instruments:Percussion:Drums			
Currently	US $99.00 (reserve not yet met)	First bid	US $99.00
Quantity	1	# of bids	1 bid history
Time left	1 days, 16 hours +	Location	SF Bay Area
		Country/Region	United States /San Francisco

If your maximum bid is equal to or greater than the reserve price, the item's current price is raised to the reserve price, and the reserve price has officially been met. If, through the course of the auction, the reserve price is *not* met, the auction ends with the item unsold.

Reserve Price Auctions, By Example

Let's look at a brief example of a reserve price auction. Suppose a seller has a leather jacket to sell that she feels is worth $50—but she wants to set a lower initial bid, to get the bidding going early. So the seller sets $25 as the initial bid, and $50 as the reserve price.

The first bidder on this item sees the $25 initial bid (the reserve price isn't displayed, of course), and bids $25. The bidder is notified that he has the current high bid, but that the reserve price has not been met. If the auction were to end right now, the item would *not* be sold—the seller is obligated to sell only if the reserve price is met.

The bidding continues, and the bid price increases until it hits $50. At that point, the last bidder is notified both that he is the high bidder, and also that the reserve price has been met. If the auction ends now—or at any point afterwards—the seller *is* obligated to sell, because the reserve price ($50) has been met.

So, in this example, any bids under $50 don't win the auction; any bids $50 and over can be winning bids.

Tips for Bidding in Reserve Price Auctions

If you want to bid in a reserve price auction, what should your strategy be? It depends on how badly you want the item.

If you really, really, *really* want the item, you should place your first bid and see if you hit the reserve price. If you didn't, place a new, higher bid, and see if *it* hits the reserve price. If you *still* didn't, repeat until your bid is high enough to guarantee a win.

For most bidders, however, this is simply a strategy to ensure writing a large check. In most cases, play a reserve price auction as you would a normal auction, and let the high bid be the high bid. If you have the high bid and the reserve price isn't met, it's no skin off your nose; it simply means that the seller set an unreasonable reserve price. You always have the option of contacting the seller post-auction to see if he/she is willing to sell at the current bid price, even though the reserve hasn't been met. The seller isn't obligated to do so, of course, but some might be willing to let the merchandise go to forgo starting a whole new auction (and paying another listing fee)—or they may be willing to negotiate a selling price somewhere in between your bid and the reserve. You never know until you ask!

Winning Quickly with Buy It Now

Some sellers choose to list their items with eBay's Buy It Now option. With Buy It Now, the item is sold (and the auction ended) if the very first bidder places a bid for a specified price. (For this reason, some refer to Buy It Now auctions as "fixed price" auctions.)

Buying an item with Buy It Now is really simple. If you see an item identified with a Buy It Now price (as shown in Figure 4.9), just enter a bid at that price. You'll immediately be notified that you've won the auction, and the auction will be officially closed.

Of course, you don't have to bid at the Buy It Now price. You can bid at a lower price, and hope that you win the auction, which proceeds normally. (The Buy It Now option disappears when the first bid is made.)

" Mike Sez "

You should only use Buy It Now if you really, really, *really* want the item; if you think the Buy It Now price is reasonable; if you fear the final price will be higher than the Buy It Now price; or if you don't want to wait for the auction to run its course to complete your purchase.

FIGURE 4.9

A Buy It Now
auction.

What to Do After You've Bid

You've made your bid on an item. What happens next?

The answer to this question is a four-letter word: *Wait*. And, as Tom Petty says, the waiting is the hardest part.

That's certainly true with online auctions.

Immediately after you place a high bid, eBay automatically sends you an e-mail notifying you of your bid status. You'll also receive an e-mail once a day from eBay, notifying you of your status in any and all auctions in which you're the highest bidder. In addition, if you get outbid on an item, eBay sends you an immediate e-mail informing you of such.

Otherwise, feel free to check in on all of your auctions in progress, just to see how things are proceeding. Remember that a watched kettle never boils—and constantly tracking your auctions doesn't make the time go any faster, either.

Keeping Track of Your Bids

You can search for all the auctions that you've recently bid on by clicking the Search link at the top of eBay's home page to display the Search page. Select the By Bidder tab, enter your own user ID in the Bidder's User ID box, and then click the Search button. eBay will now list all the active auctions in which you're a bidder.

Even better, you can use your My eBay page to automatically track all the current auctions you've bid on. See Chapter 22 for more information about My eBay.

Increasing Your Bid Amount

As you get further along in a particular auction, you might suddenly realize that your maximum bid isn't going to hold, and you want to ensure a large enough bid to win a long, hard-fought auction. How can you increase your bid—even though you're currently the high bidder?

It's really easy. Just return to the item listing page and place a new bid, making sure that your new maximum bid is higher than your old maximum bid. (You can't decrease your maximum bid!) When you enter this new bid, it replaces your previous bid.

Pretty easy, isn't it?

Oh, No! You've Been Outbid!

It happens. Your auction is progressing, and then you get that dreaded e-mail from eBay informing you that you've been outbid.

What do you do?

First, you have to decide whether you want to continue to play in this auction. If you decided up front that an item was only worth, let's say, $10, and the bidding has progressed to $15, you might want to let this one go.

On the other hand, if you hedged your bets with the earlier bid, you might want to jump back into the fray with a new bid. If so, return to the item's listing page and make a new bid. Maybe your new bid will be higher than the current high bidder's maximum bid.

Or maybe not. You don't know until you try!

> **❝Mike Sez❞**
>
> When the bidding exceeds the top level you've set for yourself, just walk away. Absolutely, positively, do *not* let yourself get caught up in a bidding frenzy—and end up paying more than the item is worth to you!
>
> Know that you're apt to generate negative feedback from the item's seller if you retract a bid. It's common courtesy—and common sense—to e-mail the seller before you retract a bid, explaining the circumstances and begging forgiveness.

Retracting a Bad Bid

Everybody makes mistakes. What happens if you place a bid in an auction that you shouldn't have placed?

Fortunately—but reluctantly—eBay lets you retract bids under certain circumstances.

When does eBay allow you to retract your bid? Well, if the seller has substantially changed the description of the item after you bid, you're free to change your mind, too. You can also retract your bid if you made a "clear error" in the amount of your bid. What's a "clear error?" Well, bidding $100 when you meant to bid $10 is clearly an error; other circumstances are left up to your judgment.

The thing is, you can always retract a bid (because you can always claim a "clear error"), but you won't win any friends doing so. In fact, if you retract too many bids, eBay will come after you and possibly kick you off the site. So retract a bid if you have to, but don't make a habit of it.

How do you retract a bid? It's actually fairly easy; just follow these steps:

1. Click the Services link on the Navigation Bar, then click Buying & Selling.

2. On the Buying and Selling Tools page, scroll down to the Buyer Tools section and click Retract My Bid.

3. When the Bid Retractions page appears, scroll down and enter your user ID, password, and the item number of the auction; you must also choose an explanation for your retraction from the pull-down list.

4. Click the Retract Bid button; your bid is now deleted from the auction in process.

Bidding in the Final Moments

It's during the last hour of most auctions that the bidding really heats up. If you wait for an e-mail to inform you when you've been outbid during an auction's final minutes, you might not have enough time to log onto eBay and make a new bid. For that reason, many bidders will log on to eBay (and onto the individual auction about to end) and manually monitor the auction's closing minutes. Just remember to hit the Refresh or Reload button on your browser frequently, to keep the item listing page up-to-date with the latest bids!

The reason for all this last-minute bidding activity is the use of a technique called *sniping*. Learn more about how to win auctions with sniping in Chapter 9.

You Won! Now What?

You've somehow waited patiently (or not) throughout the entire progress. As the clock ticked down to zero, no other viable competitors entered the arena, and your high bid stood. You won!

Now things *really* start to happen. You'll receive an e-mail from eBay notifying you that you've won the auction. You'll also receive an e-mail from the item's seller, telling you how much you need to pay, and where to send the payment. Then you'll need to reply to the seller, make your payment, and wait for the item to arrive.

To learn about the post-auction process in more detail, turn to Chapter 7, "After the Auction: Taking Care of Business."

The Absolute Minimum

Here are the key points to remember from this chapter:

- Before you place a bid, you have to be a registered eBay user—and you should check out the feedback rating and comments of the item's seller.

- You place your bid in the Bidding section of the item listing page; enter your user ID, password, and the maximum bid you're willing to make.

- eBay's proxy bidding software manages your bidding, raising your bid as necessary up to but not exceeding your specified maximum bid amount.

- If, at any point during the auction, you get outbid, you have two options: Place another (higher) bid, or walk away free and clear.

- When you win an auction, you'll be notified by eBay; you should then contact the seller to arrange payment and shipping terms.

5

SEARCHING FOR ITEMS (AND PEOPLE)

Let's get right down to it: eBay is the largest auction site on the Web, no questions asked. It's big. It's bigger than big. It's, like, really incredibly massively big. Think of the biggest thing you've ever seen, and eBay is bigger than that.

If you want to browse through the largest selection of merchandise for sale on the Internet, this is the place to go.

However, eBay's size (it's big, remember?) sometimes makes it difficult to find that *one* item you're looking for. So, how do you find that one special item among the 7 million or so items that are up for bid on eBay on any given day?

Browsing or Searching—Which One Is for You?

There are two main ways to locate items to bid on and buy on eBay. You can leisurely browse through eBay's thousands of categories and subcategories, or you can perform a targeted search for specific items.

Table 5.1 shows you what's good and what's bad about both browsing and searching.

> **" Mike Sez "**
>
> Most eBay categories are so large they're practically unbrowsable. (Do you really want to click through a hundred pages of listings to find the item you want?) I definitely recommend searching over browsing—you'll find what you're looking for a *lot* faster!

TABLE 5.1 Browsing Versus Searching—Strengths and Weaknesses

Question	Browsing	Searching
How easy is it to do?	Easy	Not as easy
How quickly can you find a specific item?	Slow	Fast
How many items will you find?	A lot	Not quite as many
Will you find the specific item you're looking for?	Not always	Yes
Can you isolate items geographically?	Yes	Yes
Can you find other bidders and sellers?	No	Yes

The bottom line: If you're not sure what you're looking for, or if you're looking for all types of items within a general category, you should browse. If you're looking for a specific item or type of item, you should search.

Browsing: the Easy Way to Find Things

eBay has more than an ever-increasing number of categories, listing all sorts of items—antiques, books, coins, collectibles, comics, computers, dolls, electronics, figures, gemstones, glass, jewelry, magazines, music, photography, pottery, sports memorabilia, stamps, toys, and many, many more. To view all the items within a specific category or subcategory, you need to browse through eBay's category listings.

eBay's main categories are listed on its home page. You can also access a complete list of eBay's categories and subcategories by going to the Site Map page and clicking Category Overview (in the Browse section).

eBay's major categories are divided into a hierarchy of subcategories. For example, if you click the Antiques link on eBay's home page, you'll see Antiquities, Architectural and Garden, Asian Antiques, and a dozen other subcategories. In fact, many of eBay's subcategories have their own subcategories—which makes them sub-subcategories, I guess!

When you access a main category page, like the one in Figure 5.1, you see a list of subcategories. (Some category pages will have a top-level subcategory list at the top of the page, and a detailed list of all subcategories at the bottom.) Click a subcategory link, and you'll either see a list of additional subcategories or a list of available items.

FIGURE 5.1

A typical eBay category page.

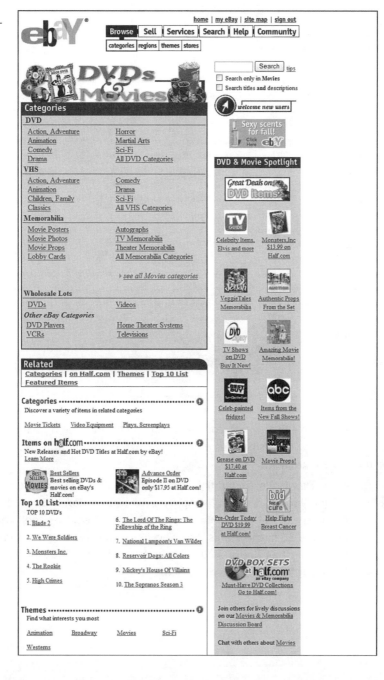

When you finally get to the list of items within a category or subcategory, the page looks like the one in Figure 5.2. At the top of the page are the Featured items (sellers pay extra for this placement); below that (or on the next page, sometimes) are the complete listings, with items ending soonest listed first.

FIGURE 5.2

eBay item listings.

All Items	Auctions	Buy It Now	⑦ Questions

Home > All Categories > Movies & Television > Video, Film > DVD > Westerns

Basic Search

☑ **only** in Westerns
☐ In titles & descriptions

[Search] Advanced Search

Show
- Gallery view
- Items near me
- Show all prices in $
- View ending times (Ends PDT)

More On eb Y
Related Items
- DVDs at Half.com
- Westerns Theme Pg
Popular Searches
- dvd
- john wayne
- western
- movies
Related Stores Stores
- PennyLaneVideo
- Sell2All
- Edith's Gallery
- OrderBox
Browse Stores

Westerns   Sell in this category
1172 items found
Show only: **current** | new today | ending today | going, going, gone

Picture hide	Featured Items - Current	Price	Bids	Time Left
	150 BRAND NEW DVD MOVIES - NO RESERVE!!	$102.50	8	21h 4m

To find out how to be listed in this section and seen by thousands, please visit this link Featured Auctions

Picture	Current Items - Current	Price	Bids	Time Left
📷	Tombstone Vista DTS DVD New! First bid wins!	$16.99 $16.99 ⁼Buy It Now	-	2d 21h 34m
📷	Man From Utah & Randy Rides Alone ~John Wayne	$1.99	-	6d 21h 05m
📷	Clint Eastwood - Guns - Western Poster	$6.99 $8.99 ⁼Buy It Now	-	6d 21h 01m
📷	GUNSLINGERS DVD-4 Movies- Van Cleef, Law	$4.95	-	6d 20h 54m
	John Wayne 2 dvd box set - New	$9.95	-	2d 20h 15m
	JOHN WAYNE-THE LUCKY TEXAN & DESERT TRAIL DVD	$4.95	-	2d 20h 15m
	JOHN WAYNE COLLECTOR SERIES DVD- 3 MOVIES!	$4.95	-	2d 20h 14m
	JOHN WAYNE - THE STAR PACKER & BLUE STEEL DVD	$4.95	-	2d 20h 14m
	Bonanza 2 dvd box set - Michael Landon	$7.95	-	2d 20h 12m
📷	Angel and the Badman dvd - John Wayne- New	$4.95	-	2d 20h 11m
	10 Classic Western dvds - J.Wayne/Lone Ranger	$39.95	-	2d 20h 11m
	YOUNG GUNS DVD Widescreen MINT!!!	$4.99	-	6d 20h 10m

Some listings have pictures or icons either before or after the title. If it's a picture, great; that means the listing has an accompanying photograph. Same thing if you see a green Picture icon.

If you see a yellow Gallery icon, that means the item is listed in eBay's Gallery. (The Gallery lets you browse through listing pictures, rather than listing text; you access the Gallery at pages.ebay.com/buy/gallery.html.) A Hot Item icon indicates that the item has received 30 or more bids. The New icon indicates that the item has been listed within the last 24 hours. And the Buy It Now icon indicates that the seller has chosen the Buy It Now option for this item.

Table 5.2 shows the various icons you might encounter.

TABLE 5.2   Listing Icons

Feature	Icon
Picture	
Gallery	
Hot Item	
New	
Buy It Now	

Searching: The Powerful Way to Find Things

You could browse through the merchandise categories listed on eBay's home page, as I just described, but given the huge number of categories, this could take forever—and, besides, you're never quite sure whether all sellers have picked the right categories for their merchandise. (Does a Batman statue belong in the **Collectibles: Comics: Figurines** category or the **Toys & Hobbies: Action Figures: Superhero** category?) In most cases, a better solution is to use eBay's built-in search engine.

Using eBay's Search Page

eBay's home page has a simple search box, but I prefer to use the more powerful Search page displayed when you click the Search link. That's because the Search page lets you search by a number of different criteria; you can search by listing title, by specific words in the listing, by item number, by location, by seller, or by bidder. You can even choose to search *completed* auctions—which is a great way to get a handle on final selling prices for various types of items.

Let's look at how you can use eBay's Search page for some of the more common types of searches.

Search by Title

To search for particular words in the listing's title, follow these steps:

1. From the Navigation Bar, click the Search link.
2. When the Search page appears, select the Search tab.

3. When the Basic Search page appears, as shown in Figure 5.3, enter one or more keywords in the Search Title box.

4. If you want to exclude listings with certain descriptions from your results, enter those keywords in the Words to Exclude box.

5. If you want to limit your search to specific categories, pull down the Search in Categories list and make a selection.

6. Click the Search button to start the search. eBay displays your results on a separate Items Matching page.

> **" Mike Sez "**
>
> All eBay search pages let you sort your results by items ending first, newly listed items, lowest-priced items, or highest-priced items. I like to display my results by ending date, with expiring auctions listed first; that way, I know what items must take priority in my bidding activities.

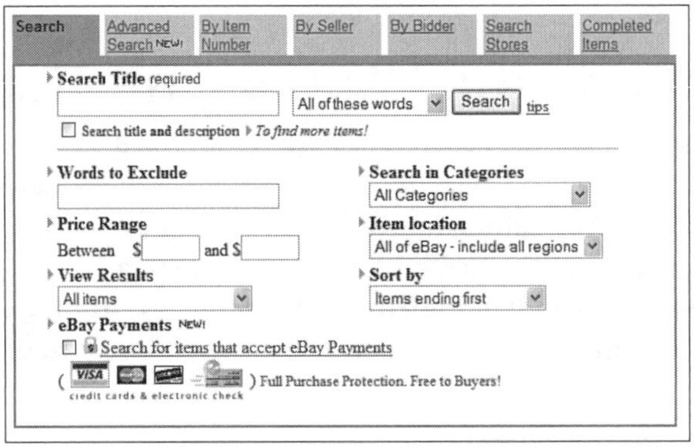

FIGURE 5.3

Searching via title and description on the Basic Search page.

Search by Description

You don't have to limit your searches to the item's title. You can also search the entire item description for any keyword that you specify. Just follow these steps:

1. From the Navigation Bar, click the Search link.

2. When the Search page appears, select the Search tab.

3. When the Basic Search page appears, enter one or more keywords in the Search Title box.

4. Check the Search Title and Description option.

5. Define other search parameters, as necessary.

6. Click the Search button to start the search. eBay displays your results on a separate Items Matching page.

Search by Price

If you're on a budget, you might want to limit your search to items within a certain price range. To perform a price-limited search, follow these steps:

1. From the Navigation Bar, click the Search link.

2. When the Search page appears, select the Search tab.

3. When the Basic Search page appears, enter one or more keywords in the Search Title box.

4. Enter the low and high prices you're willing to pay into the Price Range boxes.

5. Define other search parameters, as necessary.

6. Click the Search button to start the search. eBay displays your results on a separate Items Matching page.

Search by Location

There may be times when you only want to search for items within a certain region. Perhaps you're looking for a large item that would be too expensive to ship over long distances. Perhaps you want to limit your search to a particular geographic location. In any case, you can use eBay's regional filtering options to limit your searches to specific regions.

Follow these steps:

1. From the Navigation Bar, click the Search link.

2. When the Search page appears, select the Advanced Search tab.

3. When the Advanced Search page appears, as shown in Figure 5.4, enter one or more keywords in the Search box.

4. To limit your search to items that can be shipped to a specific country, go to the Location/International section, select the Items Available To option, and then select a region from the pull-down list.

5. To limit your search to sellers located in a specific region, go to the Location/International section, check the Items Located In option, and then select a region from the pull-down list.

6. Define other search parameters, as necessary.

7. Click the Search button to start the search. eBay displays your results on a separate Items Matching page.

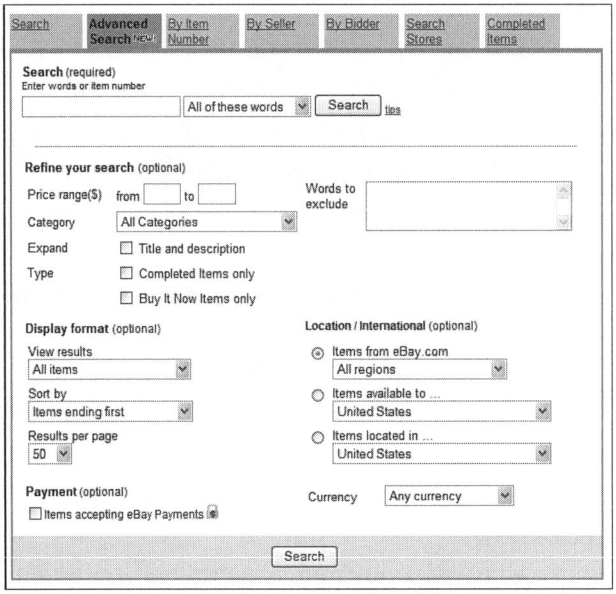

FIGURE 5.4

Use eBay's advanced search options to limit your search to specific regions.

Search for Completed Items

It's sometimes useful to search for items in auctions that have already ended. For example, you would search completed auctions if you want to find out what a certain item (or type of item) has actually sold for.

To search for completed items, use the Advanced Search page, as follows:

1. From the Navigation Bar, click the Search link.

2. When the Search page appears, select the Advanced Search tab.

3. When the Advanced Search page appears, enter one or more keywords in the Search Title box.

4. Check the Completed Items Only option (in the Refine Your Search section).

5. Define other search parameters, as necessary.

6. Click the Search button to start the search. eBay displays your results on a separate Items Matching page.

"Mike Sez"

You can also opt to display completed items after you've initiated a search. When the Items Matching page appears, go to the Show section at the left of the page, and then click the Completed Items link.

Search by Item Number

If someone has given you a specific item number to check out, you can use eBay's search function to track down and display that item. Follow these steps:

1. From the Navigation Bar, click the Search link.

2. When the Search page appears, select the By Item Number tab.

3. When the By Item Number page appears, enter the item number in the Item Number box.

4. Click the Search button to find and display the item you entered.

Search in eBay Stores

If you can't find an item for auction on eBay proper, you can opt to search items listed for sale in eBay Stores. eBay Stores is a collection of individuals and small merchants offering goods for sale at a fixed price. (Not for auction, in other words.) You can sometimes find items for sale in eBay Stores that you can't find elsewhere— including in eBay's normal auctions. Plus, all items you buy in eBay Stores can be paid for by credit card.

Follow these steps:

1. From the Navigation Bar, click the Search link.

2. When the Search page appears, select the Search Stores tab.

3. When the Search Stores page appears, enter one or more keywords in the Search Title box.

4. Define other search parameters, as necessary.

5. Click the Search button to start the search. eBay displays your results on a separate Items Matching page.

> **note**
>
> You can also access eBay stores directly at www.stores.ebay.com. Learn more about eBay Stores in Chapter 26, "Buying and Selling Right Now: eBay Stores and Half.com."

Search by Seller

Every now and then you come across a seller whom you trust, and who often has items for auction that you're interested in. You can search eBay to display all current auctions for that seller by following these steps:

1. From the Navigation Bar, click the Search link.

2. When the Search page appears, select the By Seller tab.

3. When the By Seller page appears, as shown in Figure 5.5, enter the seller's user ID in the Single Seller box.

4. Choose whether to display completed auctions—and if so, completed auctions for how many days in the past.

5. Click the Search button to start the search. eBay displays your results on a separate Items Matching page.

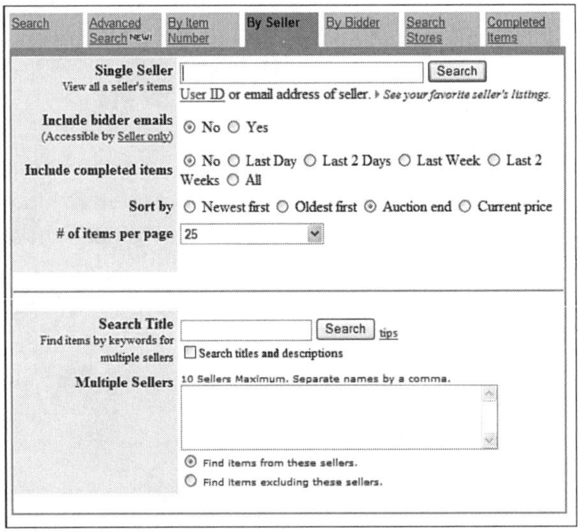

FIGURE 5.5

Searching for items listed by a specific seller.

Search by Bidder

Similarly, you can search eBay to display all auctions that have been bid on by a specific bidder. Follow these steps:

1. From the Navigation Bar, click the Search link.

2. When the Search page appears, select the By Bidder tab.

3. When the By Bidder page appears, enter the bidder's user ID in the Bidder's User ID box.

4. Choose whether to include completed items.

5. Choose whether to include items where the bidder is not the high bidder.

6. Click the Search button to start the search. eBay displays your results on a separate Items Matching page.

Complex Searches—for Simpler Results

To get the best results from your eBay searches, you need to know which commands and operators you can use in the various search boxes. You use these commands to help modify your keywords and fine-tune your searches. Table 5.3 lists the commands you can use when searching on eBay.

TABLE 5.3   eBay Search Commands

To Do This	Use This Command	Example
Search for part of a word	*	bat*
Search for either word	*(word1, word2)*	(batman,robin) (NOTE: Do not include spaces after the comma.)
Search for either word	@0	@0 batman robin (NOTE: No comma in between words.)
Include at least two of the words	@1	@1 batman robin batgirl (NOTE: No comma in between words.)
Search for an exact phrase	" "	"batman pez dispenser"
Must include a word	+	batman +pez
Must exclude a word	-	batman –pez
Most exclude two or more words	-*(word1, word2)*	-(batman,robin)
Include a year or number	#	#1972

Note that eBay automatically assumes that you want to search for items that match all the words in your query. This is the equivalent of inserting a Boolean AND between all the words in your query; a query for **batman robin** essentially looks for items that match "batman AND robin."

Practice Makes Perfect: Some Sample Searches

Let's quickly put together a few sample searches using some of the commands we've discussed.

> **caution**
>
> If you're an experienced searcher, you're probably used to using Boolean operators (AND, OR, NOT, and so on) to fine-tune your query. Well, forget your ANDs and NOTs; eBay doesn't permit the use of Boolean operators in its search function. In fact, if you enter Boolean operators in your query, eBay will treat them as keywords—and search for them!

First, say you want to look for all Batman-related merchandise. The search is simple; enter this query in the search box:

batman

That's almost too simple. What if you want to search not only for Batman, but also for Batgirl or Batmobile or Batplane or Bat*anything*? For this task, you apply the * wildcard to create this query:

bat*

Good enough. Now, let's make it more complex. You want to search for Bat stuff, but not *all* Bat stuff—just PEZ dispensers or costumes. For this search, enter this query:

bat* (pez,costume)

What if you want to look for something by title—such as the title of a movie? This is where you use quotation marks to surround the exact phrase you're searching for. If you want to search for anything associated with the movie *Batman Forever*, you enter this query:

"batman forever"

What if you want to search for Batman stuff but don't want anything related to Adam West? In this case, you use the exclude operator, in the form of a – sign, to automatically exclude any listings that include the designated word. The query looks like this:

batman –west

Conversely, if you only want to look at Batman items that had something to do with George Clooney, you use the include operator, in the form of a + sign, to search only for items that include that specific word. The query looks like this:

batman +clooney

You can also search for items in which the date of production is important. If you put a # in front of a number, eBay knows you're searching for a particular year. For example, assume you want to search for all Batman comics published in 1955. You use this query:

batman #1955

Finally, don't be afraid to string several of these commands together to create a more complex query—which will return more targeted results. Let's do a hypothetical search for all *Batman Forever* props and comics featuring George Clooney but not including Jim Carrey. (Whew!) Here's the query:

"batman forever" (prop,comic) +clooney –carrey

See how it works? It's a little like constructing an algebraic equation; you just have to think it through logically, and use all the tools you have at hand.

" Mike Sez "

Don't be surprised if you enter that complex sample query into eBay's search engine and end up with zero results. The more targeted the query you enter, the fewer results will be returned—and some queries can be so targeted that nothing matches at all.

Saving Your Searches—and Repeating Them

You've taken the time to create a complex search. You figure you'll want to repeat that search at some point in the future, to keep looking for the items you want. You don't want to reenter the query every time you perform the search.

What do you do?

When it comes to repeating your searches, eBay makes it easy. All Items Matching pages (which display your search results) include a Save This Search link, at the top right of the page. Click this link, and this search is now listed in the Saved Searches section of your My eBay page.

You can repeat a saved search by following these steps:

1. From the Navigation Bar, click the My eBay link.

2. On your My eBay Page, select the Favorites tab.

3. Click the My Favorite Searches link, or scroll down the page to the My Favorite Searches section, shown in Figure 5.6.

4. Identify the search you want to repeat and click that search's Search Now link.

The search is now executed, as originally entered.

tip

Your favorite searches are also displayed on the Favorites tab of your My eBay page.

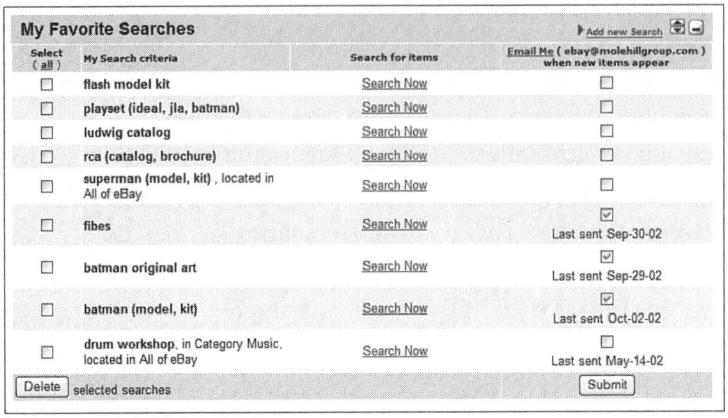

FIGURE 5.6

Saved searches
on your My
eBay page.

My Favorite Searches			Add new Search
Select (all)	**My Search criteria**	**Search for items**	**Email Me** (ebay@molehillgroup.com) when new items appear
☐	flash model kit	Search Now	☐
☐	playset (ideal, jla, batman)	Search Now	☐
☐	ludwig catalog	Search Now	☐
☐	rca (catalog, brochure)	Search Now	☐
☐	superman (model, kit) , located in All of eBay	Search Now	☐
☐	fibes	Search Now	☑ Last sent Sep-30-02
☐	batman original art	Search Now	☑ Last sent Sep-29-02
☐	batman (model, kit)	Search Now	☑ Last sent Oct-02-02
☐	drum workshop, in Category Music, located in All of eBay	Search Now	☐ Last sent May-14-02
Delete selected searches			Submit

Get Notification of New Items That Match Your Search

If you want to be automatically notified when
new items of a particular type come up for
auction, you're in luck. You can instruct eBay
to e-mail you when new items appear that
match any of your saved searches.

All you have to do is save a search, and then
navigate to the My Favorite Searches section
on your My eBay page. Check the Email Me
box next to the search you want to be notified
of, and then click the Submit button.

When you've activated this notification service, eBay will send you an e-mail (one a day)
when new items that match your search criteria
come up for auction. The e-mail contains links
for each new item in your search; click a link to
open your Web browser and display the matching item.

caution

eBay only lets you use e-
mail notification for up
to three saved searches.
Depending on your
needs, you might need to
pick and choose which three
searches you want to be notified
about—and perform periodic manual
searches for other saved searches.

" Mike Sez "

eBay's e-mail notifica-
tion service is a great
tool for active eBay bidders or for
anyone searching for that elusive
item. I love having eBay tell me
when it has something for me,
rather than having to log on and
do a manual search every day. I
highly recommend this service!

THE ABSOLUTE MINIMUM

Here are the key points to remember from this chapter:

- Browse through eBay's categories and subcategories when you're not sure of the exact item you're looking for.
- Use eBay's search pages to track down specific items for sale.
- Use wildcards and other search operators to fine-tune your item search.
- Click the Save This Search link to save your search criteria for future use—and then access your saved searches from your My eBay page.
- Activate eBay's e-mail notification service to have eBay notify you when desired items come up for auction.

6

THE BEST WAYS TO PAY

In practically all eBay auctions, the buyer has to pay before the seller ships; that's just the way it is. In effect, this means that the risk of the transaction is on the buyer; the buyer is trusting the seller to actually ship the merchandise (in the agreed-upon condition) when the payment is made.

With that in mind, how you pay is every bit as important as how much you pay. Read on to learn more about the payment options available— and to figure out which method of payment you should use.

Different Ways to Pay

How can you pay for your auction item? Well, you might not have too many choices. This is because most experienced sellers specify which methods of payment they'll accept, right up front in the item listing. So, even if you want to pay by credit card, if the seller doesn't accept plastic, you're out of luck.

tip

Always check which methods of payment are accepted by a seller before you place a bid.

Paying by Cash

Nothing could be simpler. Cram some greenbacks and a few coins into an envelope, stick a stamp on it, and you're done.

Right?

Wrong.

Paying by cash is definitely the least recommended method of payment. There are a few reasons for this, all involved with safety.

First, it's hard to hide cash in an envelope. Even if you wrap the bills in several sheets of paper and use a double envelope, there's something about a wad of cash that draws attention.

Second, it's easy to steal. Some disreputable types might see a cash-laden envelope sitting in a mailbox and make a grab for it. Easy to do.

Third, there's nothing to track. If the seller says he never received your payment, there's nothing to trace to prove otherwise. (That's why cash is the preferred method of payment for illegal drug dealers—it's virtually untraceable.)

So, unless the auction item is priced absurdly low (so low you don't care if the money gets ripped off), you should probably avoid paying by cash.

Paying by Check

The most popular method of payment is a personal check. Some sellers might not like accepting checks, for a number of reasons. Checks are too easy for the buyer to cancel, which could leave the seller in the lurch. Plus, it's difficult for a seller to verify if funds actually exist for payment.

" Mike Sez "

As much as I'd like to say otherwise, I have to admit to paying cash on a few very rare occasions, all of them in the weeks prior to Christmas, and all on very low-priced items. (And I sweated through each and every one of those transactions, until the items finally arrived!)

In addition, paying by check will probably slow down your item's shipment. That's because smart sellers wait for the check to clear before they ship your item. However, for most buyers, paying by check is just about the easiest way to go.

Let's face it. Most other methods of payment—especially cashier's checks and money orders—are a bit of a hassle. To draw a money order or cashier's check, you have to make a special trip to the bank or the post office, stand in line, pay a fee, and only *then* can you send your payment. With a personal check, you write the check from the comfort of your own desk, pop it in an envelope, and have the payment in the mail almost immediately.

Know, however, that some sellers will hold items paid for by a personal check for 1–2 weeks, until the check clears your bank. Other sellers will look at a buyer's feedback rating, and if it's strong, they'll go ahead and ship the merchandise when they receive the check. (That's one good use for eBay's feedback rating, as discussed in Chapter 24, "Understanding and Using Feedback.") But don't expect all sellers to ship immediately if you pay by personal check, especially if they haven't dealt with you before or you're a relatively new user of the auction site.

Paying by Money Order or Cashier's Check

Most sellers state that they prefer cashier's checks or money orders, and try to discourage payment by personal check. This is understandable; to the seller, cashier's checks and money orders are just like cash, but a personal check isn't good until it clears the bank.

To you, the buyer, there are three potential downsides to paying via money order or cashier's check. First, it's a hassle; you have to go to the bank or post office or credit union, wait in line, fill out a form, and then arrange funding. Depending on your local conditions, that's probably a 15- to 30-minute effort.

Second, depending on where you get your money orders, there may be a fee involved. The U.S. Postal Service, for example, charges 90 cents to cut a money order. Your bank may charge less (or more—or, in rare instances, nothing), but it's one more fee to add to what you're paying for the auction item. If you won a relatively low-priced item, the charge might not be worth it.

Finally, cashier's checks and money orders are, like cash, virtually untraceable. You get no record of the money order or cashier's check being cashed, so if the seller says he never cashed or received your payment, it's your word against his.

Paying by Credit Card

Paying via credit card is a pretty good deal for most buyers. Assuming you pay your credit card bill at the end of the month, there are no fees involved. Unlike with money orders or cashier's checks, you don't have to leave home to arrange payment.

You also have an excellent paper trail for your payment; you know almost immediately if the seller has received payment. And, unlike personal checks, credit cards ensure faster shipment; as soon as you authorize payment, the buyer receives his funds and can ship the item to you.

Unfortunately, most private individuals don't have the capability to accept credit-card payment—and most sellers on eBay happen to be individuals. Many small businesses sell items on eBay, however, and most of these firms *do* accept payment by credit card.

There is, however, a way for an individual seller to accept credit card payments—by using an online payment service. eBay recently acquired PayPal, the largest of these services, and offers payment via PayPal as an option in all of its auctions. If you see a PayPal logo in the item listing, you're in luck; that means you can use your credit card to pay, if you win.

tip

If you need an item in a hurry—around the holidays, for example—choosing a seller who accepts credit cards can be the key to a successful transaction. (If in doubt, e-mail the seller while the auction is still in progress and ask!)

Paying Cash on Delivery

You might occasionally have the option of C.O.D. (cash on delivery) payment. Although rare when buying from an individual, this is a good route to take if you can. With C.O.D. payment, you don't actually part with your money until you receive the merchandise—and you can't stiff the seller, either, because if you don't pay the delivery guy, he doesn't give you your stuff.

Using Escrow

A final option, used primarily in higher-priced auctions, is the use of an escrow service. This is a company that acts as a neutral third party between the buyer (you) and the seller, holding your money until you receive the seller's merchandise. If you don't get the goods (or the goods are unacceptable), you get your money back; the seller gets paid only when you're happy.

note

When you opt to pay for an auction via eBay Payments, you're paying by credit card—using PayPal.

Learn more about PayPal in Chapter 30, "Using PayPal and Other Payment Services."

eBay recommends using escrow for all auctions above $500.

Here's how a typical escrow transaction works:

1. At the end of an auction, you and the seller contact each other and agree to use an escrow service. The escrow service's fees can be split between the two parties or (more typically) be paid by you, the buyer. Fees differ widely from service to service.

2. You send payment (by check, money order, cashier's check, or credit card) to the escrow service.

3. After your payment is approved, the escrow service instructs the seller to ship the item.

4. You receive the item, verify its acceptability, and notify the escrow service that all is hunky-dory.

5. The escrow service pays the seller.

Although you can use any third-party escrow service, eBay offers its own escrow services as part of the end-of-auction process. Just go to Escrow.com (www.escrow.com) and follow the instructions there to initiate the escrow procedure. Escrow.com will inform you of all the details regarding the use of escrow for your transaction.

Evaluating Different Methods of Payments

Now you know how you *can* pay; you still want to know how you *should* pay.

Which Method Is Fastest?

When it comes to speed, paying by credit card (either directly or via PayPal or eBay Payments) wins hands down. The seller receives his funds a few seconds after you click the Send button on the payment page, which means that shipment can occur almost immediately.

Paying by personal check is definitely the slowest method. Not only do you have to wait for the postal service to deliver your check to the seller, but you also have to wait for the seller to wait—for your check to clear your bank. All this waiting means that the seller probably won't be able to ship your item for at least two weeks after the end of the auction, and maybe longer.

Coming somewhere in the middle are money orders, cashier's checks, and plain old cash. You still have to depend on snail-mail delivery of your payment, but when the seller receives it, he can ship your item immediately. Depending on the speed of the mail, figure anywhere from two days to a week before your item is shipped.

Which Method Is Safest?

Of course, how you pay for an item can increase or decrease your protection during a transaction; some methods of payment are safer for you than others.

The least safe method of payment for a buyer is cash; there's nothing to track, and it's very easy for someone to steal an envelope full of cash. Also considered less safe (although better than cash) are cashier's checks and money orders; like cash, they provide no money trail to trace if you want to track down the seller. Paying by check gives you a minor trail to trace, but when the check is cashed, it's still pretty much a done deal.

> **" Mike Sez "**
>
> If you have the choice (and have a credit card), my personal recommendation is to pay by plastic. You'll have a paper trail if anything goes south, as well as protection from your credit card company (above a certain amount). If payment by plastic isn't available, I pay by check if I'm not in a hurry, or by money order if I am.

A safer way to pay is by credit card. When you pay by credit card, you can always go to the credit card company and dispute your charges if the item you bought never arrived or was misrepresented. The same safety measures typically apply to credit card payments made through PayPal and other bill pay services—although you should check with the bill pay service, just to be sure.

For the ultimate protection when buying an expensive item in a person-to-person option, use an escrow service. Because the escrow service acts as a neutral third party between you and the seller, if you don't receive what you won—or are otherwise dissatisfied with the item—you get your money back, guaranteed.

Which Method Should You Use?

Use Table 6.1 to determine how you want to pay, based on several key conditions.

TABLE 6.1   When to Use Which Payment Method

Situation	Payment Method
Very low-priced item (<$5.00 total), trusted seller, no time to write a check or get to the bank	Cash
Low-priced item, no hurry for shipment	Check
Low-priced item, need fast shipment, trusted seller, don't want to use credit card	Money order/cashier's check
Higher-priced item *or* need fast shipment *or* desire fraud protection	Credit card/PayPal/eBay Payments
High-priced item, desire protection in case item doesn't meet expectations, don't mind paying additional fees	Escrow

THE ABSOLUTE MINIMUM

Here are the key points to remember from this chapter:

- Paying by cash is very unsafe, but can result in relatively fast shipping.

- Paying by cashier's check or money order is just as fast as paying by cash, and slightly safer.

- Paying by personal check is safer than cashier's check or money order and provides a nice paper trail—but can slow down shipment of your item by 1–2 weeks.

- Paying by credit card is probably the best way to go, when available (typically via PayPal); it's fast and safe.

- For really expensive items, consider using an escrow service. For a fee, the escrow service holds onto your funds until you receive the item—and are 100% satisfied.

7

AFTER THE AUCTION: TAKING CARE OF BUSINESS

You've somehow waited patiently (or not) throughout the entire auction progress. As the clock ticked down to zero, no other viable competitors entered the arena, and your high bid stood. You won!

Now things *really* start to happen.

Use the Post-Auction Checklist

When you're an auction winner, you have a bit of work to do. Work through the tasks in this post-auction checklist to make sure you've covered all the bases.

Checklist: After You've Won

- ☐ Wait for the seller to contact you
- ☐ Respond to the seller's e-mail

    or

- ☐ Use eBay's Checkout feature
- ☐ Choose a shipping method, if a choice is offered
- ☐ Decide whether you want insurance
- ☐ Choose a payment method
- ☐ Send payment
- ☐ Receive the item
- ☐ Examine the item
- ☐ E-mail the seller that you've received the item
- ☐ Leave feedback for the seller

Making Contact

The first thing that is supposed to happen after an auction ends is that eBay should send you an e-mail notifying you that you've won the aforementioned auction. I say the first thing, because sometimes eBay's system is a little slow; I most often receive notification within an hour of the auction end, but sometimes this notification doesn't come till the next day!

Figure 7.1 shows a typical end-of-auction notification from eBay.

In any case, if the seller is conscientious, he or she should send you an e-mail on their own. The seller's e-mail should tell you how much you need to pay (your high bid amount plus shipping and handling) and where to send the payment.

If you don't hear from the seller within 24 hours, you should take the initiative and send your own e-mail. Click the seller's name on the listing page to generate an e-mail message, introduce yourself, and gently inquire about shipping and handling costs and where you should send your payment.

FIGURE 7.1

Congratulations—you're a winner!

Checking Out

Many sellers opt to use eBay's Checkout service. (This isn't mandatory, and some sellers don't like—and don't use—the service.) If your seller opted to enable the Checkout service, a Checkout section appears on the item listing page at the end of the auction. (A link to this item's Checkout also appears in eBay's end-of-auction e-mail notification.)

The contents of the Checkout section will differ depending on how the seller has set up the auction. If the seller hasn't specified shipping/handling charges, you'll see a section like that shown in Figure 7.2; you'll need to click the Request Total Amount button to enter your shipping info and find out how much you owe. (Depending on how much information the seller supplied with his item listing, you might also see an option to prompt the seller to send payment information.)

FIGURE 7.2

The Checkout section of a closed auction where the seller hasn't specified shipping/handling costs.

If the seller has specified shipping/handling, you'll see a Checkout section like the one in Figure 7.3. Click the Pay Now button to provide your shipping address and specify a payment method.

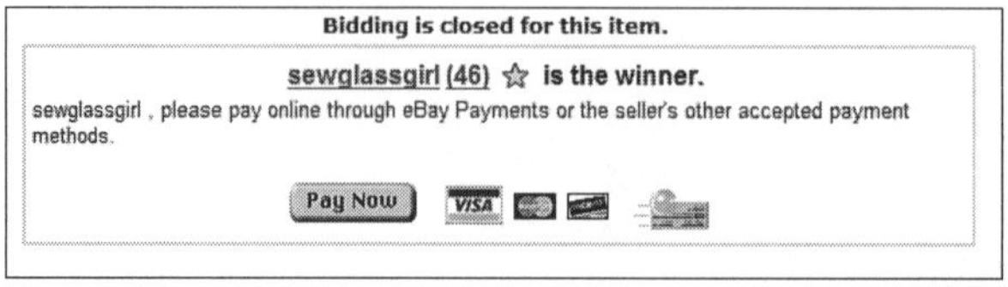

FIGURE 7.3

When you see this Checkout section, you can complete the end-of-auction process with the click of a button.

> **Bidding is closed for this item.**
>
> **sewglassgirl (46)** ☆ **is the winner.**
>
> sewglassgirl , please pay online through eBay Payments or the seller's other accepted payment methods.
>
> **Pay Now** VISA

When you enter the Checkout system, you'll be prompted to enter your shipping information and specify how you want to pay. If you decide to pay via eBay Payments or PayPal, you can enter your payment information right here; otherwise, you'll need to mail your payment, as normal. When you're finished with Checkout, eBay displays a Checkout Summary page that displays all the details of the transaction.

" Mike Sez "

It's a good idea to print the Checkout Summary page—or the completed item listing page—and send along with any payment you send via mail. This way the buyer will have detailed information on what should be shipped, how, and where.

Arranging Payment

After you've heard from the seller or used eBay's Checkout service, it's time to pay.

In most cases, the price you pay will include your high bid and a reasonable amount of shipping and handling fees. Don't be surprised if the shipping/handling actually runs a little more than what you might know the actual shipping to be; remember, the seller has to cover the costs of packaging and (in some sellers' minds) the cost of listing the item on eBay. If shipping/handling runs a few bucks more than actual shipping, don't sweat it.

You should also think about whether you need insurance on this item. In most cases buyers don't opt for insurance, but if you're buying a high-priced, rare, or very fragile item, you might want to protect yourself against damage in shipment.

note

Remember, in the world of online auctions, the buyer pays for everything—including shipping. Don't expect the seller to throw in shipping for free! Remember to mentally add the approximate shipping costs to your bid price on any item, so you're prepared for the total cost when the auction is over.

Many sellers offer several different shipping options (insurance versus no insurance, UPS versus FedEx versus USPS Priority Mail, and so on), at different costs to you. Others only ship one way. If given the choice, pick the best compromise between cost and speed. If not given the choice, live with it. If you have special shipping concerns (for example, FedEx doesn't deliver to your address), now is the time to raise them with the seller and reach some sort of agreement on how you'll get the goods and who'll absorb the costs. (That would be you, the buyer.)

Also, find out what kind of payment the seller wants. Short of receiving cash in the mail (never a good idea), most sellers prefer to be paid as fast and as securely as possible. As you learned in Chapter 6, "The Best Ways to Pay," paying by credit card is the best option, when it's available. Some sellers might strongly prefer payment by money order or cashier's check, but you might strongly prefer paying by check. In any case, verify the method of payment before you send the payment so there are no surprises. Figure out when you should receive the item shipped, and make a note to e-mail the seller if you don't receive it by that date. (Allow a few extra days of wiggle room just to be fair.)

If you're paying by personal check, now is the time to write the check and put it in the mail. If you're paying by cashier's check or money order, head to the bank or post office, cut a payment, and then put it in the mail. Remember to include your name and shipping address, along with the item number and description, with your payment.

If you're paying by credit card, payment is a little different. If you're buying from a merchant seller, you may be directed to that seller's retail Web site to arrange payment. If you're buying from a seller using PayPal, you can pay either through eBay's Checkout, or by clicking the PayPal logo on the item listing page. If your seller is using another online payment service, look for a logo to click or instructions on how to pay, somewhere on the item listing page.

> **" Mike Sez "**
>
> Insurance used to be cheap. Now you'll pay $1.30 for $50 worth of insurance at the U.S. Postal Service, which isn't a great deal. Plus, the USPS makes it a hassle to collect, if anything goes wrong. Still, depending on the price and damageability of the item, it might be worth it.

> **caution**
>
> When it comes to providing your credit card information, make sure you're working in a secure environment. That means you *don't* send your credit card numbers via e-mail (too easily hijacked), or enter it at an unsecured Web site. Look for a site that uses a secure server, or arrange to phone in your information.

Waiting for Your Doorbell to Ring...

Now you wait for the item to arrive. If the wait is too long, you should contact the seller and confirm that the item was actually shipped out on a particular date; if an item appears to be lost in shipment, the two of you can work together to track down the shipment with the shipping service.

This is also the stage of the process where some unlucky buyers discover that they're dealing with deadbeat sellers—frauds who take your money but never ship your item. If you find yourself in this situation, there are options available to you; turn to Chapter 8, "Dealing with Fraudulent Sellers," to learn more.

Receiving the Goods

In most cases the item arrives promptly. Now you should unpack the item and inspect it for any damage. If the item is something that can be tried out, you should make sure that the item actually works. If all is fine, e-mail the seller to say that you received the merchandise and that you're happy. If all isn't fine, e-mail the seller and let them know that you have a problem.

If you have a problem—or if you didn't receive the merchandise at all after a reasonable amount of time—you should first try to work out a compromise with the seller. Most sellers will bend over backwards to make you happy; some won't.

> **" Mike Sez "**
>
> When your item arrives, check it out immediately. Don't wait a month before determining that there's something wrong; find out now whether the item is in good shape and delivers what was promised.

If you can't work out anything with the seller, turn to eBay for assistance. See Chapter 8 for instructions on what to do when a deal goes bad.

Finishing Things Up and Leaving Feedback

You've made your bid, won the auction, paid the seller, and received the merchandise. Now you're done—right?

Wrong.

The last thing you need to do is leave feedback about the seller. Whether it was a good transaction or a bad one, you need to let your fellow eBay members know how things turned out.

To leave feedback, go to the listing page for the item you just bought, click the Leave Feedback to Seller link, and then fill in the resulting form. You can leave positive, negative, or neutral feedback, as well as a one-line comment about the transaction. Make sure you really want to leave the comments you've written, and then click the Leave Comment button. Your feedback will be registered and added to the seller's other feedback comments.

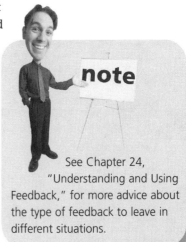

note

See Chapter 24, "Understanding and Using Feedback," for more advice about the type of feedback to leave in different situations.

THE ABSOLUTE MINIMUM

Here are the key points to remember from this chapter:

- When an auction is over, the auction site notifies both you and the seller via e-mail.
- The seller must contact you—and you must respond—within three working days.
- The seller will inform you of the total amount you owe, including shipping/handling and insurance (if you opt for it).
- Alternately, in some auctions you can use eBay's Checkout feature (located on the item listing page) to consummate your transaction.
- The buyer sends payment to the seller, normally via personal check, cashier's check, or money order.
- Upon payment, the seller packs and ships the item to you.
- After you receive the merchandise, let the seller know that you're satisfied (or not) and leave feedback on the eBay site.

8

DEALING WITH FRAUDULENT SELLERS

When you're bidding and buying items on eBay, you're pretty much in "buyer beware" territory. You agree to buy an item, almost sight unseen, from someone whom you know practically nothing about. You send that person a check and hope and pray that you get something shipped back in return—and that the thing that's shipped is the thing you thought you were buying, in good condition. If you don't like what you got—or if you received nothing at all—the seller has your money. And what recourse do you have?

Remember, when you buy something through an eBay auction, when it comes down to making the financial transaction, you're dealing with an individual—*not* eBay. And as you'll soon learn, every person you deal with behaves differently and expects different behavior of you. In the course of your eBay dealings, it's not unlikely that you might run into a shady seller who never sends you the item you purchased—or tries to pass off a lower-quality item for what was described in the item listing. What can you do to protect yourself against other users who aren't as honest as you are?

Fortunately, you can do several things to protect yourself on eBay—and, in general, shopping at eBay is no more dangerous than shopping at a local garage sale. This chapter details some of the standard guidelines and procedures you can follow to ensure that your eBay buying and selling experience is not only successful, but profitable and enjoyable as well.

Protecting Yourself Before You Buy

The first line of defense against frauds and cheats is to intelligently choose the people you deal with. On eBay, the best way to do this is via the Feedback system.

You should always check a seller's Feedback rating before you bid. If it's overwhelmingly positive, you can feel safer than if the seller has a lot of negative feedback. For even better protection, click the seller's Feedback rating in the item listing to read individual feedback comments—and studiously avoid those sellers who have a history of delivering less than what was promised.

Some buyers go to the extreme of bidding only on items listed by Verified eBay Users. Verified users (identified as such by an icon on the item listing page) have had their addresses confirmed by eBay, thus ensuring that they're probably who they say they are. The only problem with this approach is that few users go through the hassle of becoming verified; it's possible you might never encounter a verified user in the course of your auction dealings.

note

See Chapter 24, "Understanding and Using Feedback," for more information.

"Mike Sez"

eBay regards its Feedback system as the best protection against fraudulent transactions. I certainly recommend that, whether a transaction went swell or went south, you leave feedback about your partner in every transaction. I know that I check the feedback rating of every seller I choose to deal with; it really is a good way to judge the quality of the other party in your eBay transactions.

A better approach is to find out more about the person who's selling the item. To do this, click the Search link at the top of any eBay page, and then click Find Members. This displays the Find Members page, shown in Figure 8.1. From here you can view the user's ID history (shifty users sometimes change IDs frequently) and contact info. Just enter the user's ID in the appropriate box and click the Submit button.

All this info, however, still doesn't tell you a lot about the seller. If you still have doubts, e-mail the seller and ask for more info. (This is easy to do from the item listing page—just click the Ask Seller a Question link.) If the seller won't work with you—or if the information doesn't check out—then don't deal with him!

caution

You can only request user info if you're a bidder in an active auction, the winning bidder in a recently closed auction, or if you're a seller looking to check up on current bidders—or the winning bidder.

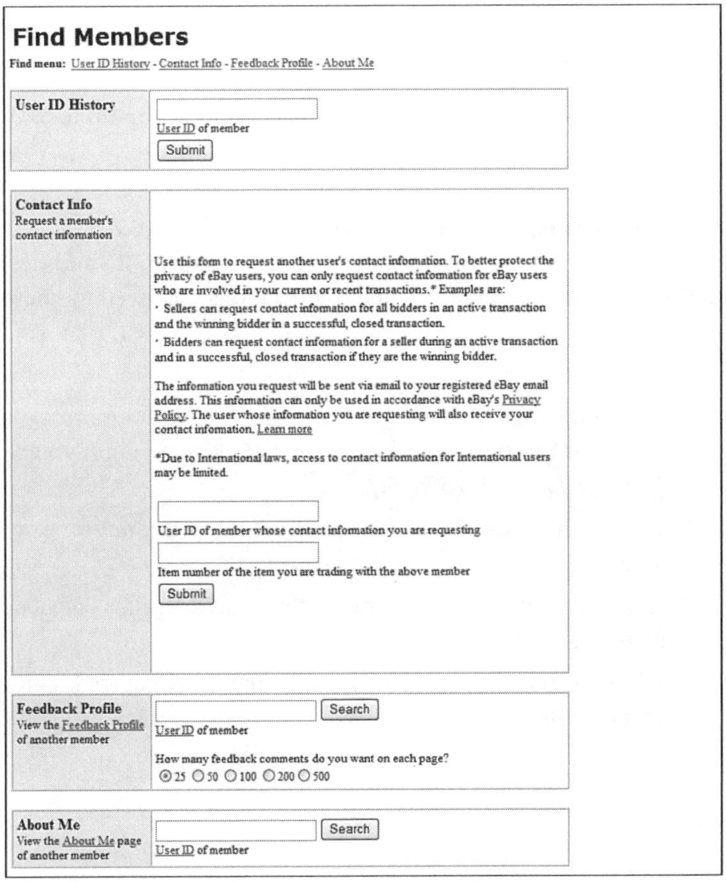

FIGURE 8.1

Use the Find Members page to learn more about any eBay user.

Find Members

Find menu: User ID History - Contact Info - Feedback Profile - About Me

User ID History

User ID of member

Submit

Contact Info
Request a member's
contact information

Use this form to request another user's contact information. To better protect the privacy of eBay users, you can only request contact information for eBay users who are involved in your current or recent transactions.* Examples are:

· Sellers can request contact information for all bidders in an active transaction and the winning bidder in a successful, closed transaction.

· Bidders can request contact information for a seller during an active transaction and in a successful, closed transaction if they are the winning bidder.

The information you request will be sent via email to your registered eBay email address. This information can only be used in accordance with eBay's Privacy Policy. The user whose information you are requesting will also receive your contact information. Learn more

*Due to International laws, access to contact information for International users may be limited.

User ID of member whose contact information you are requesting

Item number of the item you are trading with the above member

Submit

Feedback Profile
View the Feedback Profile
of another member

Search

User ID of member

How many feedback comments do you want on each page?
⊙ 25 ○ 50 ○ 100 ○ 200 ○ 500

About Me
View the About Me page
of another member

Search

User ID of member

Protecting Yourself After the Auction

What do you do if you follow all this advice and still end up receiving unacceptable merchandise—or no merchandise at all?

First, know that eBay doesn't accept any responsibility for any transactions conducted on its site. It's not the buyer or the seller, only a relatively disinterested third party.

However, that doesn't mean you shouldn't contact eBay if you're the recipient of a sour deal—

you should, and eBay encourages you to do so. At the very least, eBay will start tracking the seller's other activities and perhaps kick them off the site if a pattern of fraudulent activity can be shown. Best case scenario, eBay will actually refund some of the money you've lost.

Getting Help from eBay

eBay offers a Fraud Protection Program that protects you up to $200 (with a $25 deductible) for any auction transaction gone bad.

Understanding the Fraud Protection Program

You can participate in eBay's Fraud Protection Program if you have a feedback rating of zero or above. Here are some of the details you need to know:

- You're insured (for up to $200) on items with a final value over $25. If the item is priced under $25, you're on your own.

- There's a $25 deductible on each claim. If you submit a claim for a $35 item, you'll get $10 back ($35 minus the $25 deductible). If you submit a claim for $200, you'll get $175 back.

- You'll only be reimbursed for the final bid price, not for any other fees—such as shipping, handling, or escrow fees.

- To qualify, both your feedback rating and the seller's feedback rating have to be zero or above.

- All items that meet eBay's user agreement are covered; items that violate the user agreement aren't covered.

- You can get reimbursed if you send money to a seller and you don't receive the item. You can also get reimbursed if you receive the item, but it's significantly different than described in the auction listing. However, you won't be reimbursed if something happens to the item in transit; if the shipping company loses or damages the item, that's the company's problem to fix.

- You have to wait until 30 days after the auction to begin the complaint process—and have to file within 60 days of the auction end.

- If you paid by credit card, you can only file a Fraud Protection claim if the credit card company has denied your request for a refund—which means that you contact your credit card company first, and eBay second.

- You can file a maximum of three claims in a six-month period.

Filing a Claim

How do you get your money back if you've been burned? First, make sure you have the following information handy:

Here are the basic steps to take:

1. Somewhere between 30 and 60 days after the end of the auction, go to `pages.ebay.com/help/community/fpp.html` to access the Fraud Protection Program page. Scroll down and click the Report Suspicious Activity link, then complete the Online Fraud Reporting Complaint Form.

2. eBay will notify the seller that an Online Fraud Complaint has been filed, and suggest that the seller contact you to resolve the situation. The seller has 30 days to resolve the situation.

3. At the end of 30 days, assuming the seller doesn't do anything to resolve the situation, you now return to the Fraud Protection Program page and click the File a Protection Claim link. Follow the instructions there to access and print a copy of the Fraud Protection claim form.

4. Gather the requested information and send to the eBay Claims Administrator, per the address supplied. The information you need to provide includes the completed and signed claim form, a printed copy of the eBay item listing page, proof of payment (photocopy of the money order, personal check, charge card statement, and so on), and any other supporting paperwork.

5. Sometime in the next 45 days you will be contacted by the eBay Claims Administrator. If your claim is approved, you'll be sent a check for the disputed amount (less the $25 deductible).

I hope you'll never have to use eBay's Fraud Protection Program. But if you are the unfortunate recipient of an unscrupulous seller, it's good to know that eBay is looking out for you.

Resolving Conflicts

Sometimes a problem auction doesn't have a clear-cut good guy and bad guy. If you ever find yourself in an extreme finger-pointing situation, it might be time to engage in online dispute resolution.

eBay uses SquareTrade's Online Dispute Resolution service (www.squaretrade.com) to mediate these sticky types of disputes. If you're having trouble resolving a complaint with a seller, just go to SquareTrade's Web site and file a complaint; this automatically signs you up with the site's automated Direct Negotiation Service. This service is free, and does a good job of coming to a mutually agreeable middle ground. (Assuming, of course, that the seller agrees to participate.)

If, however, you and the seller still don't agree, you can use one of SquareTrade's human mediators to (hopefully) create a fair solution to your problem. (The use of a human mediator costs $20.) If this still doesn't resolve your problem, you can then revert to eBay's Fraud Protection Program.

Beyond eBay

Beyond eBay, you can contact other agencies if you've been disadvantaged in a deal. For example, if mail fraud is involved (which it is if any part of the transaction— either payment or shipping—was handled through the mail), you can file a complaint with your local U.S. Post Office or state attorney general's office. If you've had a large amount of money ripped off or if your credit card number was stolen, you should also contact your local police department.

You can file a complaint about any fraudulent auction transaction with the Federal Trade Commission (FTC) by contacting the FTC Consumer Response Center via phone (202-382-4357), mail (Consumer Response Center, Federal Trade Commission, Washington, DC 20580), or the Internet (www.ftc.gov). Although the FTC doesn't resolve individual consumer problems, it can and will act if it sees a pattern of possible law violations.

Reporting Inappropriate Behavior

There is a long list of activities that buyers and sellers can engage in that eBay expressly prohibits. Most of these offenses—listed in the sections following—involve blatantly manipulating auction results, whether by the seller or an overly interested bidder. If eBay catches a user doing any of these, that user will either be temporarily suspended (kind of a first warning) or permanently banned from the service.

Of course, you have to be caught before you can be punished. The main way eBay finds out about these activities is from other users—the real victims of these offensive behaviors.

If you suspect any of these bidding offenses in any specific auction (even if you yourself are not participating in the auction), you want to notify eBay at SafeHarbor@ebay.com or pages.ebay.com/help/ community/. Make sure you include all relevant information and copies of all e-mail correspondence with the suspected offender.

What activities are we talking about? The following sections discuss the most common of these bad behaviors. Remember, all of these activities are unethical and can get a user kicked off eBay permanently. Even worse, some of these activities are illegal, and can result in prosecution.

Shill Bidding

Shill bidding, quite simply, is bidding on your own item in a deliberate attempt to artificially drive up its price. A shill bid can involve the use of secondary eBay registrations, user aliases, family members, friends, or associates to pump up the price; other bidders then have to top a higher price to stay in the game.

> **note**
>
> Even though the presence of multiple user accounts is one possible factor in shill bidding, eBay does allow sellers to have more than one registration. This is subject to several provisions, chief of which is that there can never be any interaction between the registrations, especially in the areas of bidding and feedback. In addition, eBay requires that the registered user information must be identical for all accounts. (Of course, this begs the question: How can eBay tell you have multiple accounts if you enter different information for each registration?)

One of the more common ways to bid on one's own items is to create a second eBay account using a different e-mail address. Using this apparently unrelated user ID, it's easy to bid on your own items.

Bid Shielding

Bid shielding is the practice of using shill bidding (but not a shill associated with the seller) to artificially increase the price of an item temporarily, in an attempt to protect the low bid level of a third bidder. Essentially, the artificially high bid scares off other bidders, and then the shill retracts the super-high bid at the last moment, leaving the bidding wide open for the initial, lower bidder.

Bid Siphoning

Bid siphoning happens when a third party (unrelated to the seller or bidder) e-mails bidders in a currently open auction, offering a similar or identical item at a price below the current bid level. This siphons off potential sales away from the registered seller and makes an end-run around eBay's fee system.

Bid Discovery

If a bidder is losing an auction and wants to know what maximum bid level has been specified by the current high bidder (which is not divulged by eBay), he can engage in bid discovery. Bid discovery happens when the bidder places a very high bid on the item (well over the current high bidder's assumed maximum bid level) and then retracts the bid. This returns the high bid to the former high bidder, but at that bidder's maximum bid level—which wasn't previously public.

Unwanted Bidding

Sellers don't have to sell to any specific bidder. In fact, it's somewhat common for a seller to specify that he or she will refuse to sell to users with negative feedback ratings—or to e-mail specific bidders warning them away from bidding.

If you've been warned away from an auction yet persist in bidding on that seller's items, you're breaking eBay's rules. If the seller reports you to eBay, you can be indefinitely suspended from the service.

Backing Out of Transactions—*Repeatedly*

If you are the winning bidder on an item and never send payment, you create an incomplete transaction (not to mention block legitimate bidders from buying an item and keep the seller from getting paid).

If you're selling an item but you back out of the sale (without accepting payment), you also create an incomplete transaction. Of course, if you back out of the sale after you accept the buyer's money, you commit a criminal offense (as well as create an incomplete transaction!).

Although backing out of one or two transactions won't win you any friends, it also won't get you kicked off eBay. However, if you back out of a lot of transactions—as either a buyer or a seller—eBay will toss you off. It's chronic incomplete transactions that eBay notices.

Auction Interference

Another no-no still happens on occasion: One bidder sends threatening e-mails to other bidders to warn them away from a seller or an item. You're not allowed to interfere with in-process auctions—and you're *definitely* not allowed to threaten other users! eBay will bump you if they find out.

Transaction Interception

This trick is out-and-out fraud. You represent yourself as another eBay seller, intercepting the ended auctions of that seller (generally with forged e-mail messages) and convincing buyers to send you payment for the items. Getting caught at this one will cause you more trouble than just a simple eBay expulsion.

Spamming

eBay doesn't like you to send bulk e-mail (spam) to masses of other users. If eBay finds out, it'll kick you off, simple as that.

Tips for Protecting Yourself on eBay

When all is said and done, eBay is a fairly safe environment to conduct person-to-person transactions. The vast majority of eBay users are honest individuals, and you'll no doubt enjoy hundreds of good transactions before you hit your first bad one.

That said, here are some tips on how to better protect yourself when you're dealing on eBay:

- Remember that you're dealing with human beings. Be nice, be polite, and, above all, *communicate!* Send e-mails confirming receipt of payment or shipment of merchandise. Say "please" and "thank you." And don't send short, snippy e-mails in the heat of the moment. Be tolerant and friendly, and you'll be a better eBay citizen.

- Realize that, in most cases, you're dealing with individuals, not businesses. Keep that in mind if things don't go quite as smoothly as they would if you ordered from Amazon.com or L.L. Bean. Most folks don't have automated shipping systems installed in their living rooms!

- Know that experienced eBay users take the feedback system very seriously—if not obsessively. Positive feedback is expected for every successful transaction, and negative feedback should only be used in the most dire of circumstances. When in doubt, just don't leave any feedback at all.

- If you have questions about an item for sale, or about any part of the transaction, ask! E-mail the seller if you're not sure about payment or shipping terms. Good communication eliminates surprises and misinterpretations; don't assume anything.

- When the item you purchased arrives, inspect it thoroughly and confirm that it's as described. If you feel you were misled, contact the seller immediately, explain the situation, and see what you can work out. (You'd be surprised how many sellers will go out of their way to make their customers happy.)

- If the merchandise doesn't arrive in a timely fashion, contact the seller immediately. If the item appears to be lost in transit, track down the letter/package via the shipping service. If the item never arrives, it's the seller's responsibility to file an insurance claim with the carrier, and you should receive a refund from the seller.

THE ABSOLUTE MINIMUM

Here are the key points to remember from this chapter:

- Buying an item on eBay is generally about as safe as buying something from a local garage sale—with the caveat of "buyer beware."

- That said, most eBay buyers and sellers are honest and trustworthy.

- For those who aren't, eBay offers its Fraud Protection Program, which includes $200 worth of insurance per transaction for aggrieved buyers.

- You're better protected if you pay by credit card or use an escrow service.

- If you do get ripped off, contact the auction site, your local authorities, and the FTC.

- You should always leave feedback about the people you deal with—whether positive or negative.

9

SECRETS OF SUCCESSFUL BIDDERS

You want to be a player. You want to bid with the best of them. When you bid, you want to win. When you win, you don't want to overpay.

This is the chapter you've been waiting for. Discover the secrets and strategies that will help you be a successful eBay bidder!

The Guaranteed Way to Win an Auction—Be Sneaky and Snipe

If you have any experience with eBay auctions, you've seen the following phenomenon. On day one of the auction, there are a few initial bids. On day two, the number of new bids trails off. On days three through six, there are few if any bids placed. Then, on the seventh and last day of the auction, all hell breaks loose—with the heaviest bidding taking place in the auction's final hour.

What's happening here? It's simple—interested bidders are employing a technique called *sniping*, and saving their best bids for last.

Sniping is a technique used to win auctions by not bidding at all over the course of the auction, but then swooping in at the very last minute with an insurmountable bid. The thinking behind this strategy is simple. By not disclosing your interest, you don't contribute to bidding up the price during the course of the auction. By bidding at the last minute, you don't leave enough time for other bidders to respond to your bid. The successful sniper makes one bid only—and makes it count.

Sniping happens on eBay because the end time of each auction is rigidly enforced. If you know an auction ends at 12:01:30, you can time your snipe to hit at 12:01:29, leaving no time for any other bidders to trump your bid. Some other auction sites, such as Yahoo! Auctions, have flexible end times; if there is bidding within the last five minutes of an auction, the auction is automatically extended by another five minutes, giving extra time for other bidders to respond to a snipe.

Sniping: Pros and Cons

eBay management doesn't have an official position on sniping, although it has the company's tacit approval. Many experienced eBay users not only participate in sniping, but also regard it as a kind of game. (Sellers like sniping, of course, as long as it helps to drive up the prices of their items.) It's the community of less-experienced users—or those used to more traditional auctions—that is less likely to embrace sniping as a practice.

Most bidders who despise sniping say that it takes all the fun out of the auction process. Experienced snipers say that sniping itself is fun, that it can be kind of a game to see just how late you can bid and still make it count before the auction closes.

Whether you like it or not, sniping works. After all, if you place a high enough bid at the last second, there's no time for anyone to respond with a higher bid. The last high bidder always wins, and a sniper stands a very good chance of being the last high bidder.

Can a sniper lose an auction? Yes, under these scenarios:

- First, there might be another sniper in the queue who places a higher snipe than your maximum bid. A last-second bid of $35 will beat out a last-second bid of $30 any day.

- Second, your snipe might be too early, allowing time for the previous high bidder to receive an outbid notice and respond with a higher bid.

- Third, your snipe might not be high enough to beat out an existing high bid. If the current bid is $25 but the high bid (not known to you) is $35, you'd be beat if you "only" bid $30.

If you've ever been outbid on an item at the very last moment, you know that sniping can win auctions. Even if you hate sniping, the only way to beat a sniper is to snipe yourself.

Successful Sniping, Step by Step

Successful sniping requires large amounts of patience and split-second timing—but will reward you with a higher number of winning bids. Just follow these steps:

1. Identify the item you want to buy—and then *don't bid!* Resist the temptation to place a bid when you first notice an item. Make a note of the auction (and its closing time), but don't let anyone else know your intentions.

2. Five minutes before the close of the auction, make sure you're logged on to the Internet, and access the auction in question.

3. Open a second browser window to the auction in question.

4. Display the Windows clock on your desktop, and configure it to display both minutes and seconds. (Or just grab a watch with a second hand or a stopwatch.)

5. In your first browser window, enter your maximum bid and click the Submit button to display the confirmation screen. *Don't confirm the bid yet!* Wait for the confirmation screen....

6. In your second browser window, click the Refresh or Reload button to update the official auction time. Keep doing this until the time remaining until close is 60 seconds.

> **" Mike Sez "**
>
> It's a good idea to synch your Windows clock with eBay's official time. To view the current eBay time, go to `cgi3.ebay.com/aw-cgi/eBayISAPI.dll?TimeShow`.

7. Now, using either the Windows clock or your watch or stopwatch, count down 50 seconds, until there are only 10 seconds left in the auction. (You might want to confirm the synchronization midway through your countdown by refreshing your second browser window again.)

8. When exactly 10 seconds are left in the auction, click the Confirm Bid button in your first browser window to send your bid.

9. Wait 10 seconds, and then click the Refresh or Reload button in your second browser window. The auction should now be closed, and (if your sniping was successful) you should be listed as the winning bidder.

Why bid 10 seconds before close? It takes about this long to transmit the bid from your computer to the online auction site and for the bid to be registered. If you bid any earlier than this, you leave time for the auction to send an outbid notice to the previous high bidder—and you don't want that person to know that until it's too late to do anything about it.

Using Software to Snipe

If you can't personally be present to snipe at the end of an auction, check out an automated sniping program or Web-based sniping service. These programs and services let you enter the item number of the auction and your maximum bid beforehand, and then go online at precisely the right time to place a last-minute snipe—even if you're not at home or otherwise occupied.

The best of these auto-snipe programs and Web services are listed in Table 9.1.

note

For more details on these and other third-party auction programs and services, see Chapter 28, "Using Auction Software and Services.")

TABLE 9.1 Automated Sniping Programs and Web Sites

Tool	Type	Pricing	Web Site
Auction Sentry	Software	$9.95	www.auction-sentry.com
AuctionSniper	Web service	1% of final price	www.auctionsniper.com
AuctionStealer	Web service	$1/item	www.auctionstealer.com
BidNapper	Web service	$19.95–$39.95 per year	www.bidnapper.com
BidSpyder	Software	Free	www.bidspyder.com
eSnipe	Web service	1% of final price	www.esnipe.com
HammerSnipe PowerTool	Software	Free	www.hammertap.com/powertool/

Forty Sure-Fire Tips for Placing a Winning Bid— and Getting the Most for Your Money

Whether you snipe or not, you can do many other things to increase your chances of winning an auction without overpaying for the item in question. Here are my top tips that can help anyone be a more successful eBay bidder.

Tip #1: Bid in the Off Season

You already know that the final minute of the auction is the best time to place your bid. But are there specific times of the year that offer better bargains for bidders?

The answer, of course, is yes. Although there is some category-specific seasonality, the best overall time of the year to pick up eBay bargains is during the summer months. Summer is the slowest period on eBay, which means fewer people bidding—and lower prices for you.

Tip #2: Look for Off-Peak Auctions

Believe it or not, some auctions are set to end in the wee hours of the morning—when there aren't a lot of bidders awake to make last-minute snipes. Look for auctions ending between midnight and 5:00 a.m. Pacific time if you want some competition-free sniping.

Tip #3: Do Your Research

Don't bid blind; make sure you know the true value of an item before you offer a bid. Look around at auctions of similar items; what prices are they going for? Research the price of similar items offline; sometimes, you can find what you're looking for at a discount store or in a catalog or at another online site—where you'll probably get a real warranty and a better return policy. Shop around, and don't assume that the price you see at an auction is always the best deal available.

Be informed, and you won't bid too high—or too low.

Tip #4: Don't Bid on the First Item You See

Probably several other items on the same auction site are similar to the first item you saw. Look at the entire list of items before you choose which one to bid on. Seldom is the first item you see the one you really want or the best deal.

Tip #5: Know When to Say No

Be disciplined! Set a maximum price you're willing to pay for an item, and *don't exceed it!* It's okay to lose an auction.

Don't automatically rebid just because you've been outbid. It's too easy to get caught up in the excitement of a fast-paced auction. Learn how to keep your cool; know when to say no.

Tip #6: Don't Let the Proxy Bid Things Up

If two or more people are bidding on the same item, eBay's proxy bidding software can automatically (and quickly) rocket up the price until the bidder with the lower maximum bid maxes out. It's kind of an automated bidding frenzy conducted by two mindless robots.

Some bidders refuse to participate in proxy bidding. If the price is to increase, they want to do it manually. How do you defeat the automatic bidding software? Simple—make sure your maximum bid is the same price as the next incremental bid and no higher. It might take a bit more work, but it puts you in total control of the bidding process.

Tip #7: There Are Other Fish in the Sea

In 99.9% of eBay's auctions, that "one-of-a-kind" item really isn't one-of-a-kind. In fact, some sellers (especially merchant sellers) will have multiple quantities of an item, which they release to auction in dribs and drabs over time. In addition, some collectibles are bought and sold and bought and sold by multiple buyers and sellers over time, continually changing hands via new auctions. If you don't get this particular item, there's a good chance you'll get to bid on something similar soon.

Tip #8: If It Sounds Too Good to Be True, It Probably Is

A rare copy of *Action Comics* #1 for only $25? A brand-new Pentium 4 computer for only $100? There has to be a catch. That *Action Comics* is probably a facsimile reprint, and the brand-new Pentium 4 PC is actually a remanufactured unit missing some key parts. Be suspicious of improbable or impossible deals; always ask questions that confirm or reject your suspicions.

Tip #9: Ask Questions

If you're unclear about any aspect of an item you're interested in, ask the seller questions via e-mail. In addition to answering your specific questions, some sellers have additional information or pictures they can send you one-on-one. There's no excuse for ignorance; if you're not sure, ask!

Tip #10: Check the Feedback

Check out the seller's feedback rating. Make sure the seller of the item you want has a good feedback rating—and avoid any who don't. You should also click the seller's numerical feedback rating to display actual comments from other users who have dealt with this user before. The best way to avoid bad sellers is to find out that they're bad sellers beforehand.

Tip #11: Check the Seller's Past Auctions

While you're checking up on the seller, use eBay's search function to display all of the seller's completed auctions. See if the seller has sold multiples of this particular item in the past. There's no need to get into a bidding war if the same item will come up for auction again next week.

Tip #12: Check the Seller's Other Auctions

You'd be surprised how many times a seller has more than one item you're interested in. Click the View Seller's Other Auctions link to see everything else the seller has for auction—and bid accordingly!

Tip #13: Search; Don't Browse

If you know what you're looking for, don't go through the time-consuming hassle of clicking and loading and clicking and loading to access a particular item category. Using an auction's search function will find what you want a lot quicker.

Tip #14: Search Smart

Searching for an item on eBay is easy; finding what you really want is hard. You're more likely to find what you're looking for if you can use the auction site's advanced search capabilities to fine-tune your query. Some specific search tips can help you perform more effective—and efficient—searches:

- **Narrow your search.** Some of the more popular categories on eBay will list thousands of items. If you do a search on **nba**, for example, you'll be overwhelmed by the results; narrow your search within these large categories (to **nba jerseys** or **nba tickets**) to better describe the specific item you're looking for.

- **Make your queries precise—but not too precise.** When you're deciding which keywords to use, pick words that are precise, but not overly restrictive.

If you must use a very general word, modify it with a more specific word—or you're apt to generate a huge number of results that have little relevance to the specific information you're searching for. As an example, **model** is a pretty general keyword; **Star Wars Death Star model** is a much more precise query. On the other hand, if you search for an **old Star Wars Death Star model partially assembled without instructions not painted**, you probably won't return any matching results. If you get few if any results, take some of the parameters out of your query to broaden your search.

- **Get the right order.** When constructing your query, put the important stuff up front. Put keywords or phrases that describe your main subject at the start of your query; put less important words and phrases last. Search engines search for the first words first and rank results according to how they match these more important keywords.

- **Use wildcards.** If you're not sure of spelling, use a wildcard to replace the letters in question. Also, wildcards help you find variations on a keyword. For example, if you want Superman, Supergirl, and Superdog, enter **super*** to find all "super" words.

- **Truncate.** If you're not sure whether you're looking for plurals or singulars, truncate your words and use wildcards. For example, if you're looking for beanie babies, search for **bab*** to return either a single baby or multiple babies.

- **Vary your vocabulary—and your spelling.** Don't assume that everyone spells a given word the same way—or knows how to spell it properly. Also, don't forget about synonyms. What you call pink, someone else might call mauve. What's big to you might be large to someone else. Think of all the ways the item you're looking for can be described, and include as many of them as possible in your query.

- **Fine-tune your results.** Did eBay's search engine return an overwhelming number of matching items? If so, you need to fine-tune your search to be more specific. Look at the results generated from your initial search. Think about the good matches and the bad matches and why they ended up in the results list. Then, enter a new query that uses additional or different keywords and modifiers. Your goal is to make the next list of results a higher quality than the last.

- **Different day, different results.** Remember that new items are constantly added to any given auction site, and closed auctions are constantly removed from the listings. If you didn't find anything that matched your query today, try again tomorrow; you'll probably find a different list of items for sale.

Tip #15: Search for Last-Minute Bargains

When you search the eBay listings, make sure you display the results with auctions ending today listed first. Scan the list for soon-to-end items with no bids or few bids, and pick off some bargains that have slipped others' attention.

Tip #16: Don't Show Your Hand

Part and parcel of the sniping strategy; don't place an early bid on an item. That just signals your interest and attracts other bidders—which results in a higher price.

Tip #17: Watch, Don't Bid

Expanding on the previous tip, use eBay's Watch This Item feature to watch auctions in process without first placing a bid. (Just click the Watch This Item link on the item listing page, and then watch the items on your My eBay page.)

Tip #18: Use the eBay Toolbar

eBay offers a neat little add-on for your Web browser that makes it easy to track auctions you've bid on, or that are on your watch list. When you install the eBay Toolbar, it appears as part of your Web browser, underneath all your normal toolbars. (Figure 9.1 shows the eBay Toolbar as it appears in Internet Explorer.)

The eBay Toolbar also includes some other useful features, including the ability to search auction listings from the toolbar, go directly to your My eBay page, and view the top picks in selected categories. The eBay Toolbar is free, and available for downloading at `pages.ebay.com/ebay_toolbar/`.

FIGURE 9.1

Track your auctions in your Web browser with the eBay Toolbar.

Tip #19: Watch the Finish

Don't forget the downside to sniping—that you can be sniped, too. Don't get outbid at the last minute. Because most auction activity occurs at the very end of the auction, track the last hour of your most important auctions, and be prepared to react quickly to last-second snipers.

Tip #20: Get in Synch

Make sure that you're in synch with eBay's official clock (`cgi3.ebay.com/aw-cgi/ eBayISAPI.dll?TimeShow`). If you're a few seconds slow, you could lose a sniping contest!

Tip #21: Put Your Best Foot Forward

When you do bid, don't weasel around. Make your bid the maximum amount the item is worth to you, and be done with it.

Tip #22: Bid in Odd Numbers

When you bid, don't bid an even amount. Instead, bid a few pennies more than an even buck; for example, if you want to bid $10, bid $10.03 instead. That way, your bid will beat any bids at the same approximate amount—$10.03 beats $10 even, any day—without you having to place a new bid at the next whole bid increment.

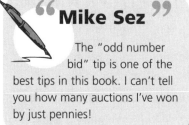

Mike Sez

The "odd number bid" tip is one of the best tips in this book. I can't tell you how many auctions I've won by just pennies!

Tip #23: Don't Be a Deadbeat

Don't bid unless you really intend to buy. Nobody likes a deadbeat—and if you do it often enough, you'll get kicked off the auction site, permanently.

Tip #24: Use My eBay

If you're a regular eBay user, the best way to track all your auction activity on a single page is by using My eBay. My eBay can also track your favorite auction categories, as well as your account status—and let you access the pages you use most often, without having to click through useless parts of the site. Personalize My eBay the way you like and then bookmark it; it's a great home page for the heavy auction trader.

note

Learn more about My eBay in Chapter 22, "Creating a Home Base with My eBay."

Tip #25: Keep Track of Your Auctions

Don't let your auction activity get away from you. Use My eBay or a third-party auction management program to look at all your auctions on a daily basis, or use auction management software to track your auctions automatically.

Tip #26: Read the Fine Print

What methods of payment can you use? What about shipping? Any other details that might impact your decision to bid? Read the entire item listing before you place your bid—so you aren't surprised by the fine print in any auction.

Tip #27: Don't Forget Shipping Costs...

When you're placing your bid, remember that you'll actually have to pay more than you bid; you have to pay shipping and handling to put the item in your hands. If S/H costs aren't detailed in the item listing, figure them out yourself, or e-mail the seller to get a reasonable estimate. That ultra-cheap $2 item looks pretty expensive if you have to add $5 shipping and handling to the base price.

Tip #28: ...But Don't Overpay for Shipping

Not only should you not get taken by surprise by shipping costs, but you also shouldn't be taken advantage of by unrealistic shipping and handling charges. Get a ballpark feel for shipping on a specific item from the seller's location to where you live. Expect a little overage on the seller's part (she has to buy packing materials, labels, and such), but not too much. If you know shipping should be in the $2 range, accept a $3 charge—but question a $5 charge.

Tip #29: Pay Quickly

Don't delay—*pay!* Look, the seller needs the money, and the sooner you pay, the sooner you'll get what you paid for.

Tip #30: Pay by Credit Card

Now that the majority of auctions are credit card enabled (via PayPal or eBay Payments), use that option. Paying via credit card is relatively safe and leaves a good paper trail—and ensures that your item will be shipped quickly.

Tip #31: Money Orders Cost Money

The seller says that money orders or cashier checks speed shipment. Depending on your bank, it might cost a few dollars to cut a money order or cashier's check. Make sure you factor these costs into your total expenditure—and question whether you really want to pay to cut a money order for a $5 item.

Tip #32: Provide All the Information Necessary

When you send your payment, make sure you include your name, shipping address, e-mail address, and item name and description. Even better, enclose a copy of the item's Checkout or listing page, with additional information written on it. (I can't tell you how many envelopes I've opened with only a check or money order inside; you gotta tell 'em who the payment is from and what it's for!)

Tip #33: Use a Middleman for Expensive Items

If you buy a high-priced item through a person-to-person auction, consider using an escrow service. Although you'll pay for the service (in the neighborhood of 5%, typically paid by you, the buyer), it's a good safety net in case the seller doesn't ship or the item isn't what was described. In addition, you can use escrow services to accept credit card payments when the seller doesn't or can't accept credit cards directly.

Tip #34: Ship It Safe

If you bought a rare or high-priced item, ask the seller to insure the item for shipping. Pay the extra cost; it's worth it in peace of mind alone.

Tip #35: Document Everything

In case something goes south, it helps to have good records of all aspects of your transaction. Print copies of the confirmation e-mail, plus all e-mail between you and the seller. Make sure you write down the seller's user ID, e-mail address, and physical address. If the transaction is ever disputed, you'll have all the backup you need to plead your case.

Tip #36: Keep a Log

Not only should you document all the correspondence for an individual auction, you should also keep a log of all the auctions you've won. If you do a lot of bidding, it's all too easy to lose track of which items you've paid for and which you've received. You don't want to let weeks (or months!) go by before you notice you haven't received an item you paid for!

Tip #37: If You Win It, Inspect It

When you receive the item you paid for, open it up and inspect it—*immediately!* Don't wait a month before you look at it and then expect the seller to rectify a situation that was long considered closed. Okay the item, and then send the seller an e-mail saying you got it and it's okay. If you sit on it too long, it's yours—no matter what.

Tip #38: If You Get Ripped Off, Tell eBay About It

If you have a problem with a seller, first try working it out between the two of you. If things don't get resolved, contact eBay with your grievance; you can use eBay's Fraud Protection Program to register your complaint and (hopefully) get reimbursed for your loss. (And don't forget to leave negative feedback on the snake who did you wrong!)

Tip #39: Communicate!

Don't assume anything; communicate what you think you know. If you have questions during an auction, ask them. When the auction is over, e-mail the seller. When the seller e-mails you, e-mail him or her back to confirm. E-mail the seller when you send payment and again to confirm receipt of the item. The more everyone knows, the fewer surprises there are.

Also, remember that not everyone reads his e-mail daily, so don't expect immediate response. Still, if you don't receive a response, send another e-mail. If you're at all concerned at any point, get the seller's phone number or physical address from the auction site and call or write her. A good phone conversation can clear up a wealth of misunderstandings.

Tip #40: Be Nice

You're dealing with another human being, someone who has feelings that can be hurt. A little bit of common courtesy goes a long way. Say please and thank you, be understanding and tolerant, and treat your trading partner in the same way you'd like to be treated. Follow the golden rule; do unto other auction traders as you would have them do unto you.

The Absolute Minimum

Here are the key points to remember from this chapter:

- Sniping—a literal last-second bid—is the most successful tool for winning eBay auctions.

- Keep track of items you haven't yet bid for by using the Watch This Item and My eBay features.

- When you place your bid, make it the highest amount you're willing to pay—and then walk away if the bidding goes higher.

- The best time of year to pick up good deals is during the summer.

- You can sometimes win an auction by bidding in an odd amount—$20.03 instead of $20.00 even, for example.

- The faster you pay, the faster you'll receive the item you won!

PART III

EBAY FOR SELLERS

10

SELLING 101: A TUTORIAL FOR BEGINNING SELLERS

You've poked around eBay some. Maybe you've bid on an item or two; maybe you've even been fortunate to be the high bidder in an auction for something you really wanted. Now you're looking at your collection of... well, whatever it is you collect, and you're thinking that maybe you ought to be getting some of that online auction action.

In other words, you're ready to put your first item up for bid on eBay.

Getting Ready to List

Before you list your first item, you need to get all your ducks in a row. That means determining what you're going to sell and for how much, as well as how you're going to describe and promote the item. If you try to list an item "cold," you'll find yourself stopping and starting as you move through the listing process; you'll be constantly running around trying to gather more information or make important listing decisions on-the-fly. Better to prepare for these decisions up front, as described in the following checklist:

Checklist—Before You List an Item for Auction

☐ Make sure the item exists and is at hand, and has been cleaned up and spruced up as much as possible. (This includes putting the item in the original box, if you have it.)

☐ Determine what you think the final selling price will be, and then choose an appropriate minimum bid price.

☐ Take a picture or a scan of the item and prepare a JPG-format file for uploading.

☐ Determine if you want to use eBay's Checkout feature—and if so, change your selling preferences to activate Checkout.

☐ Determine what listing options you might want to purchase—such as bold-facing the title or placing the item in the Gallery.

☐ Think up a catchy yet descriptive headline for the item.

☐ Write out a detailed description of the item.

☐ Determine what payment options you'll accept. (If you haven't yet signed up with PayPal, now is the time.)

☐ Determine how you want to ship the item.

☐ Weigh the item, and then try to determine the actual shipping costs. Use that information to set an upfront shipping/handling charge, if you want.

☐ If you haven't yet registered as an eBay user and entered your credit card information, do that now.

☐ Determine what day of the week—and what time of the day—you want your auction to end.

When all this is done, *then* you can create your listing!

Before You List—Think About Checkout

You first learned about eBay's Checkout feature back in Chapter 7, "After the Auction: Taking Care of Business." Checkout is a way to automate the end-of-auction process, with your buyer being directed back to the eBay site to enter shipping and payment information.

Many sellers like Checkout, as it reduces the number of after-auction e-mails they have to deal with, and takes some of that end-of-auction burden off their shoulders. Other sellers can't stand Checkout, as it works to eliminate direct contact between buyer and seller—and inserts the eBay site back into a process that eBay doesn't necessarily need to be a part of. (These same detractors claim that Checkout is nothing more than a ploy to force buyers to use eBay's built-in payment services—and there's more than a little truth to that, despite eBay's denials.)

Love it or hate it, you have to configure your seller settings so that eBay knows whether or not you want to use Checkout. If you choose to use Checkout (and there's no charge to do so), eBay will insert a Checkout button into your after-auction item listing pages. If you choose not to use Checkout, no buttons are inserted anywhere, and you're on your own when an auction ends.

To configure your Checkout preferences, follow these steps:

1. Click the My eBay link above the Navigation Bar.
2. When your My eBay page opens, select the Selling tab.
3. Click the Update Checkout Preferences link, found in the Billing/Payment area of the Selling-Related Links section.
4. When the Checkout Preferences page appears, check either Yes or No in the Allow Checkout section.
5. If you choose to use Checkout, enter your contact name and address in the Payment Address section, and then check the Remember My Payment Address option.
6. Click the Submit button when done.

Any changes you make on the Checkout Preferences page do not apply to any auctions currently in progress. Changes you make will be applied to new, relisted, and revised auction items.

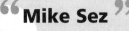

"Mike Sez"

My personal preference is *not* to use Checkout. I'm perfectly capable of managing my end-of-auction activity on my own (or via an auction management program), thank you very much.

Getting Started: Creating an Item Listing

Remember that before you can list an item for sale, you have to be a registered eBay user. It also helps to have your credit card on file, so that you can pay the fees you will soon incur. (If you need to do either of these things, turn immediately to Chapter 3, "Joining Up and Getting Started.")

Assuming you're registered and filed, now what do you do? Well, listing an item for sale on eBay is pretty simple; all you have to do is work through the following series of steps.

Step 1: Get Ready to Sell

This is the easiest thing you'll do in the whole process. All you have to do is click the Sell link in the Navigation Toolbar found at the top of any eBay page.

Step 2: Choose the Type of Auction

eBay now displays the Choose Selling Format page, shown in Figure 10.1. You can choose from three different types of selling formats:

- If you want a traditional eBay auction for your item, select Sell Item at Online Auction.

FIGURE 10.1

Decide whether you want a regular auction or a fixed-price sale.

- If you want to sell your item at a fixed price, select Sell at a Fixed Price. (Items listed in eBay's Fixed Price Format appear in all item listings and searches, but users can't bid on them; they can only use the Buy It Now option.)
- If you want to create a real estate listing (instead of a typical auction), select Advertise Your Real Estate.

Most users will choose the Sell Item at Online Auction option. Click the Continue button to proceed.

Step 3: Choose Your Category

When the Select Category page appears, as shown in Figure 10.2, select the category and subcategory for your item. Start by selecting a major category in the 1) list; when you select a category, eBay displays available subcategories in the 2) list. Select a subcategory and eBay displays more subcategories (if available) in the 3) list, and so forth. Make your selections in each list, and then click Continue.

note

Items listed in the Fixed Price Format are charged the same insertion and final value fees as regular auction items.

FIGURE 10.2

Select the category— subcategories— for your item.

Sell Your Item: Select Category

1 Category 2 Title 3 Pictures 4 Payment 5 Review
               & Description & Details & Shipping & Submit

If you already know your category number, enter it below.

Click in the boxes below starting with Box 1 until you have found the appropriate category. When the boxes turn gray, click the **Continue** button at the bottom of the page.

Main category
Not sure where to list your item? View descriptions of all top level categories.

Music ->CDs, Records, & Tapes ->CDs ->...

1)
Jewelry, Gems & Watches ->
Movies & Television ->
Music ->
Photo & Optics ->
Pottery & Glass ->
Real Estate ->

2)
CDs, Records, & Tapes ->
Music Memorabilia ->
Musical Instruments ->
Sheet Music, Music Books ->

3)
CDs ->
Records ->
Tapes ->
Wholesale Lots ->
Other

4)
Big Band, Swing
Blues
Childrens
Christian
Classical
Comedy

5)

6)

Click here if you are having trouble viewing the category selector above.

Main category # [   ]
Number will appear when you have completely selected your category.

Choose a second category (optional)
List your item in two places for greater visiblity. Learn more.
Insertion and most listing upgrade fees will be doubled. Final value fees will **not** be doubled.

Select a top level category
No second category
Antiques
Art
Books
Business & Industrial
You will select a subcategory on the next page.

or Enter a
Second category # [   ]
(optional)

[< Back]   [Continue >]

If you want to list your item in more than one category, scroll down to the Choose a Second Category section and make a selection from the Select a Top Level Category list. Each selection you make will lead you through the available subcategories.

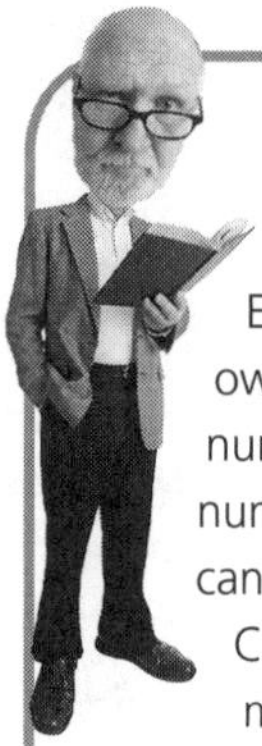

tip

Each subcategory has its own specific identifying number. If you know the number of a category, you can enter it in the Main Category # box, instead of making selections in the lists.

Step 4: Describe Your Item

When the Describe Your Item page appears, as shown in Figure 10.3, enter a title for your item in the Item Title box. (The title must be 45 characters or less.) You can then enter a description—of any length—into the Item Description box.

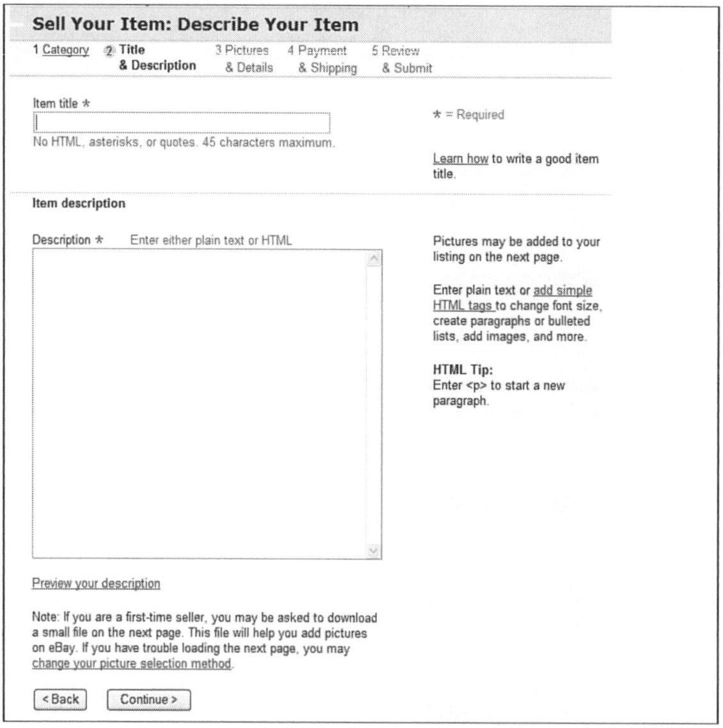

FIGURE 10.3
Provide a description for your item.

Some categories require you to enter specific information in addition to your general description. For example, if you're selling event tickets, you'll need to select how many tickets you're selling, for what particular event, on which date. If you're prompted to enter specifics of this type, do so now.

Click Continue to proceed.

Step 5: Fill in the Details

When the Provide Pictures & Item Details page appears, shown in Figure 10.4, you have a lot of entering to do. You'll need to provide the following details:

- **Duration**. Choose from 3, 5, 7, or (for ten cents extra) 10 days.

- **Start Time.** By default, your auction starts as soon as you finish creating the listing. If you want your auction to start (and thus end) at a different time, select the Schedule to Start On option and select a date and time from the pull-down lists. (You'll pay $0.10 to use this feature.)

- **Quantity.** In most cases you have a single item to sell, so you enter 1. If you have more than one identical item to sell, enter the number you have—which means you'll be holding a Dutch auction, as described later in this chapter.

- **Starting Price.** Enter the price you want bidding to start at.

- **Reserve Price.** If you want to hold a reserve price auction (discussed later in this chapter), enter the minimum price you'll accept for the item here.

- **Buy It Now Price.** If you want to add the Buy It Now option to your auction, enter the lowest price you'll accept into this box.

- **Private Auction.** If you're selling a confidential or potentially embarrassing item, choose to hide all bidders' names by selecting this option.

- **City, State.** Enter where you'll be shipping the item from. (This helps potential buyers determine approximate shipping costs to their location.)

- **Item Location.** Pull down the list and select the nearest metropolitan area. (This lets you list your item in eBay's local auctions—great for large and hard-to-ship items.)

note

The Item Title field must contain standard numbers and text, and *cannot* contain any HTML code. The Item Description field, on the other hand, *can* contain HTML code; see Chapter 16, "Creating a Great-Looking Listing" for more information.

"Mike Sez"

The most common duration for an eBay auction is 7 days. Unless you're in a rush for cash (or are up against some other deadline), there is no reason to go for any auction lasting less than a week. On the other hand, 10 days is overkill, given that so much bidding takes place in the auction's final minutes. The best option is the 7-day auction, which exposes your item to a week's worth of bidders.

■ **Country.** This is the United States by default; if you live elsewhere, use the pull-down menu and select your country.

■ **Add Pictures.** If you have a picture of your item and want eBay to host the picture for you, select the eBay Picture Services option and then select a layout: Standard (one picture, no charge), Slide Show (multiple pictures, $0.75), Supersize Pictures (one or more bigger pictures, $0.75), or Picture Pack (up to six pictures, $1.00).

If you want to host your pictures on another Web server, select the Your Own Web Hosting tab and enter the file's Web address in the Picture URL box.

If you're using listing creation software (discussed in Chapter 28, "Using Auction Software and Services") that includes a picture as part of the listing, select the option "The Description Already Contains a Picture URL for My Item."

FIGURE 10.4

Select all manner of listing options.

Sell Your Item: Provide Pictures & Item Details

1 Category   2 Title   3: Pictures   4 Payment   5 Review
              & Description & Details   & Shipping   & Submit

Title   CD: Laura Nyro NEW YORK TENDABERRY   * = Required

Pricing and duration

Duration *   7 days

Start time   ⦿ Start listing when submitted (Free)   Learn more about
                 ○ Schedule to start on: scheduled listings and
$0.10 fee applies for   Date   Time   PDT   eBay Time.
scheduled listings

Quantity *   1   Learn more about Multiple Item
                                                           Auctions (Dutch Auctions)
Starting price * $ Learn more about starting price.

Reserve price $ A reserve price is the lowest
(optional)   price you're willing to sell the
Variable fee applies   item for. Learn more.

Buy It Now price $ Sell to the first buyer who
(optional)   Note: You can't use Buy It now if you sell a   meets your specified price.
$0.05 fee applies.   quantity greater than 1.   Learn more.

☐ Private Auction   When to use Private Auctions.
Keeps bidders' User IDs from being displayed to others.

Item Location   Minimize

City, State *   Carmel, IN

Region *   IN-Indianapolis   Increase your exposure for free
                                                           by listing locally. Learn more.

Country *   United States
                 [edit]

Add pictures

eBay Picture Services   Your own Web hosting   Want to know more about
Let eBay host your pictures   Enter your picture URL   adding pictures to your listing?
                                                           See our photo tutorial.
Picture URL (Web address)
http://   Try our free full
For example, URLs ending in .jpg or .gif   featured version with
                                                           crop, rotate and
☐ The description already contains a picture URL for my item.   more.

                                          ⊕ Live help

Increase your item's visibility

Gallery picture URL (Web address)

`http://`

(jpg, bmp or tif images only, no gif)

⊙ No Gallery picture			See examples of Gallery and Gallery Featured.
○ Gallery	$0.25	Add a picture preview to your listings and search results, and be on display in the Gallery!	
○ Gallery Featured	$19.95	Get all the benefits of Gallery plus showcase your item in the Featured section of Gallery.	

Listing upgrades - make your item stand out

☐ Bold	$2.00	Attract buyers' attention and set your listing apart -- use **bold** .	See example of a bold listing.
☐ Highlight	$5.00	Make your listing stand out with a colored band.	See example of a highlighted listing.
☐ Featured Plus!	$19.95	Show off your listing in the Featured area of category listings and search results.	See example of Featured Plus! listing.
☐ Home Page Featured	$99.95	Get maximum exposure! Appear in our Featured area and your item may appear on the Home page.	See example of Home Page Featured listing.
Great Gift icon [Not Selected ▾]	$1.00	Let buyers know that your item makes a great holiday or special occasion gift. Add a fun gift icon to your listing.	Learn more about Great Gift icons.

Free page counter

○ Do not add a counter	○ Green LED `1234`	Andale counters show how often your item has been viewed. Learn more.
⊙ Andale Style `1234`	○ Hidden `Thanks for looking!`	
	Only seller can see page views	Learn more about hidden counters.

[< Back] [Continue >]

- ■ **Gallery Picture.** If you want to include a picture of your item in the Gallery, enter the URL for your picture in the Gallery Picture URL box and check the Gallery option. If you don't want to use the Gallery, make sure that the No Gallery Picture option is selected.

- ■ **Listing upgrades.** Select or deselect any of the following for-a-charge listing upgrades: Bold, Highlight, Featured Plus, Home Page Featured. If you think your item would make a nice gift, select an icon from the Great Gift Icon list.

- ■ **Free Page Counter.** To display a hit counter (free, from Andale) at the bottom of your listing, scroll down to the Free Page Counter selection and select either Andale Style, Green LED, or Hidden.

note

Listings with pictures are more successful than those without; turn to Chapter 15, "Using Pictures in Your Listings," to learn more about creating and inserting pictures for your item listings.

(Hidden counters can only be seen by you—not other users.) If you don't want to display a counter, select Do Not Add a Counter.

These options are all discussed in more detail in Chapter 13, "Choosing the Right Listing Options." Click Continue when you're ready to proceed.

Step 6: Enter Payment and Shipping Info

When the Enter Payment & Shipping Page appears, as shown in Figure 10.5, select which payment methods you'll accept. You can opt for payment by PayPal, Money Order or Cashiers Check, Personal Check, COD, or Other Online Payment Services. You can also leave all the other options unchecked and select See Item Description instead; if you choose this option, make sure you describe your payment options in the Description section of your item listing.

FIGURE 10.5

Choose your payment and shipping options.

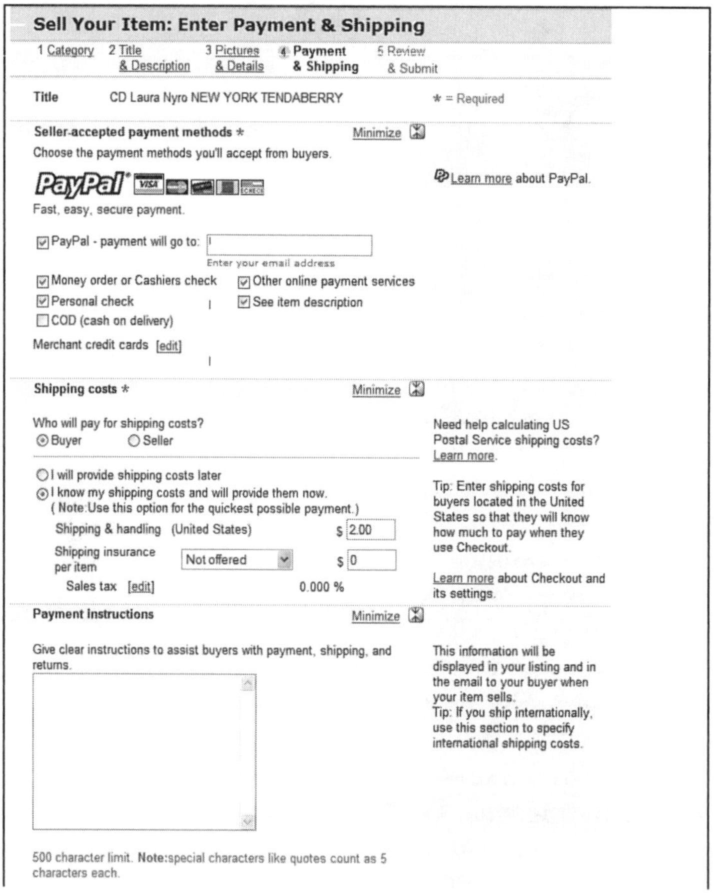

You can opt to accept payment via PayPal even if you don't currently have a PayPal account. Just enter your e-mail address in the Payment Will Go To box, and PayPal will contact you if the buyer chooses to pay via PayPal. At that point PayPal will walk you through creating a PayPal Premier account, so you can receive your funds.

If you already have a PayPal account, enter the e-mail address you use for that account into the Payment Will Go To box. (PayPal identifies members by their e-mail addresses.) With this information entered, eBay can route any credit card payments to the correct PayPal account—*yours*.

Next up on the page is the Shipping Costs section. Start by selecting who will pay shipping costs (the Buyer, in most cases), and then enter what the shipping/handling charges will be, if you know. (If you don't, check the I Will Provide Shipping Costs Later option.)

Enter any specific payment instructions into the Payment Instructions box. If your Checkout preferences did not include your payment address, you'll also see a Payment Address section; enter your address here. If your Checkout preferences *did* include your payment address, there won't be a Payment Address section on this page.

Next you need to select whether you'll ship to the U.S. only, worldwide, or to the U.S. and specific countries. Finally, select whether you'll accept escrow payments for this item, and then click Continue. Click Continue to proceed.

note

Learn more about determining shipping costs in Chapter 19, "Shipping It Out—Cheaply and Safely."

Step 7: Preview Your Listing

The next page, shown in Figure 10.6, provides a preview of your listing page and the options you've selected. If you see something that needs to be changed, click the Edit link next to that item. (For example, to edit the title you'd click the Edit Title link.) If everything looks right, click the Submit Listing button.

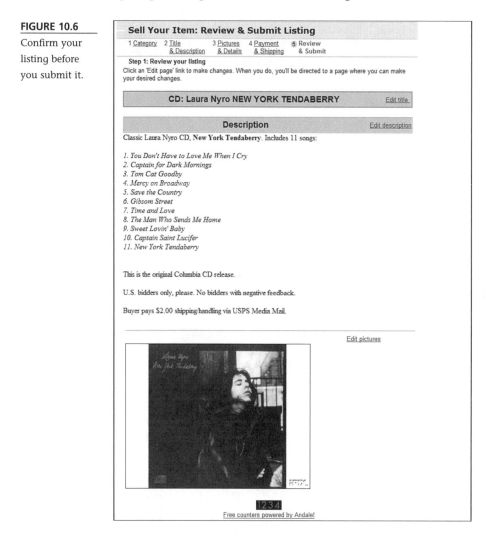

You're Done!

When you're all done, eBay displays the Congratulations page. This page confirms your listing and presents you with important details about your auction—including your item listing's URL, in case you want to publicize your auction elsewhere on the Internet.

After you see the Congratulations screen, your completed listing should appear immediately on the eBay Web site—although it might take a few hours to be listed in the appropriate category listings.

Dealing with Different Types of Auctions

As you work your way through eBay's item listing process, you discovered that there are four variations on the main auction theme—and that's not counting those high-priced real estate auctions! The four variations, which you first learned about in Chapter 4, "Bidding 101: A Tutorial for Beginning Bidders," are Reserve Price, Dutch, Private, and Buy It Now auctions. We'll look at each in turn.

Set a Higher Minimum with a Reserve Price Auction

A reserve price auction is one in which your initial bid price really isn't the minimum price you'll accept. Even though bids might exceed the initial bid price, if they don't hit your reserve price, you don't have to sell.

> **note**
>
> Learn more about real estate auctions in Chapter 27, "Buying and Selling Wheels and Walls: eBay Motors and Real Estate."

Many buyers—especially those just getting started—don't like reserve price auctions, and shy away from them. That's probably because they appear more complicated than regular auctions (and they are, just a little), and also because the reserve price is never disclosed to bidders. In this case, lack of familiarity definitely breeds contempt, at least from a certain class of bidders.

But there's something to the confusion factor. Let's say you set a minimum price of $5 for an item (really low, to get a buzz going and attract some early bidders) but a reserve price of $50 (because that's what you believe the item is really worth). If the high bidder bids $25, that bid doesn't win—because it's less than the $50 reserve. Unfortunately, bidders have no idea how much more to bid to hit the undisclosed reserve price. Messy and confusing, eh?

Why, then, would you opt for a reserve price auction? There are two possible scenarios:

- When you're unsure of the real value of an item—and don't want to appear to be asking too much for an item—you can reserve the right to refuse to sell the item if the market value is below a certain price.

- When you want to use a low initial bid price to get the bidding going more quickly than if the true desired minimum price (now the reserve price) was listed; the reserve price still guarantees that you won't have to sell below a minimum acceptable price.

If you insist on running a reserve price auction, it's easy enough to do. On the Provide Pictures & Item Details page, make sure you enter a price (higher than your Starting Price) in the Reserve Price box. That's all you have to do; after that, the auction runs as normal—or as normal as a reserve price auction gets.

Remember, if no one bids the reserve price or higher, no one wins.

Sell Larger Quantities with a Dutch Auction

When should you place a Dutch auction? Simple—when you have more than one copy of an item to sell.

Dutch auctions are those in which you have more than one quantity of an identical item to sell. It's great if you have a dozen Scooby Doo PEZ dispensers, 10 copies of *Lord of the Rings* on DVD, or a hundred units of white extra-large boxer shorts to sell.

To set up a Dutch auction, all you have to do is enter a quantity greater than 1 in the Quantity box on the Provide Pictures & Item Details page. When you do this, eBay automatically registers your auction as a Dutch auction.

The way Dutch auctions work is a little complicated, so I'll refer you to the explanation in Chapter 4. Suffice to say that the highest bidder always wins something—but doesn't always have to pay the highest price. To be precise, all bidders pay the lowest winning price, even if they bid higher. (I told you it was complicated!)

tip

If your auction ends and the high bid is below your reserve price, you don't have to do anything—you are not obligated to sell the item. However, you may want to use the Second Chance link on the item listing page to contact the high bidder and see if he/she is willing to pay the reserve price for the item, or perhaps you can negotiate a fair price in between the high bid and your reserve. If you don't want to do this, you can always *relist* the item in a new auction, in the hope that a new round of bidders will push the price up to what you expect to receive. If you do relist, however, you might want to edit the item's description to make it more appealing, or even rethink your reserve price to make the item more affordable.

" Mike Sez "

I personally don't like reserve price auctions, and only run them on the rarest of occasions. My experience is that you turn a lot of potential bidders off by using a reserve price; it's better to create a regular auction with a higher minimum bid price, and be upfront about everything.

In any case, eBay handles all the details automatically as long as you specify multiple quantities.

Keep It Anonymous with a Private Auction

The next oddball auction type is relatively simple, compared to the others. If you're auctioning off something that is a little delicate, sensitive, or downright embarrassing, choose a Private auction and none of the bidders' names will ever be revealed publicly. It's great for items in the Adult category, although some bidders on ultra-high-priced items might also want to remain anonymous.

caution

You can't make a Dutch auction private.

To activate a Private auction, all you have to do is check the box next to the Private Auction option on the Provide Pictures & Item Details form.

End It Quick with Buy It Now

eBay's Buy It Now (BIN) option lets you add a fixed-price option to your auction listings. The way BIN works is that you name a fixed price for your item; if a user bids that price, the auction is automatically closed and that user is named the high bidder. Note, however, that the BIN price is active only until the first bid is placed. If the first bidder places a bid lower than the BIN price, the BIN price is removed and the auction proceeds normally.

Why would you add the BIN feature to your auction? I find that most sellers who use BIN just happen to be retailers with a lot of similar inventory. That is, they're likely to place the same item up for auction week after week; in this scenario, the BIN price becomes the de facto retail price of the item.

You might also want to consider BIN around the Christmas holiday, when buyers don't always want to wait around seven whole days to see if they've won an item; desperate Christmas shoppers will sometimes pay a premium to get something *now*, which is where BIN comes in.

You activate BIN on the Provide Pictures & Item Details page. Just enter your BIN price into the Buy It Now Price box. And remember—your BIN price should be higher than your Starting Price.

> **" Mike Sez "**
>
> There's no sense using Buy It Now if you're not going to make any more money from it than you would a normal auction. If you want to use Buy It Now, set a BIN price 20% or so *above* your most wildly optimistic selling price. (So, if you think your item might possibly, if all the stars align properly, sell for $10, set a BIN price of $12.) That way if an enthusiastic buyer does end your auction prematurely, you'll be well compensated for it.

Managing Your Item Listing

When your listing is complete, the auction itself begins. But what if, for whatever reason, you need to make a change to your listing—or cancel the auction altogether?

Adding to and Editing Your Listing

One thing I heartily recommend doing is to give your ad a good look over after you've posted it. Maybe you like it—great. Maybe you don't—not so great. If you don't like your listing, there are two things you can do—edit the basic item description, or add to the description.

If you haven't received any bids yet, your best option is to edit the listing. eBay lets you edit your title, description, and pictures—as long as no one has placed a bid yet. To edit your listing, go to your item listing page and click the Revise Item link (located in the Seller Services section). This eventually sends you to an editing screen where you can change whatever information you want.

After that first bid is in, however, you can't change a thing. (eBay doesn't want to disadvantage early bidders if you dramatically change the information about the item you're selling.) What you can do, however, is add more information to your description. When you do this, know that your original description remains as is; the addition does not change or delete anything you've done previously.

To add to your description, go to eBay's Site Map and click the Add to My Item Description link. When the next page appears, enter the item number of the auction and click the Revise Item button. When the Add to Description page appears, enter the text you want to add. As with any description text, you can enter plain text or HTML-coded text—or URLs for additional pictures for your listing. Click the Save Changes button when done.

Canceling an Auction

What if your auction starts and you decide you really don't want to sell that item? You need a good excuse, but you *can* cancel eBay auctions.

Canceling an auction is a two-step process:

1. **Cancel any existing bids on your item.** Go to the Bid Cancellation page (cgi.ebay.com/aw-cgi/eBayISAPI.dll?CancelBidShow—or go to the Site Map page and click Cancel Bids on My Item) and cancel the first bid on your item. Then return to this page as many times as necessary to cancel all the outstanding bids.

2. **Officially end your auction.** (You can't end an auction that has open bids, which is the reason you had to cancel all the bids first.) Go to the Ending Auction page (cgi3.ebay.com/aw-cgi/ eBayISAPI.dll?EndingMyAuction—or go to the Site Map page and click End My Auction Early) and enter the auction item number. Click the Continue button to proceed, and then click the End Auction button to officially cancel your auction.

Blocking Buyers

Here's something else you'll eventually run into. Not every member of eBay is worth dealing with. When you run into a deadbeat bidder or otherwise slimy customer in one of your auctions, you don't want to have to deal with that person *again*. The best way to remove this person from your life is to block that bidder from all your future auctions.

> **"Mike Sez"**
>
> You can also use the bid canceling feature to delete bids from undesirable bidders. Let's say you stipulated in your item listing that your auction is for U.S. bidders only, and you discover that someone from Japan has placed a bid. Just cancel the bid. (And maybe e-mail the bidder and tell him why…). Or maybe you stated that you only wanted bidders with positive feedback, and a no-feedback newbie (or below-zero slime) places a bid anyway. Just cancel the bid. (And no e-mails are necessary!)

To block a bidder, you have to add that user to your Blocked Bidder/Buyer List. Follow these steps:

1. From the Site Map page, click the Blocked Bidder/Buyer List link (or go directly to pages.ebay.com/services/buyandsell/biddermanagement.html).

2. When the Bidder/Buyer Management page appears, scroll to the Blocked Bidder/Buyer List section and click Continue.

3. When the Blocked Bidder/Buyer List page appears, add the buyer's user name to the list; separate multiple names with commas.

4. Click the Submit button when done.

You can remove blocked buyers from your list at any time. Just return to the Blocked Bidder/Buyer List page and delete the user name you want to unblock, and then click Submit.

Relisting an Item

This is maybe getting a little ahead of things, but it's a good place to talk about it. What happens if your auction ends—and you don't have any bidders?

The answer is simple—if at first you don't succeed, try, try again!

eBay lets you relist any unsold item, with no additional insertion fee, if the following conditions are met:

- You didn't receive any bids on a regular (no-reserve) auction.
- For a reserve price auction, you didn't receive any bids that met or exceeded your reserve price.
- You are relisting an item within 30 days of the closing date of the first auction.
- If you're relisting a reserve price auction, the new reserve price is the same or lower than the original reserve price.

One last thing. If your item *doesn't* sell the second time, eBay won't waive the insertion fee. In other words, if you have a real loser item, eBay won't give you a free ride!

To relist an item, follow these steps:

1. Go to the item listing page for your completed auction and click the Re-list This Item link.

2. Proceed through the normal listing creation procedure. Your information from the previous listing will be already entered, although you can make any changes you want for this new listing.

caution

You can't take advantage of the relisting offer if you tried to sell a fixed-price item at Half.com or eBay Stores.

"Mike Sez"

If your item didn't sell the first time around, there was probably a good reason for it—maybe the starting price was too high, or the description sucked, or you didn't include a picture. When you relist an item, take the opportunity to spruce up the listing, revisit the pricing, and so on, to try to make the item more attractive to potential bidders.

eBay won't charge you a listing fee for this item the second time, although you will be charged a final value fee if it sells. If your item *doesn't* sell the second time around, there's no third chance.

The Auction's Over! Now What?

The days go by, and finally, your auction is over. If you're fortunate, you've received a high bid that far exceeds your opening bid or reserve price—which means that you have a buyer.

The question is, now what do you do?

You've sat around watching the bidding for seven days or so, but now it's time to go to work. You need to contact the high bidder, figure out the final selling price (including shipping and handling), deal with the payment process, pack the darned thing up and ship it out, sit around for another couple of days hoping it gets to where it's going in one piece, and then leave feedback for the buyer. Whew! That sounds like a lot of hard work—and it is.

To learn about the post-auction process in more detail, turn to Chapter 18, "After the Auction: Concluding Your Business." To learn more about how to ship items to buyers, turn to Chapter 19, "Shipping It Out—Cheaply and Safely." And for some really useful advice on how to make selling easier—and more profitable—turn to Chapter 21, "Secrets of Successful Sellers."

THE ABSOLUTE MINIMUM

Here are the key points to remember from this chapter:

- Before you sell an item, you have to be a registered eBay user and have a credit card on file.

- To start an auction for an item, click the Sell link on the Navigation Bar, and work your way through the Sell Your Item pages.

- You can choose from 3-, 5-, 7-, or 10-day auctions—although the default 7-day auction is the most popular.

- You can opt for four major auction variations—reserve price, Dutch, private, or Buy It Now.

- When the auction is over, you'll be notified by eBay; you then should contact the buyer and communicate payment and shipping terms and information.

11

DETERMINING WHAT TO SELL—AND FOR HOW MUCH

Selling your first item on eBay can be a real rush—and a genuinely stressful experience. What's the right price to set? What category should it go into? What do I do if it doesn't sell—or if it does? As you gain more experience selling, you still run into a lot of these same issues. Pricing is always a guessing game, as is category placement. But as you sell more and more items on eBay, you run into a new issue—where do you get more stuff to sell?

Now, to anyone with a garage full of junk, that might not seem like a real issue. You want more stuff to sell? Just go out to the garage and grab something! For those of you who want to make some big bucks, however, you need to find a constant flow of merchandise to put up for auction. The more you have to sell, the more money you can make!

Finding Items to Sell

Most eBay users get started by selling items they find in their attics, garages, and basements. (Makes you think of eBay as a giant garage sale, doesn't it?) But what do you do when you've completely cleaned out the attic?

There are many different places to find quantities of items to sell on eBay. We'll discuss a few of the more popular ones here—although it's likely you have a few ideas of your own. Just remember that you need to buy low and sell high—so be on the lookout for places where you can buy stuff *cheap*.

You should also be on the lookout for *trends*. Just because something's hot today doesn't mean it's going to be hot tomorrow. You wouldn't have wanted to be the proud owner of a garage-full of Pokemon cards just as the Poke-bubble burst, would you? So, when you're hunting for merchandise you can auction on eBay, try to stay on top of the coming trends—and don't buy in at the tail end of an old trend.

Of course, it's difficult to stay on top of the trends in thousands of different categories. For that reason, many eBay power sellers specialize in a half-dozen or fewer types of merchandise. You can track the trends in a handful of categories (by watching the current auctions—and the current selling prices); you can't be as aware of the trends in a larger number of categories.

So specialize, stay on top of trends, and keep your eyes open!

Garage Sales and Yard Sales

If eBay is like a giant garage sale, you might as well start with the bona fide original source. Many eBay sellers scrounge around their local garage and yard sales, looking for any merchandise that they can sell for more money on eBay. It isn't difficult; you can pick up a lot of stuff for a quarter or a dollar, and sell it for 5 or 10 times that amount online. Just make sure you get to the sale early, or all the good bargains will be picked over already!

Flea Markets

Flea markets offer similar merchandise to what you find in garage sales. The bargains might be a little less easy to come by, however, but if you keep a sharp eye you can find some items particularly suited for eBay auction.

Estate Sales

Not to be insensitive, but dead people provide some of the best deals you can find. It's the equivalent of raiding somebody else's garage or attic for old stuff to sell. Check out the weekly estate sales and auctions in your area, be prepared to buy in quantity, and see what turns up.

Live Auctions

Any live auction in your area is worth checking out, at least once. Just don't let yourself get caught up in the bidding process—you want to be able to make a profit when you resell the merchandise on eBay!

Vintage and Used Retailers

Head down to the funky side of town and take a gander at what the various "vintage" and used merchandise retailers have to offer. These are particularly good sources of collectibles, although you might have to haggle a little to get down to a decent price.

Thrift Stores

Think Goodwill and similar stores here. You can typically find some decent merchandise at low cost—and help out a nonprofit organization, to boot.

Discount and Dollar Stores

These "big lot" retailers are surprisingly good sources of eBay-ready merchandise. Most of these retailers carry overruns and closeouts at attractive prices. You can pick up merchandise here cheap, and then make it sound very attractive in your eBay listing. ("Brand new," "last-year's model," "sealed in box," and so on.)

Closeout Sales

You don't have to shop at a cheap retailer to find a good deal. Many mainline merchants offer terrific deals at the end of a season or when it's time to get in next year's merchandise. If you can get enough good stuff at a closeout price, you have a good starting inventory for your eBay sales.

Going Out of Business Sales

Even better, look for a merchant flying the white flag of surrender. When a retailer is going out of business and says "everything must go," that means that bargains are yours to be had—and don't be afraid to make a lower-priced deal, if you can.

Classified Ads

This isn't as good a source as some of the others, but if you watch the classifieds on a regular basis, you might stumble over some collectibles being sold for less than the going price online. Just buy a daily newspaper and keep your eyes peeled.

Friends and Family

You can sell stuff you find in your garage—what about your neighbor's garages? Think about cutting a deal as a "middleman" to sell your friends and family's stuff on eBay, especially if they're ignorant of the process themselves. (And remember to keep a fair share of the profits for yourself; you're doing all the work, right?)

eBay!

This leads us to the final place to look for items to sell on eBay—eBay itself! Yes, it's possible to make money buying something on eBay and then turning around and selling it to someone else on eBay at a later date. The key is timing. Remember, you have to buy low and sell high, which means getting in at the start of a trend. It's possible—although it takes a lot of hard work, and not a little skill.

Picking the Right Category

This one sounds simple. You have an item, you find the category that best describes the item, and you're done with it. To be fair, sometimes it is that simple. If you have *Singin' in the Rain* on DVD, you put it in the **Movies & Television: Video, Film: DVD: Musicals** category, no questions asked.

What if you have an old advertisement for a Major Matt Mason astronaut toy? Does it go in the **Collectibles: Advertising: Other Advertising** category or the **Toys & Hobbies: Robots, Monsters, Space Toys: Space Toys: Vintage (Pre-1970)** category?

Where you put your item should be dictated by where the highest number of potential bidders will look for it. In the Major Matt Mason example, if there are more bidders traipsing through the Advertising category, put it there; if there are more potential buyers who think of this as a vintage Space Toy thing, put it in that category. (In reality, you'll probably find listings for this sort of item in both categories.) Think like your potential buyers, and put it where you would look for it if you were them.

If you really can't decide—if your item really does belong in more than one category—eBay lets you list your item in two categories. It costs a whole ten cents more, but it potentially doubles your exposure.

> **note**
>
> If you're selling items in one of eBay's adult-oriented categories (presumably because the item contains graphic nudity or sexual content), you have to be at least 18 years old, have a valid credit card, and complete a waiver stating that you're voluntarily choosing to access adult-only materials.

Just scroll down to the Choose a Second Category section on the Category page, and enter a second category. Your item listing will show up in both categories, just like that.

Setting the Right Price

How should you price your item? If you set your minimum price too high, you might scare off potential buyers. If you set your minimum price too low, you'll probably get more interested bidders, but you might end up selling your item for less than you want or than what it's worth.

So, what's the right starting price?

Set It Low Enough to Be Attractive...

I like setting a price that's low enough to get some interested initial bidding going, but not so low that it won't get up to the price I think the item can really sell for. So, how do you know what the final selling price will be? You don't. But you can get a good idea by searching eBay for completed auctions of similar items. eBay keeps most auctions on file for thirty days, so if anything similar has sold in that period of time, you can find it from eBay's advanced search page.

At the very least, you want to be sure you're not setting the starting bid higher than the similar items' final selling price. If you do a search for completed auctions and find that *Star Wars* laserdiscs have been selling between $4 and $6, don't put a $10 starting price on the *Star Wars* laserdisc you want to sell. Ignore precedence and you won't get any bids. Instead, gauge the previous final selling prices and place your starting price at about a quarter of that level. (That would be a buck or so for our *Star Wars* example.)

Of course, you can always go the reserve price auction route—where you get to set a low initial price and a high selling floor. In our *Star Wars* example, that might mean starting bidding at a penny (very attractive to potential bidders), but setting a reserve price of $4 or so. But when you run a reserve price auction, you run a very real risk of scaring away a lot of viable bidders. If you want to run that risk, fine; reserve auctions do let you get bidding started at a very attractive level, while protecting you if bids don't rise to the price you're looking for.

caution

Don't waste your time searching auctions still in progress. Because so much bidding takes place in the last hour of the auction (that's sniping, remember?), a mid-auction price is likely to bear no relation to the final price—which you can find by searching completed auctions.

...But Don't Set It So Low That It's Not Believable

In some instances you need to worry about setting the starting price too *low*. If you set too low a minimum bid for your item, some potential bidders might think that something is wrong. (It's the old "if it's too good to be true, it probably is.") Although you might assume that bidding will take the price up into reasonable levels, too low a starting price can make your item look too cheap or otherwise flawed. If you start getting a lot of e-mails asking why you've set the price so low, you should have set a higher price.

Make Sure You Recover Your Costs...

Another factor in setting the starting price is what the item actually cost you. Now, if you're just selling some junk you found in the attic, this isn't a big concern. But if you're selling a large volume of items for profit, you don't want to sell too many items below what you paid for them. Many sellers like to set their starting price at their item cost—so if the item cost you $5, you set the minimum bid (or reserve price) at $5, and see what happens from there.

...But Not So High You Pay Too High a Listing Fee

Of course (and there's always another "of course"), if you set a higher starting price, you'll pay a higher insertion fee. Here's where it helps to know the breaks—in eBay's fee schedule, that is. Table 11.1 shows the fee breaks as of fall of 2002.

TABLE 11.1   eBay's Insertion Fee Breaks

Price Point	Fee
$0–$9.99	$0.30
$10.00–$24.99	$0.55
$25.00–$49.99	$1.10
$50.00–$199.99	$2.20
$200.00 and up	$3.30

Let's think about what this means. At the very least, you want to come in just below the fee break. Which means you want to list at $9.99 (which incurs a 30-cent fee) and not at $10.00 (which incurs a 55-cent fee). That extra penny could cost you 25 cents!

It's in your best interest to minimize any and all fees you have to pay. If you're almost positive (based on completed auction activity) that your item will sell in the $20 range no matter what you price it at, price it as low as is reasonable. And remember—if you set the starting price for anything under $10, you only pay a 30-cent listing fee!

Make Sure You Can Live with a Single Bid

What happens if you set the starting price at $5 and you only get one bid—at $5? Even if you thought the item was worth twice that, you can't back out now; you have to honor all bids in your auction, even if there's only one of them. You can't e-mail the bidder and say sorry, I really can't afford to sell it for this price. If you listed it, you agreed to sell it for any price at or above your minimum. It's a binding contract. So if the bidding is low, you better get comfortable with it—it's too late to change your mind now!

"Mike Sez"

As a rule of thumb, I set item pricing at 10%–25% of what I think the final selling price will be. When faced with a choice, I almost always opt for a lower, rather than a higher, starting price.

The Absolute Minimum

Here are the key points to remember from this chapter:

- You can find items to sell on eBay just about anywhere, from garage sales to estate auctions to dollar stores. Just remember to buy low and sell high!

- When it comes time to pick the item category, think about where the most potential buyers would think to look for that item. If you can't decide between two categories, pay ten cents extra to have eBay list the item in two categories.

- Setting the starting price for an auction is more of an art than a science. In general, lower prices are best—if you can live with an item actually selling for the minimum price.

12

DECIDING ON YOUR PAYMENT METHODS

When you're listing an item for auction on eBay, you can choose which types of payment you'll accept from the winning bidder. This may seem like an easy decision, but each different type of payment needs to be handled differently on your end.

This chapter talks about the different types of payment you can choose to use. As any experienced eBay seller will tell you, not all dollars are worth the same; a dollar paid by one method might actually be worth less (or be more risky) than a dollar by another method. And you *do* want the biggest dollar, don't you?

Fortunately, you're not forced to use any one payment method. For example, you can limit your payments to credit cards only; there's no law that says you have to accept cash or checks. So, read on to learn which types of payment provide the biggest return for your efforts!

Paying by Cash

As a seller, there's nothing better than opening up an envelope and finding a few crisp new bills inside. Unfortunately, sending cash through the mails is not one of the smartest things a buyer can do; cash is too easily ripped off, and virtually untraceable. You can ask for cash payment (not that you should, of course), but unless the selling price is extremely low (under $5), don't expect buyers to comply.

Paying by C.O.D.

Cash on delivery (C.O.D.) might sound good on paper. You ship the item, with the stipulation that the deliveryman (or woman) collect payment when the item is delivered.

There are problems with this method, however. What happens if the buyer isn't home when the delivery is made? What if the buyer is at home, but doesn't have the cash? What if the buyer refuses to pay—and rejects the shipment? I've heard stories of up to 25% of all C.O.D. orders being refused, for one reason or another.

Even worse, C.O.D. service often comes with a high fee from the carrier—and it's a fee that you, the seller, have to pay. The additional fee alone rules out C.O.D. for many sellers.

All things considered, it's easy to see why few eBay sellers offer C.O.D. payment. The problems with this payment method tend to outweigh the benefits, and I can't recommend it.

Paying by Personal Check

The most common form of payment is personal check. Buyers like paying by check because it's convenient, and because checks can be tracked (or even canceled) if problems arise with the seller.

Sellers like personal checks a little less, because they're not instant money. When you deposit a check in your bank, you're not depositing cash. That $100 check doesn't turn into $100 cash until it tracks back through the financial system, from your bank back to the buyer's bank, and the funds are both verified and transferred. That can take some time, typically 10 business days or so.

> **" Mike Sez "**
>
> If you ship an item on immediate receipt of a personal check and then a week later you get a notice from your bank that the check has bounced, you deserve to lose every single penny of that transaction. Eager shippers and personal checks just don't mix—and you *will* learn from your mistake.

Because buyers prefer paying by check, you should probably be prepared to handle this payment method. When you receive a check, deposit it as soon as possible—but do *not* ship the item. Wait until the check clears the bank (two weeks if you want to be safe—longer for checks on non-U.S. banks) before you ship the item. If, after that period of time, the check hasn't bounced, it's okay to proceed with shipment.

If you are on the bad end of a bounced check, all hope is not lost. The first thing to do is get in touch with your bank and ask them to resubmit the check in question. Maybe the buyer was just temporarily out of funds. Maybe the bank made a mistake. Whatever. In at least half the cases, bounced checks unbounce when they're resubmitted.

caution

If a check bounces, the depositor (you) will likely be assessed a fee from your bank. (The writer of the bad check will also have a fee to pay.) If the buyer who wrote the check offers to make good on the payment, make sure they reimburse you for your bad check fee, over and above the final auction price.

Whether you resubmit the check or not, you should definitely e-mail the buyer and let him know what happened. At the very least, you'll want the buyer to reimburse you for any bad check fees your bank charged you. The buyer might also be able to provide another form of payment to get things moving again. (Credit cards are nice—as are money orders.)

Paying by Money Order or Cashier's Check

Money orders and cashier's checks are, to the seller, almost as good as cash. You can cash a money order immediately, without waiting for funds to clear, and have cash in your hand. When you receive a money order or cashier's check, deposit it and then ship the auction item. There's no need to hold the item.

The only bad thing about money orders and cashier's checks is that you have to wait for them to arrive. Even if the buyer puts payment in the mail the very next day, you'll still wait anywhere from 3–5 days after the auction to receive payment. Still, there's not a lot not to like about this method of payment—it's hard to get burned with either a money order or cashier's check.

Paying by Credit Card—Or PayPal

Until very recently, if you wanted to accept credit card payment for your auction items, you had to be a real retailer, complete with merchant account and bank-supplied charge card terminal. This limited the number of sellers who could accept credit card payment, which probably cut down on potential bidders, because many buyers like the convenience and relative safety of paying by credit card.

Today, however, there are several options available to any online auction seller that enable you to accept credit card payments for your auction items—the most popular of which is offered by several online payment services. These online payment services let any auction seller easily accept credit card payments, with little or no setup hassle. These services, led by PayPal, enable buyers to pay *them* by credit card, and then send you a check or deposit funds directly to your bank account.

Using an Online Payment Service

To use one of these online payment services (as a seller), you need to sign up for the service (no charge) and create an account. When it comes time to list an item, you include information about the service in your item listing. At the end of the auction, you send the winning bidder an electronic invoice (via e-mail) that contains instructions for credit card payment. The buyer uses the information contained in that invoice to log on to the online payment site and enter his or her credit card information. The online payment site then charges the buyer's credit card, and notifies you that you've been paid. Upon this notification, you then ship the item, and contact the online payment site to either cut you a check or transfer the funds into your normal bank account.

Almost all of these services charge the seller a percentage of the final value of the transaction—including shipping and handling charges. (PayPal charges either 2.2% or 2.9% of the total price, depending on the type of account you have.) So, if a seller sells an item for $5 and tacks on $4 for shipping and handling, the online payment service will base their fee on the total $9 payment.

And these fees can add up. When you consider that you have to pay eBay's listing fee and final value fee, paying another few points for the convenience of accepting credit cards can really sock it to a small seller—or anyone selling a low-priced item. You should definitely research the payment service's fees before you sign up.

Choosing an Online Payment Service

Today the largest online payment service is PayPal (www.paypal.com), which is now owned by eBay. You can deal with PayPal separately from eBay, or choose to let eBay integrate PayPal into your auction listings and Checkout when you list your item. (This last option is a good one; you can select to accept PayPal payments by checking a single box when you're creating a new item listing.)

Other services similar to PayPal include:

- **BidPay** (www.bidpay.com). Enables buyers to send sellers Western Union money orders for auction payment.

- **Payingfast** (www.payingfast.com). Enables buyers to send money orders to sellers; buyers can pay via check or credit card.

- **Yahoo! PayDirect** (paydirect.yahoo.com). Yahoo's proprietary online payment service, available to all Web users.

Which Way Is Best?

The more payment options you offer, the more potential bidders you'll attract. Still, some methods are better than others for different types of sellers; use Table 12.1 to determine which methods work best for you.

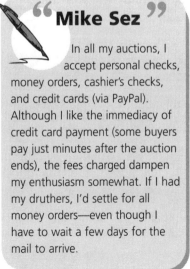

note

Previous to acquiring PayPal, eBay owned another electronic payment service, Billpoint. Billpoint lost the marketplace war to PayPal, however, and has since been phased out.

Learn more about PayPal in Chapter 30, "Using PayPal and Other Payment Services."

❝Mike Sez❞

In all my auctions, I accept personal checks, money orders, cashier's checks, and credit cards (via PayPal). Although I like the immediacy of credit card payment (some buyers pay just minutes after the auction ends), the fees charged dampen my enthusiasm somewhat. If I had my druthers, I'd settle for all money orders—even though I have to wait a few days for the mail to arrive.

TABLE 12.1 Payment Methods Rated

Payment Method	Pros	Cons
Cash	Fast payment, no hassles	Unattractive to buyers
C.O.D.	Cash payment	High noncompletion rate; lots of paperwork
Personal check	Convenient for buyers	Slow, have to wait to clear
Money order/ cashier's check	Fast payment, like cash	Hassle for buyers
Credit cards	Fees involved	Fast payment, buyers like online payment services

THE ABSOLUTE MINIMUM

Here are the key points to remember from this chapter:

- The fastest way to get your money is via credit card (or credit card payment via PayPal or another online payment service). You'll pay for the privilege, however.

- The slowest way to get your money is via personal check—even though most buyers prefer this method.

- If you do accept payment by personal check, remember to wait at least 10 business days for the check to clear before you ship the merchandise.

- The best compromise between speed and hassle is payment via cashier's check or money order. (And there are no fees involved.)

13

CHOOSING THE RIGHT LISTING OPTIONS

Back in Chapter 10, "Selling 101: A Tutorial for Beginning Sellers," you learned how to use the various forms on the eBay site to create an auction item listing. At the time, I told you about the various listing options available on the Provide Pictures & Item Details page, but I didn't go into a lot of detail.

Well, now it's time to fuss over all those particulars.

All the options I talk about in this chapter are found on the Provide Pictures & Item Details page, in eBay's Sell Your Item section. To be specific, this is the third page you encounter after you click the Sell link on eBay's home page.

Choosing the Right Length

The first listing option you encounter is one of Duration. eBay lets you choose from four different lengths for your auctions: 3, 5, 7, or 10 days. The first three options come at the standard listing price; 10-day auctions cost you an additional ten cents.

When eBay first started out, it only offered a single length: 7 days. This is still the default length, and the length chosen by the majority of sellers. What's nice about a 7-day auction is that it guarantees that your item is listed over a weekend; a 3- or 5-day auction won't necessarily hit the busy weekend days, depending on the day you start the auction.

Thinking about heavy weekend traffic, some users prefer a 10-day auction, starting on a Friday or Saturday, to get *two* weekends into the bidding schedule. There's some logic in that; just one extra bid will probably offset the extra ten-cent cost. However, a longer auction like this also means that you have to wait longer before you collect your money, so that needs to be figured in, as well.

If you really need your money quickly, go with a 3- or 5-day auction, but try to time the listing so that you get in a bidding weekend. Also know that some buyers expect and plan on 7-day auctions, so you might not get as much last-minute sniping if you opt for the shorter length.

> **tip**
>
> More bidders log on to eBay on Saturday and Sunday than on any other days of the week—probably because more users are home from school and work.

> **" Mike Sez "**
>
> I opt for the 7-day auction for all my items. It's what users expect, and it allows for bidding on each day of the week—without taking *too* long to get the process over with.

Choosing a Different Start Time

eBay also lets you choose a specific start time for your auction—which, of course, also becomes your auction's end time. By default, an eBay auction starts as soon as the item listing is placed, so if you placed your listing at 10:00 a.m., that's when the auction starts and ends. However, you can pay an extra $0.10 and schedule your auction to start (and stop) at a specified time different from when you created the item listing.

This is an okay option if you have to create your auction listings at what would otherwise be a bad time to end an auction—in the morning or early afternoon, for example. It's better to end an auction during the evening, when more users are at home. So, if you can't launch your auctions of an evening, spend the extra ten cents so that eBay can automatically schedule the start of your auction for you.

To Reserve—Or Not to Reserve

After you decide on the duration of your auction, how many units you're selling, and your starting price, you run into the Reserve Price option. As you learned in Chapter 10, a reserve price auction is one where you set a low starting price to get the bidding started, but keep a higher, hidden reserve price that serves as the lowest price you'll sell the item for. For example, you might start bidding at $1, but have a reserve price of $10. You don't actually sell the item until you get a bid at $10 or above; a high bid of $9.99 wouldn't be a winning bid.

On the up side, reserve price auctions let you set however low a starting price as you want—and low starting prices get a lot of buyer attention, and get the bids flowing. You're not obligated to sell at that low price, of course; that's why you have the reserve, as protection in case the bids don't go high enough.

> ## "Mike Sez"
>
> Using eBay to schedule a start time for your auctions may be a necessary evil if you're not at home, at your computer, at the time of day you want your auctions to end. It may be better, over the long run, to use an auction management program or service that includes this type of listing scheduling at a lower (or zero) additional cost.
>
> I hardly ever use the reserve price option; my auction-of-choice is the standard, non-reserve model. The only exception is when I have an item that should have a relatively high basement price (above $100), even though similar auctions are starting at much lower prices. For example, I might list an item that will probably sell in the $200 range with a $20 starting price. It's this kind of differential that makes you think about setting a reserve price.

On the down side, reserve auctions confuse a lot of potential bidders—newer users, in particular. They also foster a bit of suspicion from bidders, because you're not telling them the whole truth. (The reserve price is always hidden.) So you're apt to have fewer bidders on a reserve price auction, in spite of the lower starting price.

My advice is, in most cases, not to use the reserve price option. If there's an absolutely positively minimum price you have to get out of a particular item, set that price as your starting bid price. There's no need—and little to be gained—by setting a hidden reserve.

In case you're wondering, you don't save on eBay fees if you have a lower starting price in a reserve price auction. That's because if you've chosen the reserve price option, eBay bases your listing fee on the reserve price you set—not on the lower starting price. So there's no getting around it; there's no way to cheat eBay out of their fees!

Sell It Now?

The next option on the Provide Pictures & Item Details page is the Buy It Now (BIN) price. Buy It Now is the option that lets you sell your item to the first bidder who offers a specific fixed price. If the first bidder bids lower than the Buy It Now price, the Buy It Now option disappears and the auction continues as normal.

Should you use Buy It Now? The downside is that BIN adds to an auction's confusion factor, possibly scaring some users away. (The presence of a high BIN—relative to the starting price, in any case—is apt to tell some buyers that you're asking more for your item than it's worth, or that similar items are selling for.) The upside is that if you set a high enough BIN price and some chump ponies up, you get your money sooner than if you'd allowed the auction to continue to its natural conclusion.

If you're going to use Buy It Now, make sure that it's worth your while. You definitely *don't* want to set a BIN price lower than what you think your item will eventually sell for. For example, if you know that similar items have been selling for $20 on eBay, the absolute lowest you want to set your BIN price is $20. If you set the BIN price at $15, for example, some sharp buyer is going to swoop in and pay you $15 for an item that probably would have sold for $20.

In fact, if you use the BIN option, you probably want to set the BIN price at some point *higher* than the expected high bid price. Taking our $20 example, you might set the BIN at $25. If somebody wants to buy it now, they'll pay you a $5 premium for the privilege. If not, bidding will proceed as normal until a (presumably lower) high bid is realized.

> **"Mike Sez"**
>
> I know I might be walking away from some quick bucks, but I typically don't use Buy It Now in my auctions. My feeling is that it scares away potential bidders—and I'm in the business of attracting bidders, not driving them away.

Public or Private?

Just below the Buy It Now option is the Private Auction option. When you choose this option, the bidders' names don't show up on the item listing page; bidders' identifications remain private.

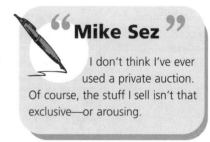

Mike Sez

I don't think I've ever used a private auction. Of course, the stuff I sell isn't that exclusive—or arousing.

The worth of a private auction comes when you have something controversial to sell—something that others might be embarrassed to be found bidding on. Although most private auctions are for adult-only items, it's easy to imagine an auction for an exclusive high-priced item where bidders don't want (or need) the publicity. So, if you're selling either dirty pictures or items that John Travolta might be interested in, going private is worth consideration.

Local Is Good

You should always fill in your city and state on the Provide Pictures & Item Details page, as this information helps bidders determine approximate shipping cost from your location to theirs. But there's a second location option on the Provide Pictures & Item Details page, called Region. What exactly is this option, and how does it work?

The Region option is actually a list of eBay local auctions. When you select a region, you ensure that your listing will be visible to any users browsing or searching your specific local auction. (And, wonder of wonders, listing your item in a local auction is that rare eBay phenomenon—a totally free option!)

Choosing to list in your local auction is as easy as making a selection from the Region list. If you don't make a selection, your item won't be listed locally—even if you fill in the city and state fields.

When users perform a search for an item, they have the option of searching by region. In addition, when users click the Browse link on the Navigation Bar, they can then select the Regions link, which displays the Go Local! page. (You can also access this page directly, by going to pages.ebay.com/ regional/hub.html.) The Go Local! page contains direct links to more than 60 regional listing pages, like the one shown in Figure 13.1. Users can then search for local listings in particular categories.

Mike Sez

Listing locally is a particularly good idea if you're selling a large or hard-to-ship item—one that's more easily carted across town than shipped across country. And, because local listings are free, there's no reason *not* to select a region on the Provide Pictures & Item Details page.

FIGURE 13.1

When you select a region for your item listing, your listing now appears in your local Go Local! listing page.

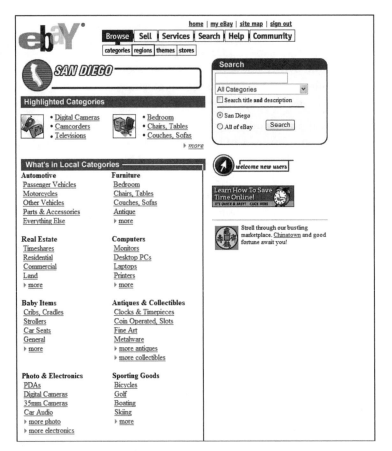

A Pretty Picture

I devote an entire chapter of this book (Chapter 15, "Using Pictures with Your Listings") to including pictures with your eBay listings, so I won't go into a lot of detail here. Suffice to say that listings with pictures are more successful than listings without pictures. Whether you use eBay's picture hosting services or your own Web hosting, you'll increase your sell rate *and* your average final price when you add a picture to your text.

"Mike Sez"

Unless there's a good reason *not* to include a picture (like you don't have a camera), I always recommend including at least one picture with your item listings. You should know, however, that using eBay's picture hosting service can get expensive; they charge for every picture of yours (past the first one) that they host on their servers.

Go for the Gallery?

The Gallery is a section of eBay that displays listing pictures, along with titles, as shown in Figure 13.2. It's a great way to browse through the listings if your shopping style is particularly visual. Buyers access the Gallery by clicking the Gallery link on the Site Map page, selecting Gallery View in the Show section on any search results or category page, or going direct to pages.ebay.com/buy/gallery.html. Items listed with the Gallery option are also displayed (with photo) in any browsing category page, as shown in Figure 13.3.

FIGURE 13.2

Browsing items for auction in the Gallery.

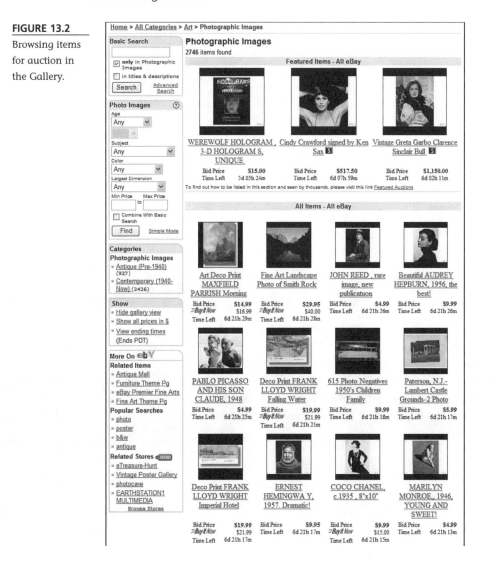

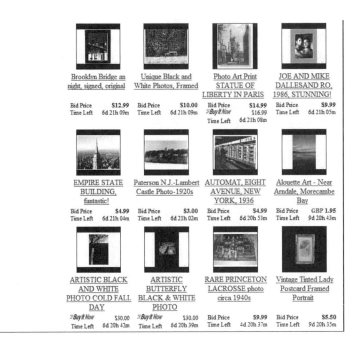

FIGURE 13.3
Gallery items are
highlighted—
with picture—on
browsing cate-
gory pages.

eBay also offers a second Gallery option, called
Gallery Featured. When you pay for this option,
your item will periodically show up in the special
Featured section above the general Gallery.

Pricing for the standard Gallery listing is just 25
cents. Pricing for the Gallery Featured option is
$19.95.

" Mike Sez "

Even though a basic
Gallery listing is cheap
(just a quarter!), I tend not to utilize this option. My personal experience shows that few users
actually venture to the Gallery (it's
kind of hidden on eBay's site),
which makes this a good-sounding
option that seldom pays for itself.

Grab Attention with Listing Upgrades

Next we come to that list of nickel and dime (and higher!) marketing devices that eBay calls "listing upgrades." These options are designed to make your listing stand out from the hundreds or thousands of similar listings in any particular category.

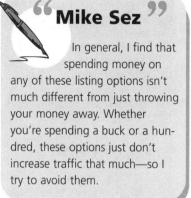

Bold

This option, which costs $2.00, displays your item title in bold in any category or search results listings. A boldfaced item listing is shown in Figure 13.4.

FIGURE 13.4

Two item listings—the first one in bold.

Goldberg Anniversary Piper R/C Airplane Model	$73.00	7	1d 00h 58m
R/C Airplane 3 Blade Prop Propeller Vintage	$2.00	1	1d 02h 19m

Highlight

What's more attention-getting than a bold title? How about a *shaded* item listing?

When you select the Highlight option, your listing (on any category or search results page) is displayed with a colored shade, as shown in Figure 13.5. This little bit of color will cost you $5.00.

FIGURE 13.5

Two item listings—the first one enhanced with the Highlight option.

BUTTON made NEW YORK for USSR army 1942 #305	$9.00	-	11m
Venezia Jeans button down denim shirt 26/28	$6.19	2	12m

Featured Plus!

The Featured Plus! option displays your item in the Featured Items section of its category, and in the Featured Items section of any search results page. This option will set you back a whopping $19.95.

Home Page Featured

Ever wonder how much it costs to have your item featured on the main eBay home page? Here's the answer: $99.95. (And it doesn't even guarantee how often your item will pop up. What a deal—*not*.) All you have to do is select the Home Page Featured option, and your item will *periodically* be displayed on the home page. (And for the same low price, your item is also displayed in the Featured Items section of normal category and search results pages.)

Great Gift Icon

Think your item would make a great gift for a specific occasion? Then pony up $0.25 to add one of several Great Gift icons beside your item's listing. Figure 13.6 shows a listing enhanced with one of these icons.

FIGURE 13.6
An item
enhanced with a
Great Gift icon.

| Great Christmas Gift for the Doll Collector | $35.00 | - | 14h 18m |

Count 'em Up

The final option you can select on the Provide Pictures & Item Details page is the free page counter. When you opt to put a counter at the bottom of your listing page (like the one in Figure 13.7), you and (in most cases) potential bidders can see how many other users have visited the page. The more page visitors, the more likely it is that you'll receive a substantial number of bids.

FIGURE 13.7
An Andale
counter at the
bottom of an
eBay listing
page.

00032
Free Counters powered by Andale!

You can choose from three different types of counters, all supplied (free of charge) by Andale, a third-party service firm. The Andale Style counter is a black-and-white "odometer"-type counter; the Green LED Counter is a little more colorful, displaying bright green "digital" numbers against a black background; and the Hidden counter is hidden to bidders but visible to you, the seller. Choose one of these three, or the Do Not Add a Counter option—no payment necessary!

" Mike Sez "

If you think you're going to get a lot of traffic to your item listing page, by all means display a counter. A high number on a counter will make bidders think they have to bid *now* to get in on the action. If, on the other hand, you don't want to tip your hand as to how many potential bidders you might have, go with the hidden counter. After all, it doesn't matter if you have 2 or 200 visitors, as long as you have one really good bid!

THE ABSOLUTE MINIMUM

Here are the key points to remember from this chapter:

- eBay offers a variety of listing enhancements on the Provide Pictures & Item Details page.
- Most of these listing enhancements cost money.
- Few of these listing enhancements are worth the money.
- Having an item that a lot of buyers want will produce many more bidders than you'll get by using these expensive listing options.

14

WRITING A LISTING THAT SELLS

Did you know that only about half the items listed on eBay at any given time actually sell during the current auction? That's right; in about half the current auctions, no one meets the minimum bid.

How do you increase the odds of *your* item selling? It's all about creating a powerful, effective item listing—in both the title and the item description.

Write a Title That SELLS!

Let's start right at the top, with the title of your item listing. You can use up to 45 letters, numbers, characters, and spaces, and you need to accomplish two things:

- You have to include the appropriate information so that anyone searching for a similar item will find your item in his search results.

- You have to make your title stand out from all the other titles on those long listing pages.

Do those two things, and you significantly increase your chances of getting your item noticed and sold.

Include Key Information

Let's tackle the first point first. You have to think like the people who will be looking for your item. Most users will be using eBay's search feature to look for specific items, so you want to put the right keywords into your item title, to make your item pop up on as many search results pages as possible.

As an example, let's say you have an original 1964 Superman model kit, manufactured by Aurora, still in its shrink-wrapped box. How do you list this item?

You have to make sure you get all the right keywords in your title. For this example, it's obvious that **Superman** should be a keyword, as should **Aurora** and maybe **1964**. Then, it gets iffy-er. Should you call it a **model kit** or a **plastic model kit** or a **plastic model**? Should you call it **unassembled** or **still in box** or **original condition**?

When dealing with collectibles, you often can use accepted abbreviations and acronyms. (I'll list some of these acronyms later in this chapter.) In this case, you could use the abbreviation **MISB**, which stands for *mint in sealed box*. True collectors will know what this means, and it saves precious "real estate" in your title. (By the way, if this model wasn't in the box but was instead already assembled, you could use the abbreviation **BU**, for *built-up*.) Continuing this example, a title that included all the keywords users might search on would be **1964 Superman Aurora Plastic Model Kit MISB**. (This comes in just under 45 characters!)

tip

If you're unsure how best to word the title for your item listing, check out auctions for similar items and "borrow" their wording.

Note the inclusion of the year in the title. That's a good thing, as it helps to narrow down or better identify the item. Someone looking for a 1964 Superman model is not going to be interested in the 1978 or 2001 reissues, so including the date helps to narrow down your prospective customers.

If your item has a model number or series name, that's definitely something to include. As an example, you might be selling a **14" Pearl Export Select Snare Drum with Case**. In this case, Pearl is the manufacturer and Export Select is the series or line. Another example might be a listing for a **1956 Gibson ES-175 Red Jazz Guitar**. This title gets in the year (1956), the manufacturer (Gibson), the model number (ES-175), the color (Red), and a brief description of what it is (a jazz guitar)—which pretty much covers all the bases.

Make Your Title Stand Out

Beyond including as many relevant facts as possible in your title, how do you make your title POP off the page and STAND OUT from all the other boring listings? Obviously, one technique is to employ the judicious use of CAPITAL LETTERS. The operative word here is *judicious*; titles with ALL capital letters step over the line into overkill.

You can also try a lot of nonalphanumeric characters, such as **!!!** or **###** or ******* at the beginning or end of your title, although I don't recommend it. That's because eBay's search engine sometimes ignores titles that include too many of these nonsense characters—which is the exact opposite of what you want to accomplish. Plus, these nonsense characters waste valuable space that could be better used to tell more about your item.

Instead, I advise you to think like an advertising copywriter. What words almost always stop consumers in their tracks? Use attention-getting words such as **FREE** and **NEW** and **BONUS** and **EXTRA** and **DELUXE** and **RARE**—as long as these words truly describe the item you're selling and don't mislead the potential bidder.

Try this one on for size: Which would you rather bid on, a **1964 Superman Model Kit** or a **RARE 1964 Superman Model Kit**? I'm betting you go for the second one—and mentally prepare yourself to pay more for it, too!

In short, use your title to both inform and attract attention—and include as many potential search keywords as possible.

What to Avoid

You already know that you should probably avoid nonsense characters—especially if you can use that space to better effect. You should also avoid using "hot" words that don't have anything to do with your item—words designed to mislead eBay's search engine and potential bidders.

In our Superman example, some enterprising sellers might create a title like this: **Superman Model NOT Batman Spider-Man**.

Okay, what's wrong with this? It's not a lie; the Superman model definitely is *not* a Batman or Spider-Man model. But that's not why the seller put those words in the title. He put those words there so that anyone searching for a Batman or Spider-Man model would find his listing in their search results. He might think he's increasing the visibility of his listing, but what he's really doing is ticking off potential buyers of Batman and Spider-Man merchandise. What at first seems clever is annoying and misleading, and should be avoided.

One other thing, which I touched on previously—DON'T TYPE IN ALL CAPS! It's okay to capitalize a word or two in your title or description, but don't type an all-cap title. (And *definitely* don't capitalize your entire item description!) All caps makes it look like you're shouting, and while you might think that would be good for grabbing buyers' attentions, it actually has just the opposite effect; it turns them off.

Write the Right Description

If the listing title is the headline of your ad, the listing description is your ad's body copy. Which means it's time to put on your copywriter's hat, and get down to the nitty-gritty details.

Take All the Space You Need

What makes for good copy? First, you have all the space you need, so say as much as you need to say. Unlike the title description, you don't have to scrimp on words or leave anything out. If you can describe your item adequately in a sentence, great; if it takes three paragraphs, that's okay, too.

When you're writing the description for your ad, make sure you mention anything and everything that a potential bidder might need to know. Note any defects or imperfections of the item. Include your desired payment terms and your preferred shipping methods. If the object is graded or evaluated in any way, include that assessment in your description. In other words, include everything you can think of that will eliminate any surprises for the buyer.

First Things First

However, you should probably put the most important and motivating information in your initial paragraph because a lot of folks won't read any further than that. Think of your first paragraph like a lead paragraph in a newspaper story; grab 'em with something catchy, give them the gist of the story, and lead them into reading the next paragraph and the one after that.

The Bare Necessities

There are certain key data points that users expect to see in your item description. Here's the bare minimum that you should include:

- Name (or title)
- Condition
- Age
- Original use (what you used it for)
- Value (if you know it)
- Any included accessories (including the original instruction manual, if you have it)
- Any known defects or damage

If you don't know any of this stuff, that's okay—as long as you admit it. If you're not that familiar with the type of merchandise you're selling, just say so. Better to plead ignorance upfront than to have a more savvy buyer cause problems for you after the sale.

Describe It—Accurately

Because other users will be bidding on your item sight unseen, you have to make the process as easy as possible for potential bidders. That means describing the item as accurately as possible, and in as much detail as possible. If the item has a scratch or blemish, note it. If the paint is peeling, note it. If it includes a few non-original parts, note it. Bidders don't have the item to hold in their hands and examine in person, so you have to be their eyes and ears. That means describing the item in painful detail, and being completely honest about it.

If you're *not* honest in your description, it will come back to haunt you—in the form of an unhappy and complaining buyer.

Stress Benefits, Not Features

Although you need to be descriptive (and in some collectibles categories, you need to be *obsessively* so), it doesn't hurt to employ a little marketing savvy and salesmanship. Yes, you should talk about the features of your item, but it's even better if you can talk about your product's *benefits* to the potential buyer.

Let's say you're selling a used cordless phone, and the phone has a 50-number memory. Saying "50-number memory" is stating a feature; saying instead that the phone "lets you recall your 50 most-called phone numbers at the press of a button" is describing a benefit. Remember, a feature is something your item has; a benefit is something your item does for the user.

Break It Up

You should include as much descriptive copy as you need in your listing, but you should also make sure that every sentence sells your item.

If your listing starts to get a little long, you can break it into more readable chunks by using a little HTML. When you want to start a new paragraph, press the Enter key on your keyboard, type **<P>**, and then press Enter again. This inserts a paragraph break into your text, which should provide a blank line between the first paragraph and the next.

Don't Forget the Fine Print

Breaking up your description enables you to put a *lot* more info into your description. When it comes to informing potential buyers, it's impossible to be too complete. (And if you don't define a detail, the buyer will—in his or her mind.) Don't assume that buyers know *anything*; take the time to spell out all the details about payment and shipping and the like.

Here is some of the "fine print" you might want to include at the bottom of your item description:

> **tip**
>
> When you enter plain text into the Description box, eBay formats it as plain text on your item listing page. However, you can enter HTML code as part of your description, and make your listing look as lively as a page on the World Wide Web. To learn more about using HTML to spice up your otherwise-boring listings, turn to Chapter 16, "Creating a Great-Looking Listing."

- Bidding restrictions, such as "No bidders with negative feedback," "Bidders with positive feedback of at least 10 only," "U.S. buyers only," and the like.
- Payment restrictions, such as "U.S. funds only," "No personal checks," "Personal checks take two weeks to clear," and so on.
- Shipping/handling charges (if you know them) and restrictions, such as "Buyer pays shipping/handling," "Shipping via USPS Priority Mail only," and so forth.
- Information about the condition of the item, in painful detail.
- If your item has been graded (discussed later in this chapter), include the grade.
- Information about your other auctions.

Include the Alternates

The very last things you can put into your listing, at the very bottom, are some extra words. Remember, not every person uses the same words to describe things.

If you're selling a plastic model kit, for example, some users will search for **model**, others for **kit**, still others for **statue** or **figure** or **styrene**. Although you can't put all these variations into the item title, you *can* throw them in somewhere in the description—or, if all else fails, at the bottom of the item description. (Remember, they'll be picked up by eBay's search engine if they're *anywhere* in the description area.)

While you're at it, throw in any alternate spellings you can think of. For example, you might know that the correct spelling of **Spider-Man** includes the hyphen in the middle, but other users might search for the unhyphenated **Spiderman**. Whichever variation you use in your title, throw the other one in at the bottom of the description.

Making the Grade

When you're selling items on eBay, it helps to know what kind of shape your items are in. For many categories of merchandise, that means grading the item's condition—according to some very formal rules.

Grading is a way of noting the condition of an item, according to a predetermined standard. Collectors use these grading scales to help evaluate and price items within a category. If you know the grade of your item, you can include the grade in the item's title or description, and thus more accurately describe the item to potential bidders.

You should know, however, that there is no such thing as a "universal" grading system for all items; different types of collectibles have their own unique grading systems. For example, trading cards are graded from A1 to F1; stamps are graded from Poor to Superb.

Many collectible categories use a variation of the Mint grading system, as shown in Table 14.1.

TABLE 14.1 Mint System Grading

Grade	Abbreviation	Description
Mint	MT, M, 10	An item in perfect condition, without any damage or imperfections.
Very Fine	VF	Similar to mint.
Near Mint	NM, 9	An item with a very minor, hardly noticeable flaw. Sometimes described as "like new."
Near Fine	NF	Similar to near mint.
Excellent	EX, 8	An item considered above average, but with pronounced signs of wear.

TABLE 14.1   Continued

Grade	Abbreviation	Description
Fine	F	Similar to excellent.
Very Good	VG, 7	An item in average condition.
Good	GD, G, 6	An item that has clear indications of age, wear, and use.
Fair	F	An item that is heavily worn.
Poor	P, 5	An item that is damaged or somehow incomplete.

Degrees between grade levels are indicated with a + or -. (For example, an item between Fine and Very Fine would be designated as F+.) Naturally, the definition of a Mint or Fair item differs by item type.

Other Ways to Describe Your Item

There are some other grading-related abbreviations you can use in your item listings. As you can see in Table 14.2, these abbreviations help you describe your item (especially in the title) without wasting a lot of valuable space.

TABLE 14.2   Grading-Related Terms

Abbreviation	Description	Meaning
BU	Built up	For models and other to-be-assembled items; indicates that the item has already been assembled
CC	Cut corner	Some closeout items are marked by a notch on the corner of the package
CO	Cut out	Closeout item
COA	Certificate of authority/ authenticity	Document that vouches for the authenticity of the item; often found with autographed or rare collectible items
COH	Cut out hole	Some closeout items are marked by a small hole punched somewhere on the package
HC	Hard cover	Used to indicate hardcover (as opposed to softcover, or paperback) books
HTF	Hard to find	Item isn't in widespread circulation

Abbreviation	Description	Meaning
MIB	Mint in box	Item in perfect condition, still in the original box
MIMB	Mint in mint box	Item in perfect condition, still in the original box—which itself is in perfect condition
MIP	Mint in package	Item in perfect condition, still in the original package
MISB	Mint in sealed box	Item in perfect condition, still in the original box with the original seal
MOC	Mint on card	For action figures and similar items, an item in perfect condition still in its original carded package
MWBMT	Mint with both mint tags	For stuffed animals that typically have both a hang tag and a tush (sewn-on) tag, indicates both tags are in perfect condition
NOS	New old stock	Old, discontinued parts in original, unused condition
NR	No reserve	Indicates that you're selling an item with no reserve price
NRFB	Never removed from box	An item bought but never used or played with
NWT	New with tags	Item, unused, that still has its original hanging tags
OOP	Out of print	Item is no longer being manufactured
RR	Re-release	Not the original issue, but rather a reissue (typically done for the collector's market)
SC	Soft cover	A paperback (non-hard cover) book
SS	Still sealed	As it says, still in the original sealed package

The big problem with any grading system is that grading is subjective. Although there may be guidelines for different grading levels, the line between very good and excellent is often a fine one. You should be very careful about assigning your own grading levels; even better, supplement the grade with a detailed description and photographs, so bidders can make up their own minds as to your item's true value.

THE ABSOLUTE MINIMUM

Here are the key points to remember from this chapter:

- Your item title needs to be no more than 45 characters long—and can include letters, numbers, characters, and spaces.

- Pack as much info into your title as possible, using common abbreviations and grading levels.

- The description of your item can be as long as you want—so take the space to include as much detailed information as is practical.

- Include an accurate description of the item's condition, including any flaws or damage.

- Include all necessary fine print for your transaction at the bottom of the item description.

- Use grading (Fair, Good, Mint, and so on) to describe the condition of your item.

15

USING PICTURES IN YOUR LISTINGS

A picture in your listing greatly increases the chances of actually selling your item—and also increases the average price you will receive.

Knowing that, you'd think more eBay ads would include pictures. The fact that they don't is because adding a picture to an eBay listing requires more work than checking a check box. Basically, you have to go through four separate steps to insert a picture into your item listing:

1. Take a picture of your item.

2. Convert that picture to a digital graphics file.

3. Edit the image file (so that it looks pretty).

4. Upload your image file to a server somewhere on the Internet—or use eBay's picture listing service.

We'll look at each of these steps individually, but first, here's a checklist of what you need to take effective pictures for your eBay listings:

Checklist—eBay Pictures

- ☐ Digital camera
- ☐ Lighting (built-in flash can work)
- ☐ Tripod
- ☐ Clean space with plain black or white background
- ☐ Scanner (for flat items)
- ☐ Graphics editing software
- ☐ Web picture hosting service (optional)

❝Mike Sez❞

Is there any time when you *don't* want to include a picture of an item? If the item is nothing more than a black box—or a blank book cover—there's not a lot of point in showing it. However, don't think that if an item is damaged you shouldn't show it; just the opposite! You want bidders to know what they're getting into, regarding damage and flaws, and showing a picture is the best way to do this.

Take a Picture—Or Make a Scan

It all starts with a picture. But it better be a darned good picture, or potential bidders won't find it much use. Although this really isn't the place for a basic photography lesson, I can give you a few tips on how to take the right kinds of pictures to use in your eBay listings:

- **Use a digital camera.** Although you can take pictures with a normal film camera, develop the film, and have your film processor transfer your photos to graphics files on a photo CD, it's a lot easier if you start with digital at the source—especially if you plan on listing a lot of items on eBay. You can pick up a low-end digital camera for well under $200 these days, and going direct from camera-to-computer-eBay is a lot easier than any other method.

caution

Whatever you do, resist the temptation to simply copy someone else's picture file to use in your listing. Not only is this unethical, but it misrepresents the exact item you're selling. You could also find yourself on the wrong side of a copyright lawsuit if the owner of the photo takes particular offense.

■ **Shoot in strong light.** One of the worst photographic offenses is to shoot under standard indoor room light. Although you can touch up the photo somewhat afterwards (see the "Edit the Image File" section, later in this chapter), you can't put in light that wasn't there to begin with. Open all the windows, turn on all the room lights, use a flash (but judiciously—you want to avoid glare on your item), or just take the item outdoors to shoot—do whatever it takes to create a well-lighted photograph. (Figures 15.1 and 15.2 show the same item shot in low light and with stronger lighting; Figure 15.2 definitely works best.)

⁶⁶Mike Sez ⁹⁹

When you go shopping for a digital camera, look for one with a macro mode, so you can take close-ups of any small objects you might be selling. Also, invest another dozen bucks in a tripod, so you can take steady pictures in low light.

FIGURE 15.1

An item shot in low lighting— bad.

- **Avoid glare.** If you're shooting a glass or plastic item, or an item still in plastic wrap or packaging, or just an item that's naturally shiny, you have to work hard to avoid glare from whatever lighting source you're using. (This is one reason why I typically don't recommend using a single-point flash—without any fill lighting, it produces too much glare.) You avoid glare by adding fill lighting (to the sides of the object), diffusing the lighting source (by bouncing the light off a reflector of some sort), or just turning the item until the glare goes away. A simpler solution is to shoot in an area with strong natural light—like outside on a nice day.

- **Shoot against a plain background.** If you shoot your object against a busy background, it detracts from the main point of the photograph. Hang a white or black sheet (or t-shirt) behind the item; it'll make the main object stand out a lot better.

- **Focus!** Okay, this one sounds obvious, but I see a lot of blurry pictures on eBay. Make sure you know how to focus your camera, or how to use the auto-focus function. Also—and this is particularly important if you're shooting in low-light conditions—remember to hold the camera steady. A little bit of camera shake makes for a blurry photo. Either learn how to steady the camera, or buy a cheap tripod to hold the camera for you.

■ **Frame.** To take effective photographs, you have to learn proper composition. That means centering the item in the center of the photo, and getting close enough to the object so that it fills up the entire picture. Don't stand halfway across the room and shoot a very small object; get close up and make it *big!* (Figures 15.3 and 15.4 show an item framed poorly and then framed correctly.)

FIGURE 15.3
An item framed poorly.

FIGURE 15.4
The same item, framed correctly—it fills up more of the picture.

- **Take more than one.** Don't snap off a quick one and assume you've done your job. Shoot your item from several different angles and distances—and remember to get a close-up of any important area of the item, such as a serial number or a damaged area. You may want to include multiple photos in your listing—or just have a good selection of photos to choose from for that one best picture.

Mike Sez

When you're scanning compact discs, take the CD booklet out of the jewelcase to scan.

Of course, if you're selling relatively flat items (books, comics, CDs, and so on), you might be better off with a scanner than a camera. (And remember that boxes have flat sides that can be scanned.) Just lay the object on a flatbed scanner and scan the item into a file on your computer. It's actually easier to scan something like a book or a DVD case than it is to take a good steady picture of it!

Convert a Picture to a Digital Graphics File

If you took your pictures with a digital camera, all your pictures are in digital format, ready to transfer to your computer for editing. You can now skip to the next section.

If your pictures were shot on film, you have to get those film images into digital format. This is done by running your photograph (or negative) through a scanner, which digitizes the image and stores it in a computer graphics file. You can buy your own flatbed scanner for $100 or so, you can ask a friend with a scanner to scan your photo for you, or you can pay around $10 to have Kinko's or some similar establishment do the job professionally.

When you have the scanned images on a disk or CD, you can then copy them to your computer, and get ready to edit them.

note

There are several different file formats you can use for your graphics files. The preferred format is the JPG format; most cameras and scanners will save files in this format.

Edit the Image File

After your photograph has been converted to a JPG file (the graphics file type of choice on the Internet), you can then do a little editing to "clean it up" for eBay use.

Things to Edit

What kind of editing are we talking about? Here's a short list:

- Lighten up photos shot in low light.
- Correct the color in poorly shot photos.
- Crop the picture to focus only on the subject at hand (Figure 15.5 shows a picture being cropped in the Adobe Photoshop Elements program).
- Resize the image to fit better in your eBay listings. (Too big a picture won't fit within a normal Web browser window.)
- Decrease the resolution or color count to produce a smaller-sized file. (Files that are too big will take longer to load onto a bidder's PC—and may even be rejected by eBay.)

FIGURE 15.5

Cropping a photo in Adobe Photoshop Elements.

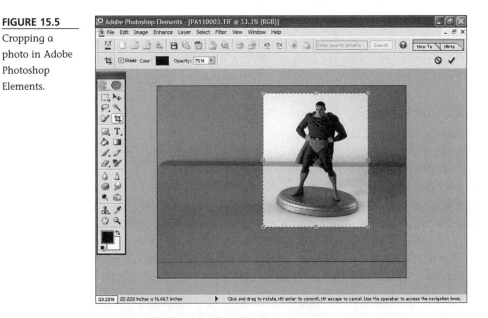

Graphics Editing Software

How do you do all this? You need an image-editing program. Although hard-core picture fanatics swear by the extremely full-featured (and very expensive) Adobe Photoshop, there are a number of lower-cost programs that perform just as well for the type of editing you'll be doing. These programs include:

- Adobe Photoshop Elements (www.adobe.com)
- CorelDRAW Essentials (www.corel.com)
- Micrografx Picture Publisher (www.micrografx.com)

- PaintShop Pro (www.jasc.com/products/psp/)
- Microsoft Picture It! Photo
  (pictureitproducts.msn.com/)
- PhotoSuite (www.roxio.com)

If you'd rather not muck around with this sort of
picture editing, you can always have somebody
else do it for you. Here again, Kinko's is a good
place to start.

Resizing Your Photos

While you're editing, remember to resize your
photo to best fit within your eBay listing. (Most pictures you take in a digital camera will come out too
big to fit on a Web page without scrolling.) eBay
recommends that you size your image to no more
than 300 pixels wide by 300 pixels tall.

Resizing Your Files

You should also reduce the amount of detail in
your picture to keep the file size small—no more
than 50KB for each picture. This keeps the loading
time for each photo down to a reasonable level.

There are three ways to reduce the size of an image file. You can reduce the dots per
inch (dpi); you can resize the width and height; or you can reduce the number of
colors used. Depending on your pictures, you may need to use some or all of these
techniques to get the file down to a workable size. Most image editing software lets
you perform all three of these operations.

tip

You might already have
one or more of these pro-
grams (or a similar graphics
program) installed on your
PC; check your Windows
Start menu to see what's
there.

" Mike Sez "

Personally, I find
300×300 pictures to be
a tad on the small side. I see no
harm in going up to 600×600,
especially if viewing the detail of
the object is important.

Upload Your Image File to the Internet—Or Use eBay's Picture Hosting Service

When you have your photos ready, you need to do one of two things: Upload the
photos to your own personal Web site (or picture hosting service), or get ready to add
these photos to your new eBay item listing.

You see, when it comes to photos, eBay gives you a choice. They can host your photos for you, or you can have someone else host your photos. Which one is the right
solution for you?

Using eBay Picture Services

When you have eBay host your photos, you have some choices to make. If you only want to show one picture, and you don't mind it just kind of sitting at the bottom of your page (like the one shown in Figure 15.6), you're okay with eBay. If you want to show more than one photo, or if you want to show larger photos, you can still use eBay—you'll just have to pay for it.

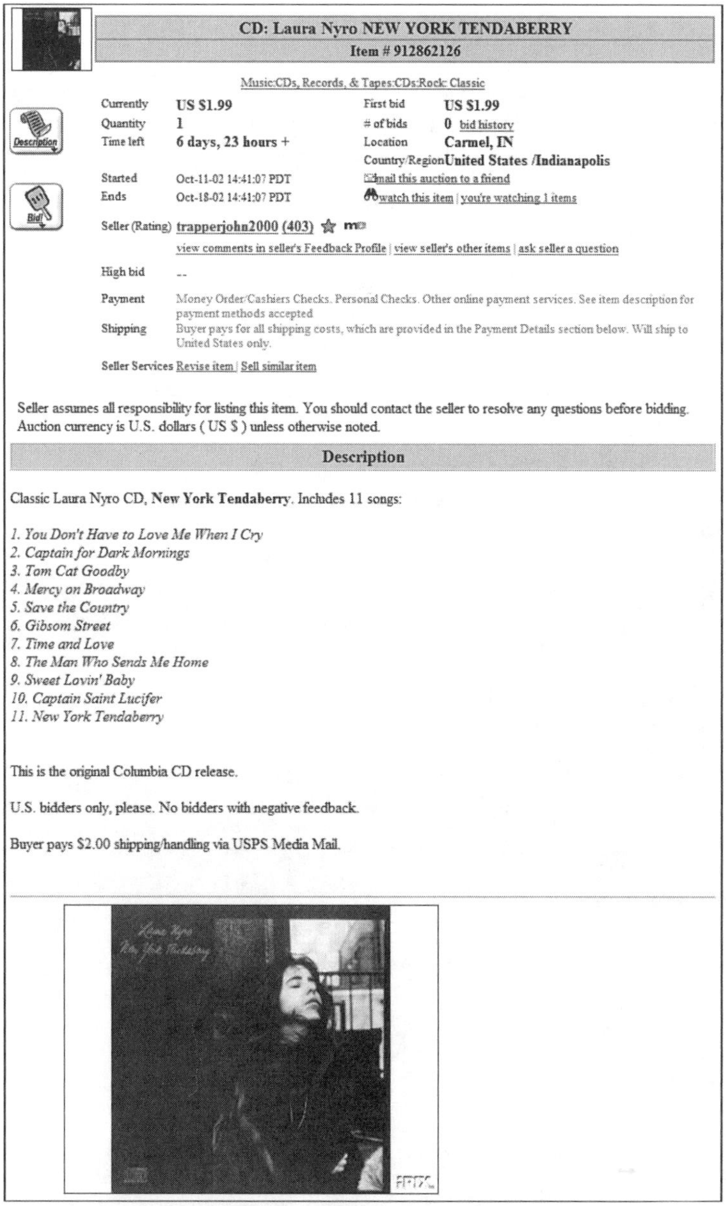

FIGURE 15.6

The standard photo offered free of charge by eBay Picture Services.

This is another case of eBay nickel and diming you to death on the little things. Here's how their fee structure works:

- First photo: free.
- Each additional picture (up to six, total): 15 cents each.
- Slide show (multiple pictures in a flip format): 75 cents.
- Supersize pictures (allow users to click a photo to display at a larger size): 75 cents
- Picture pack (up to six pictures, supersized, with Gallery display): $1.00

You can see how the costs start to add up. Let's say you have two pictures of your item (front and back, perhaps) that you want to display large. You'll pay 90 cents for this privilege (15 cents for the second picture, plus 75 cents for supersizing).

It might be cheaper for you to find another site to host your pictures, which we'll talk about next. But don't dismiss eBay's Picture Services, which is relatively easy to use, especially for beginners. Here's how you do it.

1. Start the process to create a new item listing, and work your way to the Provide Pictures and Item Details page.
2. Scroll down to the Add Pictures section and select the eBay Picture Services tab, as shown in Figure 15.7.

FIGURE 15.7

Using eBay Picture Services to insert photos in your item listing.

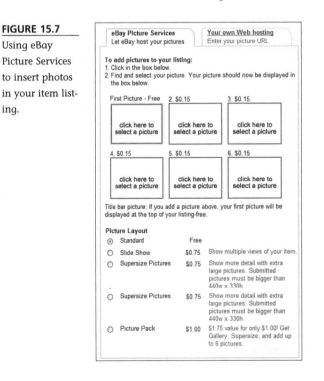

3. Click the First Picture-Free box. An Open dialog box now appears on your computer desktop; use this dialog box to locate and select the photo you want to use. Click the Open button when done—and the photo you selected now appears on the Provide Pictures and Item Details page.

4. To insert an additional picture (for 15 cents extra), click the second box and follow the instructions in step 3.

5. To insert even more pictures, click the next box(es) and follow the instructions in step 3.

6. In the Picture Layout section, select which options you want—Standard (single picture), Slide Show, Supersize Pictures, or Picture Pack.

tip

One plus to using eBay Picture Services is that you get a free picture of your item in the title bar of your item listing page.

That's it. eBay will automatically upload the pictures from your hard disk to their picture hosting server, and automatically insert those pictures into your item listing.

Using Another Web Host

Many users are less than thrilled with eBay's picture hosting service. It's better than nothing (which is what eBay had up until a few years ago), but it can be somewhat expensive (if you want to show a lot of pictures) and somewhat limited. For example, any pictures you insert via this method are displayed below and to the left of the item description—which doesn't have a lot of visual impact.

A better solution for some users is to use another Web hosting service to host your files. Here you have a lot of options.

First, if you have your own personal page on the Web, you can probably upload your pictures to that Web server. For example, if you have a personal page on Yahoo!, GeoCities, or Tripod, you should be able to upload your images to that site.

If you don't have a personal page but *could* have a personal page (via America Online or your Internet service provider), that's a potential place for you to upload picture files. If your company has a Web server, there's a chance it'll let you use a little space there.

If you don't have any other options, you can go to a site that specializes in storing image files for eBay users. Some of these sites include:

■ Andale (www.andale.com)

■ AuctionDesigner.com (www.auctiondesigner.com)

■ AuctionWatch (www.auctionwatch.com)

■ ImageHosting.com (www.imagehosting.com)

■ ManageAuctions.com
(www.manageauctions.com)

■ MyItem.com (www.myitem.com)

■ PennyThings.com (www.pennythings.com)

■ Picturetrail (www.picturetrail.com)

■ PixHost (www.pixhost.com)

■ Pongo (www.pongo.com)

■ Prosperpoint (www.prosperpoint.com)

■ Twaze.com (www.twaze.com)

Most of these sites charge some sort of fee for hosting your pictures, either on a monthly basis for a certain amount of storage space, or on a per-picture basis. Compare the fees at these sites with what you'll pay at eBay, and then make the smart choice.

After you have your pictures uploaded, you can then add them to your new item listing. Just follow these steps:

1. Start the process to create a new item listing, and work your way to the Provide Pictures and Item Details page.

2. Scroll down to the Add Pictures section and select the Your Own Web Hosting tab, as shown in Figure 15.8.

3. Enter the full URL (including the **http://**) for the picture into the Picture URL box.

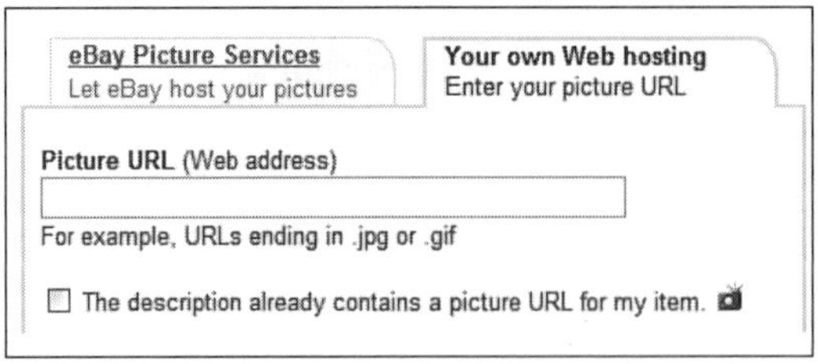

caution

The only problem with using a third-party Web hosting service in this manner is that eBay only lets you insert *one* picture into your listing. If you want to insert multiple photos, you either have to use eBay Picture Services, or insert your own picture links using HTML, as discussed in the following section.

" Mike Sez "

I'm not a big fan of eBay's picture hosting service. I don't like the way they incorporate photos into the listings (at the bottom!), and I don't like the fees if I have a lot of photos. I much prefer uploading my own pictures (using the same hosting service that hosts my personal Web site) and inserting those pictures into my item listings with HTML code, as described next. It's a little extra work, but it's free and looks great.

FIGURE 15.8

Pointing to a picture file uploaded to another hosting service.

eBay Picture Services	Your own Web hosting
Let eBay host your pictures	Enter your picture URL

Picture URL (Web address)

For example, URLs ending in .jpg or .gif

☐ The description already contains a picture URL for my item. ▣

Adding a Picture Within Your Item Description

There's another picture option available for more advanced users—especially if you're comfortable adding a little HTML code to your item descriptions. This option lets you insert images directly within your item description. (And eBay won't charge you for it, either!)

As you'll learn in Chapter 16, "Creating a Great-Looking Listing," you can include HTML code in your item descriptions—and you can use this code to link to pictures you've already uploaded to a picture hosting service. This process isn't as hard as it sounds, assuming you've already found a hosting service, uploaded your picture file, and obtained the full URL for the uploaded picture. All you have to do is insert the following HTML code into your item description, where you want the picture to appear:

```
<img src="http://www.webserver.com/picture.jpg">
```

Just replace *www.webserver.com/picture.jpg* with the correct URL for your picture.

If you opt for this method, you'll need to tell eBay that your description includes a picture, so that the picture icon will still display beside your item listing. You do this on the Provide Pictures and Item Details page, in the Add Pictures section. Just check the following option: The Description Already Contains a Picture URL for My Item.

And that's that. Your item will now display with the picture(s) you've selected—and you can expect the bids to start pouring in!

THE ABSOLUTE MINIMUM

Here are the key points to remember from this chapter:

- Adding a picture to your item listing will increase the number of bids you receive—and the value of those bids.
- The easiest way to take pictures of the items you want to sell is with a digital camera—unless you have a small, flat item, in which case scanning is probably better.
- Take the best picture possible, and then edit the picture (in a graphics editing program) to make it look even better.
- Make sure the picture will fit on your item listing page, and that the file size of the picture isn't too large.
- You can choose to let eBay host your pictures (with some potential cost), or you can find a third-party hosting service (that might also charge a fee).
- You add photos to your listings when you're creating the item listing, on the Provide Pictures and Item Details page.

16

CREATING A GREAT-LOOKING LISTING

Most of the item listings on eBay look the same—a paragraph or two of plain text, maybe a picture unceremoniously dropped in below the text. That's how a listing looks when you enter a normal, plain-text description for your item listing.

But then there are those ads that shout at you with colored text and different font faces and sizes and multiple columns and sizzling graphics and… well, you know the ones I'm talking about. How do you go about creating a dynamic listing like that?

Those colorful, eye-catching listings are created with Hypertext Markup Language (HTML). HTML is the engine behind every Web page you've ever viewed, the coding language that lets you turn on and off all sorts of different text and graphic effects.

Here's a secret known to successful sellers: eBay lets you use HTML in your item listings; all you have to do is know which HTML codes to enter in the Description box when you're creating your item listing. And it isn't that difficult, not really. This isn't a secret that only power sellers can use; it's a relatively common technique that *any* eBay seller can use to spruce up an eBay item listing.

caution

eBay lets you insert HTML code into your item's description, but forbids the use of HTML in the item's title.

Crack the Code: An HTML Primer

HTML coding might sound difficult, but it's really pretty easy—something you can do yourself. (It's not nearly as complicated as a fancy computer programming language, such as BASIC or C++, trust me.) HTML is really nothing more than a series of hidden codes. These codes tell a Web browser how to display different types of text and graphics. The codes are embedded in a document, so you can't see them; they're only visible to your Web browser.

All Web pages are created with HTML—as are all eBay listing pages. HTML isn't even limited to the Web; many e-mail programs let you send and receive HTML e-mail, and Microsoft Word even lets you save its word processing documents in HTML format. And any page or document created with HTML can have all the fancy features you find on the Web: different font sizes, hyperlinks to other Web pages, graphics, sound, video, and even embedded applets.

The first thing you need to know is that HTML is nothing more than text surrounded by instructions, in the form of simple codes. Codes are distinguished from normal text by the fact that they're enclosed within angle brackets. Each particular code turns on or off a particular attribute, such as boldface or italic text. Most codes are in sets of "on/off" pairs; you turn "on" the code before the text you want to affect and then turn "off" the code after the text.

For example, the code **<h1>** turns specified type into a level-one headline; the code **</h1>** turns off the headline type. The code **<i>** is used to italicize text; **</i>** turns off the italics. (As you can see, an "off" code is merely the "on" code with a slash before it, **</like this>**.)

Any text not surrounded by code uses HTML's default formatting—normal Times Roman text. It's the same with tables and other elements; if no code is applied, they default to standard formatting.

To create state-of-the-art item listings, then, you need to learn some of the basic HTML codes. Although I can't teach you all there is to know about HTML in a single chapter, I can show you enough basic HTML to help you create some stunning eBay ads. (And if dealing with a few angle brackets makes you nervous, know that you can use third-party programs and services to create the HTML code for you—see the "Let Somebody Else Do the Coding: Prepackaged HTML for Your Item Listings" section, later in this chapter.)

Codes for Text Formatting

Using HTML formatting codes is the fastest and easiest way to add spice to your item listings. If you do nothing else, boldfacing important words in your description will add selling power to your ad—and you can do that with a pair of simple HTML codes.

Here are some of the common HTML codes that format the way selected text looks in your listing:

<h1>formats text as the largest headline**</h1>**

<h2>formats text as the second-largest headline**</h2>**

<h3>formats text as the third-largest headline**</h3>**

****boldfaces text****

<i>italicizes text**</i>**

<u>underlines text**</u>**

<tt>creates monospaced, or typewriter-style text**</tt>**

<center>centers text**</center>**

<pre>displays "preformatted" text to preserve line breaks and such**</pre>**

Insert the "on" code right before the text you want formatted, and insert the "off" code right after the selected text. For example, if you want to boldface a single word in a sentence, make it look just like this:

This is the sentence with the ****highlighted**** word.

It's really that simple; just add the **** and **** codes around the text you want boldfaced. The rest of your item description looks as normal as it did before.

> **note**
>
> I present only a handful of the huge number of HTML codes available to you. If you want to learn more about these and other HTML codes, I recommend that you go to the HTML Goodies (`www.htmlgoodies.com/tutors/`) or WebMonkey (`hotwired.lycos.com/webmonkey/authoring/html_basics/`) Web sites. You can also pick up a copy of Que's *Absolute Beginner's Guide to Creating Web Pages*, available wherever good books are sold; this book is a great primer for creating your own Web pages with HTML.

One common design technique is to use the **<h1>** code for any major headings within your listing and then use **<b>** and/or **<i>** to highlight important words or phrases within your description. You can also use the **<center>** code for any text or graphics you want centered in your description. Figure 16.1 shows how an eBay listing looks with this type of formatting.

FIGURE 16.1

An eBay item listing with headline, bold-face, and italic text—all centered.

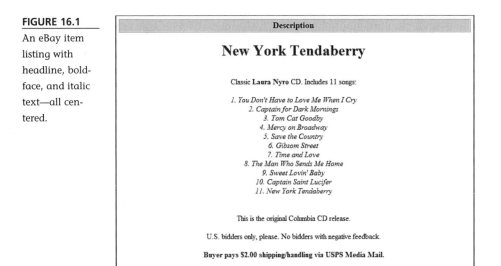

> **Description**
>
> # New York Tendaberry
>
> Classic **Laura Nyro** CD. Includes 11 songs:
>
> *1. You Don't Have to Love Me When I Cry*
> *2. Captain for Dark Mornings*
> *3. Tom Cat Goodby*
> *4. Mercy on Broadway*
> *5. Save the Country*
> *6. Gibsom Street*
> *7. Time and Love*
> *8. The Man Who Sends Me Home*
> *9. Sweet Lovin' Baby*
> *10. Captain Saint Lucifer*
> *11. New York Tendaberry*
>
> This is the original Columbia CD release.
>
> U.S. bidders only, please. No bidders with negative feedback.
>
> **Buyer pays $2.00 shipping/handling via USPS Media Mail.**

Codes for Fonts

You don't have to settle for the standard Times Roman font used in every other eBay listing; you can make your ad stand out with your own choice of font.

To specify a different font for a piece of text, use the following code:

```
<font face="xxxx">text</font>
```

Replace *xxxx* with the name of the font you want. For example, if you want to change the font to Arial, enter this code:

```
<font face="Arial">text</font>
```

If you want to change the size of your text, use this code:

```
<font size="xx">text</font>
```

Replace the *xx* with the size you want, from -6 to +6, with -6 being the smallest, +6 being the biggest, and 0 (or no size specified) being "normal" size type.

That's right—you don't specify the exact point size, just the *relative* size displayed onscreen. For example, if you want really tiny type, go with size 1 and enter this code:

```
<font size="-1">text</font>
```

You can also string these font codes together. Let's say you want to change your text to the largest possible Times Roman; enter this code:

```
<font face="Times Roman" size=6>text</font>
```

Be careful about changing fonts within your description. Combining too many different fonts looks garish. This might be something you want to set at the beginning of your description and leave the same throughout the entire listing. (If so, just remember to put the **</font>** code at the very end of your description.)

Codes for Color

Adding color to your text works pretty much the same as changing the font or size. The code you use looks like this:

```
<font color="#xxxxxx">text</font>
```

Replace the six *x*s with the code for a specific color. Table 16.1 lists some basic color codes.

caution

Just because you have a specific font installed on your computer doesn't necessarily mean that all the other Web users who'll be viewing your ad have the same font installed on their PCs. If you change fonts in your listing, change to a common font that is likely to be preinstalled on all Windows computers. Arial and Times Roman are always safe bets; choosing something more obscure could ensure an unpredictable display for your listing on many computers around the world.

TABLE 16.1   Common HTML Color Codes

Color	Code
White	FFFFFF
Red	FF0000
Green	00FF00
Blue	0000FF
Magenta	FF00FF
Cyan	00FFFF
Yellow	FFFF00
Black	000000
Light gray	DDDDDD

tip

For a complete list of the literally hundreds of different HTML color codes, go to the Webmonkey Color Codes Reference (hotwired.lycos.com/ webmonkey/reference/ color_codes/).

As an example, suppose you want to color some text red. You use this code:

```
<font color="#FF0000">red text</font>
```

Color is a good way to highlight important parts of your listing. You can put headings or subheadings in a different color or highlight selected words or phrases in the same manner. Don't use too many colors, however; if your ad looks like a rainbow, the color loses its ability to impact.

Codes That Insert Things

So far, I've shown you codes that format text. Other codes insert items into your document. These codes don't have "on/off" pairs; they're freestanding. These types of codes include

- **<p>** inserts a paragraph break
- **
** inserts a line break
- **<hr>** inserts a horizontal rule

If you want to separate two paragraphs, you insert a **<p>** between the two blocks of text. If you want to put a line between the two paragraphs, you insert a **<hr>**. Sometimes, it's good to use horizontal rules between different sections of your listing.

Codes for Graphics

As you learned in Chapter 15, "Using Pictures in Your Listings," adding pictures and other graphics to your listings really brings some excitement to the normally plain-text world of eBay. You can add pictures the eBay way (described in Chapter 15), which puts all your pictures at the end of your text description—or you can put a picture *anywhere* in your text, using HTML.

Before you can insert a graphic into your listing, you need to know the address of that graphic (in the form of a Web page URL). Then you use the following code:

`<img src="URL">`

No "off" code is required for inserted graphics. Note that the location is enclosed in quotation marks—and that you have to insert the **http://** part of the URL.

As an example, if your graphic is the file **graphic01.jpg** located at `www.webserver.com/mydirectory/`, you insert this code:

`<img src="http://www.webserver.com/mydirectory/graphic01.jpg">`

The nice thing about inserting graphics this way is that you can include more than just pictures—you can add logos, starbursts, you name it. (And you can put the graphics *anywhere* in your text description.) You use the same technique to link to any graphic image anywhere in your item listing.

Codes for Links

Web pages are all about hyperlinks to other Web pages. Why should your eBay item listing be any different?

If you want to include a hyperlink to another Web page, use the following code:

`<a href="URL">this is the link</a>`

The text between the on and off codes will appear onscreen as a typical underlined hyperlink; when users click that text, they'll be linked to the URL you specified in the code. Note that the URL is enclosed in quotation marks and that you have to include the **http://** part of the address.

Here's what a representative hyperlink code looks like:

```
<a href="http://www.webserver.com/mydirectory/mypage.htm">Click for
   my Web page</a>
```

You can also create a "mail-to" link in your listing; users would be able to send e-mail to you by simply clicking the link. Here's the code for a mail-to link:

```
<a href="mailto:yourname@domain.com">click here to e-mail me</a>
```

If you want to include a mail-to link to my e-mail address (books@molehillgroup.com), the code looks like this:

```
<a href="mailto:books@molehillgroup.com">Click here to e-mail the
author</a>
```

You can include links in your listing to your own personal Web pages (a great idea if you have additional images of this specific item) or to related sites. Many sellers also like to provide a direct e-mail link in case potential bidders have questions they need answered.

Codes for Lists

If you have a lot of features to list for your item, you might want to format them in a bulleted list. Using HTML codes, it's easy to create a neatly bulleted list for your ad.

First, you enclose your bulleted list with the **<ul>** and **</ul>** codes. Then, you enclose each bulleted item with the **<li>** and **</li>** codes.

The code for a typical bulleted list looks like this:

```
<ul>
   <li>item one</li>
   <li>item two</li>
   <li>item three</li>
</ul>
```

Bulleted lists are great ways to run through a list of attributes or specifications; it's a lot cleaner than just listing a bunch of stuff within a long text paragraph.

Code for Tables

In addition to making pretty text and inserting links and graphics, one of the other interesting things you can do with HTML is add a table to your item listing.

Okay, so tables sound boring—and complicated. In reality, however, they let you break up your ad into two or more columns and add color backgrounds behind your text. And they're not *that* hard to do.

You start by enclosing your table with **<table>** and **</table>** codes. Then, you enclose each individual row in the table with **<tr>** and **</tr>** codes and each cell in each row with **<td>** and **</td>** codes.

A basic table with two rows and two columns (four cells total) is coded like this:

```
<table>
   <tr>
      <td>row 1 cell 1</td>
      <td>row 1 cell 2</td>
   </tr>
   <tr>
      <td>row 2 cell 1</td>
      <td>row 2 cell 2</td>
   </tr>
</table>
```

Within any individual cell, you can insert any type of item—plain text, formatted text, bulleted lists, background shading, and even graphics. One neat effect is to use a simple two-column, one-row table to create the effect of two columns on your page. You can even shade the background of one of the cells or columns to set it off; it's a nice way to include more detailed information about your item.

You can format both the table as a whole and the cells within a table, to some degree:

- To dictate the width of the table border, use the **<table border="*xx*">** code, where ***xx*** is in pixels. (A border value of "1" is common.)

- To shade the background of a cell, use the **<td bgcolor="#*xxxxxx*">** code (which works like the color code for text).

note

If you already know a little HTML, you're probably wondering why I don't discuss the HTML codes you need to start and set up an entire HTML document (codes such as **<HTML>**, for example). The reason is that eBay already sets up the HTML page. When eBay generates an item listing page, that page includes all of eBay's "startup" HTML coding; your description is just inserted into the middle of the preset page. In fact, if you tried to insert the startup HTML codes in your listing code, you'd really mess up the coding for the entire listing page. So, don't worry about setting up the page, and concentrate on formatting your description as effectively as possible.

■ To dictate the width of a cell, use the **<td width="xx%">** code, where **xx** is a percentage of the total table width. (For example, **<td width="50%">** specifies a cell that is half—50%—of the total table width.)

These codes gang together with the standard **<table>** and **<td>** codes in the table.

Code You Can Use, for Real

Let's look at two examples of fancy ads created with simple HTML codes. You can use these codes exactly as printed in your own listings; just copy the code—word for word and character for character—into the Description box in the Sell Your Item page, and insert your own description in place of my generic sample text.

Second-Column Details

The first example is an all-text example, using a simple two-column, single-row table. The left column is designed to hold the ad's headline and the bulk of the descriptive copy; the thinner right column holds a bulleted list of item details and features.

Now, I said that you use a table to create this listing; the listing itself, however, doesn't really look like a table. Why is that? It's simple; I set the border code (**<border="x">**) to **0**—totally eliminating the border from the table. This way, you only see the two cells, which look like a two-column document. (Pretty sneaky, eh?)

Figure 16.2 shows what the completed listing looks like. 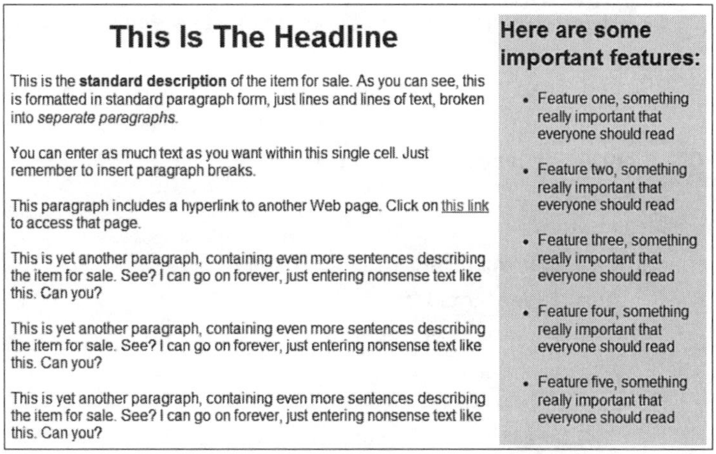

FIGURE 16.2

A two-column ad, with bulleted copy in the subsidiary shaded column.

This Is The Headline

This is the **standard description** of the item for sale. As you can see, this is formatted in standard paragraph form, just lines and lines of text, broken into *separate paragraphs*.

You can enter as much text as you want within this single cell. Just remember to insert paragraph breaks.

This paragraph includes a hyperlink to another Web page. Click on this link to access that page.

This is yet another paragraph, containing even more sentences describing the item for sale. See? I can go on forever, just entering nonsense text like this. Can you?

This is yet another paragraph, containing even more sentences describing the item for sale. See? I can go on forever, just entering nonsense text like this. Can you?

This is yet another paragraph, containing even more sentences describing the item for sale. See? I can go on forever, just entering nonsense text like this. Can you?

Here are some important features:

- Feature one, something really important that everyone should read

- Feature two, something really important that everyone should read

- Feature three, something really important that everyone should read

- Feature four, something really important that everyone should read

- Feature five, something really important that everyone should read

Here's the code you use to create that ad:

```
<table border="0">
   <tr>
      <td width="70%">
         <font face="Arial">
         <center><h1>This Is The Headline</h1></center>
         <p>
         This is the <b>standard description</b> of the item for sale.
          As you can see, this is formatted in standard paragraph form,
          just lines and lines of text, broken into <i>separate
          paragraphs</i>.
         <p>
         You can enter as much text as you want within this single cell.
          Just remember to insert paragraph breaks.
         <p>
         This paragraph includes a hyperlink to another Web page. Click on
         <a href="http://www.molehillgroup.com">this link</a> to access
         that page.
         <p>
         This is yet another paragraph, containing even more sentences
         describing the item for sale. See? I can go on forever, just
         entering nonsense text like this. Can you?
         <p>
         This is yet another paragraph, containing even more sentences
         describing the item for sale. See? I can go on forever, just
         entering nonsense text like this. Can you?
         <p>
         This is yet another paragraph, containing even more sentences
         describing the item for sale. See? I can go on forever, just
         entering nonsense text like this. Can you?
         </font>
      </td>
      <td bgcolor="#DDDDDD" width="30%">
         <font face="Arial">
         <h2>Here are some important features:</h2>
         <p>
         <ul>
            <li>Feature one, something really important that everyone
             should read</li>
```

```
      <p>
      <li>Feature two, something really important that everyone
       should read</li>
      <p>
      <li>Feature three, something really important that everyone
       should read</li>
      <p>
      <li>Feature four, something really important that everyone
       should read</li>
      <p>
      <li>Feature five, something really important that everyone
       should read</li>
     </ul>
     </font>
    </td>
   </tr>
 </table>
 </font>
```

Looks cool, doesn't it?

Before we go on, I want you to notice just a few things about the HTML code for that listing.

First, you can put as much text as you like into either of the two cells, including paragraph breaks and bulleted lists and graphics and whatnot.

Second, in this kind of format, I find that it works best to use the thinner cell for a bulleted list of features and put your main text and graphics in the left cell.

Third, I used a light gray background color for the right column, to set it off visually from the rest of the text. I also used a second-level headline (**<h2>**) in the right column, so as not to compete with the first-level headline (**<h1>**) in the left column.

Finally, notice that I changed the font face for all the text within each cell by using the **<font face="Arial">** code right after each **<td>** code. This affected all the text until the **</font>** code before each **</td>** code. (You can change the text for each cell individually, but you can't change the text for the entire table all at once.)

Big Picture, Colored Background

The next example is even easier than the first. You create another two-column, one-row table, but don't bother to set the column widths. This way, the columns size naturally, based on their contents.

The contents in this ad are pretty simple. The left column contains a picture of your item, and the right column contains a brief description (in large text). The table background is all blue, and you reverse the text out of the background by coloring the text white.

The whole thing is preceded by a large colored headline above the table. The completed ad looks like Figure 16.3.

FIGURE 16.3

Another table ad, with the picture on the left and the description on the right.

```
<h1><center><font color="#FF0000">This Is The Headline
<br>
On Two Lines, In Color!</font></center></h1>
<p>
<table bgcolor="#0000FF">
   <tr>
      <td>
         <img src="http://www.webserver.com/picture.jpg">
      </td>
      <td>
         <center><h2><font color="#FFFFFF">Look at this item!
         <p>
         It's really cool!
         <p>
         You should buy it!
         <p>
         Send me all your money <i>now!</i></font></center></h2>
      </td>
   </tr>
</table>
```

Can you get any simpler than that? Again, you can put as much text as you want in the right cell. You can also add text to the left cell, either before or after the graphic. You can even add more regular text *after* the table—a good place, in fact, to put a link to your own personal Web page or a mail-to link to your e-mail address.

Easier HTML Editing

Most users enter HTML code directly into the Description box on the Sell Your Item page. This is okay if you only have a limited amount of coding (a few boldfaces and italics, a paragraph break or two). If you have a lot of HTML code, however, it might be easier to create the code in another application and then cut and paste it into the Description box. The only thing you have to remember is that the pasted code must be in plain-text format—you can't paste a Word document into the box.

I typically use Windows Notepad to create short amounts of HTML code. I'll actually save some boilerplate code in a Notepad file and then edit it for my individual ads. It's very easy to cut from Notepad and then paste into the Description box.

Let Somebody Else Do the Coding: Prepackaged HTML for Your Item Listings

If all this talk of angle brackets and on and off codes leaves your head spinning, you have some options that won't leave your hands dirty with raw HTML.

There are many software programs and Web-based services available that let you create great-looking eBay item listings without having to enter a line of HTML code. Most of these programs and services let you choose a design, fill in some blanks, and then automatically write the HTML code necessary to create the listing. They're easy to use, even if they do come at a cost.

" Mike Sez "

Want another tip? Use these examples as templates, and then experiment, adding your own codes to see what happens!

note

People who develop Web pages for a living typically use dedicated HTML editing programs, such as Microsoft FrontPage, to create their pages. The HTML coding you might do for an eBay listing isn't complex enough to warrant the use of such a program; if you want to create really complicated item listings, you're better off going with a listing-creation program, as discussed next.

Perhaps the most popular listing creation software is that offered by eBay itself. eBay offers two different programs, eBay Seller's Assistant Basic and eBay Seller's Assistant Pro, both of which are available at `pages.ebay.com/sellers_assistant/`. Basic (priced at $4.99 per month) is the best program for casual sellers; Pro ($15.99 per month) is designed for high-volume power sellers. Both programs not only create item listings, but also manage the progress and completion of your auctions.

I'll talk more about these and other third-party auction management programs in Chapter 28, "Using Auction Software and Services." For now, however, you can check out the following sites to see if any of these programs or services are right for you:

- Andale (`www.andale.com`)
- Auction Lizard (`www.auction-lizard.com`)
- Auction Wizard 2000 (`www.auctionwizard2000.com`)
- AuctionDesigner.com (`www.auctiondesigner.com`)
- AuctionHelper (`www.auctionhelper.com`)
- AuctionWatch (`www.auctionwatch.com`)
- AuctionWorks (`www.auctionworks.com`)
- Auctiva (`www.auctiva.com`)
- ManageAuctions (`www.manageauctions.com`)
- My AuctionMate (`www.myauctionmate.com`)
- Virtual Auction Ad Pro (`www.firstdesign.com/vadpro/`)

> **"Mike Sez"**
>
> I've used a lot of different ad creation software and services—especially when they all used to be free!—but have gravitated back to eBay Seller's Assistant Basic. The price is okay (if you do a large enough number of auctions each month), it's easy to use, and it offers a wide variety of listing templates. There are more versatile programs around, but they cost more.

THE ABSOLUTE MINIMUM

Here are the key points to remember from this chapter:

- eBay lets you use HTML code to customize the appearance of your item's description. (But *not* the item title!)

- HTML codes typically come in "on" and "off" pairs that either format surrounded text or insert special elements, such as graphics or hyperlinks.

- You can use HTML tables to create complex page designs with simple coding.

- If you don't want to do the HTML coding yourself, you can use special Web sites or software programs to automatically create HTML listing code.

17

MANAGING THE AUCTION PROCESS

After you've placed your item listing and your auction is underway, you can just sit back and count the bids for the next seven (or so) days, right?

Wrong.

There's plenty for a motivated seller to do over the course of an eBay auction. Not only can you keep track of the current bids, but you might also have to answer questions from bidders, update your item listing, cancel bids from questionable bidders, and—on rare occasions—cancel the entire auction.

Auctioning an item on eBay is *work!*

Keeping Tabs on Your Current Auctions

When you're only running one or two auctions at a time, it's relatively easy to go directly to the item listing pages to check the status of those auctions. But what do you do if you're running a half-dozen, or a dozen, or several dozen auctions simultaneously?

If you're a busy seller, you need some way to consolidate all the information from all your auctions-in-process—the number of bidders, the high bids, and the time left until the auction ends. Fortunately, there are several tools available to you for just this purpose.

Receiving Daily Updates from eBay

One of the most convenient ways to keep track of your in-process auctions is to let eBay do it for you. You can configure eBay to send you an e-mail message every morning, containing key information about all your open auctions—as well as all the auctions in which you're currently bidding.

To automatically receive eBay's Daily Status report, follow these steps:

1. Click the My eBay link above the Navigation Bar, select the Preferences tab, and click Change My Notification Preferences to display the Change Your Notification Preferences page.

2. Check those e-mails you want to receive, and uncheck those you don't. (In particular, check the Bidding and Selling Daily Status option.)

3. Check whether you want to receive these messages as simple text-only e-mail or more appealing HTML e-mail.

4. Scroll down and select which *other* items you do or don't want to receive— including product surveys, special promotions (spam), direct (snail) mail, and telemarketing calls(!).

5. Click the Save My Changes button.

As you can see on the Change Your Notification Preferences page, eBay has lots of different e-mail messages that you can choose to receive. These messages include:

- Outbid notices (notification that you've just been outbid in a specific auction)
- End of item notices (notification for unsuccessful bidders that an auction has ended)
- Second-chance offer notices (offers from the seller on items you have bid on but not won)
- Bid notices (confirmation that you've completed a bid on an item)

- Bidding and selling daily status (daily update on all items you're selling or bidding on)
- Item watch reminder (daily notification of all items on your watch list that end within 36 hours)
- Listing confirmation (confirmation that you've successfully listed an item for sale)

Using My eBay

eBay's Daily Status Report is a nice auction management tool—especially because eBay does all the work and e-mails you the results once a day. But

note

You can't opt *not* to receive end-of-auction notices.

what if you want to check the current status of your auctions in the middle of the afternoon, or late at night? If you want the latest auction information, you need a tool that accesses current auction information at any hour of the day.

One way to gather this live information is to perform a search on your user name. eBay will display all your open auctions as the results of this search.

But typing in your user information every time you want to check your auctions is unnecessarily time-consuming. Better to go to a single page that automatically displays all your auction info.

You can find such a page in My eBay. As you'll discover in Chapter 22, "Creating a Home Base with My eBay," this page displays key information about all your eBay activities—including items you're selling, watching, and bidding on, as well as recent feedback you've received.

When you click the My eBay link above eBay's Navigation Bar, you're taken to your My eBay page. If it's not already selected, click the Selling link to display the Selling page.

The Items I'm Selling section of this page displays the item number, title, current price, number of bids, and time left for each of your open auctions. By default, this page sorts your auctions by the time left, with the items ending first shown first in the list. You can change the sort order by clicking any item heading; for example, if you want to sort by current high bid, click the Current Price heading.

tip

Display the latest up-to-the-second bid information by clicking the Refresh or Reload button in your Web browser.

Using Auction Management Software and Services

If you're a high-volume individual seller or a merchant selling a ton of items on eBay, it gets really tedious really fast handling each and every auction—the listing, the ad creation, the auction management, the e-mail notifications—one auction at a time. Automating some of your auction-management tasks would make the process easier.

Many users choose to outsource their auction management to an outside service, or utilize dedicated software programs to do the management for them. These programs and services not only track the progress of in-process auctions, but also manage all manner of post-auction activity.

One of the most popular of these auction-management programs is eBay's very own eBay Seller's Assistant Basic (pages.ebay.com/ sellers_assistant/). (Yes, this is the same software you can use to create your auction listings, as discussed back in Chapter 16, "Creating a Great-Looking Listing.") It only costs $4.99 a month (others cost a lot more), and is relatively easy to use for casual sellers—less than a dozen listings a week. Of course, if you only list a few items a month, even $4.99 a month is cost prohibitive; you can probably manage that number of auctions manually, anyway.

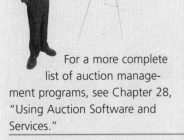

note

For a more complete list of auction management programs, see Chapter 28, "Using Auction Software and Services."

Andale is *not* pronounced "an-dale"; it's pronounced "an-da-lay."

For higher-volume sellers, I like Andale (www.andale.com). It's a bit expensive ($0.20 for each item listed and another $0.20 for each buyer using Andale's Checkout system), but the management and e-mail functions are both more sophisticated and easier to use. Andale, like many similar services, automatically sends high bidders an end-of-auction e-mail directing them to a special checkout page on the Andale site. The buyer fills in all the information at Andale, saving you the trouble of manually managing the end-of-auction process. (The only thing you have to do manually is handle check or money order payments, and ship and pack the item!) Similar services include Auctiva (www.auctiva.com) and AuctionWatch Sales Manager (www.auctionwatch.com).

Editing In-Process Auctions

Sometimes you have to do more than just track your auctions. Sometimes you actually have to change an item listing.

Updating Your Auction Listing

Maybe you've received additional information about the item you're selling. Maybe a bidder has asked a question and you feel that question (and your answer) should be part of your item listing. Maybe you flat out made a mistake in your original listing and want to offer a correction in the item listing.

Whatever your reason might be, eBay makes it relatively easy to update your item listing.

If your listing hasn't received any bids yet, you can actually edit the original listing. eBay lets you edit your title, description, and pictures—as long as no one has yet placed a bid. To edit your listing, follow these steps:

1. Navigate to the item listing page.
2. Click the Revise Item link (located in the Seller Services section of the listing).
3. Follow the onscreen instructions to access the listing editing screen.
4. Make the appropriate changes to your listing and then click the Submit button.

What do you do if you need to update your listing and you've already received a bid or two on the item? In this instance, the Revise Item link doesn't appear, so you have to take a different tack.

Your option here is to append new information to the end of your current listing. The original listing will display unchanged, but the new information you add will appear underneath the main item description.

To add new information to your item description, follow these steps:

1. Navigate to eBay's Site Map page and click the Add to My Item Description link.
2. When the next page appears, enter the item number of the auction you want to update and click Revise Item.
3. When the Add to Description page appears, as shown in Figure 17.1, enter the text you want to add. As with any description text, you can enter plain text or HTML-coded text—or URLs for additional pictures for your listing.
4. Click the Save Changes button when done.

FIGURE 17.1

Adding new text
to your item
description.

Add to Description

Item title
World History of Sicence Fiction HC ANTHOLOGY

Add to your description in the box below, then click "Save Changes".
Remember: You can only add to, not change, your current
description.
View your current description

To add Item Specifics to your
listing, please use the Revise
Your Item process.

Add to description   Enter either plain text or HTML

If you enter plain text only,
your description may not be
formatted. but you can use
HTML to add images and
format your text.

HTML Tip: Enter <p> to start
a new paragraph.

Preview your revised description

Cancel Changes   Save Changes >

Deleting Unwelcome Bidders

What do you do if a known deadbeat bidder makes a bid in one of your auctions?
Although you could just sit back and pray that the deadbeat gets outbid, a better
approach is to cancel that user's bid—and block that user from ever bidding in one
of your auctions again.

Here's what to do:

1. Start by canceling the bid in question. Go to
   the Site Map page and click the Cancel Bids
   on My Item link. When the Bid Cancellation
   page appears, cancel that user's bid.

2. Now you want to block the bidder from any
   future auctions. Go to the Site Map page
   and click the Blocked Bidder/Buyer List link.
   When the Bidder/Buyer Management page
   appears, scroll to the Blocked Bidder/Buyer
   List section and click Continue.

3. When the Blocked Bidder/Buyer List page
   appears, add the buyer's user name to the
   list; separate multiple names with commas.

4. Click the Submit button when done.

note

You can ferret out
deadbeat bidders by exam-
ining the feedback rating and
comments for the high bidders in
each of your auctions.

Now you don't have to worry about that questionable bid, and the deadbeat bidder won't be able to bother you again.

Canceling an Auction

One last little bit of auction maintenance—what do you do if you need to cancel an auction completely?

It happens, you know. Maybe you have an unexpected trip come up, so you won't be home when your auction ends (and when the item will need to ship). Maybe you discover you really don't have the item you thought you have. Maybe you drop the item and break it into a zillion pieces. Or maybe someone comes along with a better offer and you decide to sell the item outside of eBay.

In any case, if you need to cancel an auction, eBay will accommodate you—as long as you have a good excuse, and don't make a habit of it.

Here's how to cancel an auction in process:

1. Go to the Site Map page and click the Cancel Bids on My Item link. When the Bid Cancellation page appears, cancel the first bid on your item. Then return to this page as many times as necessary to cancel all the outstanding bids.

2. After you've canceled all the bids, go to the Site Map page and click the End My Listing Early link. When the Ending Auction page appears, enter the auction item number. Click the Continue button to proceed, and then click the End Auction button to officially cancel your auction.

> **caution**
>
> Frequent early cancellations may cause eBay to cancel your membership.

Answering Bidder Questions

Over the course of a popular auction, chances are a few potential bidders will ask questions about your item or your auction. eBay lets bidders e-mail sellers during the course of an auction, so don't be surprised if you get a few e-mails from strangers asking unusual questions.

These questions will come to the e-mail account you specified when you became an eBay member. Bidders can send these e-mails by clicking the Ask Seller a Question link on the item listing page.

> **note**
>
> You reply to the question by using the Reply feature of your e-mail software. The reply goes directly to the other member, without looping back through eBay.

When you receive a question from a potential bidder, answer that question promptly, courteously, and accurately. It's in your best interest to make the questioner happy; after all, that person could turn out to be your high bidder.

Promoting Your Auctions

Here's something else you can do after you've started your auction—tell people about it!

Yes, it's allowable (and encouraged) to promote your auction outside of eBay. You can drop notes about the item you're selling in newsgroups, message boards, and mailing lists; you can e-mail your friends and family and colleagues and let them know about your auction; you can even include links to your auctions on your own personal Web page.

When you mention your auction, make sure you include the URL for your item listing page. It should look like this:

```
http://cgi.ebay.com/ws/
eBayISAPI.dll?ViewItem&item=xx
```

All you have to do is replace *xx* with the actual auction item number for your particular item, and you've created a direct link to your auction page.

tip

An easier way to obtain the link to your auction is to navigate to the item listing page and copy the URL from the address box in your Web browser.

"Mike Sez"

A good way to create a permanent link to *all* your eBay auctions is to link to your About Me page. (You'll learn about About Me in Chapter 23, "Creating Your Own Personal About Me Page.") This page includes all sorts of information, including your current auction listings and recent feedback.

THE ABSOLUTE MINIMUM

Here are the key points to remember from this chapter:

- Configure eBay so that you receive a daily status report for your open auctions in each morning's e-mail.

- You can use My eBay for up-to-the-minute tracking of all your open auctions.

- Some users prefer to use a third-party program or service to manage their in-process auctions and post-auction activity.

- When a potential bidder asks you a question about your auction, answer it—promptly and accurately.

- If you need to, you can update or append your item listing in the middle of an auction, as well as cancel individual bids, block unwanted bidders, and cancel the entire auction.

- Promote your auctions by linking to the URL of your item listing pages on your personal Web page, in e-mail correspondence, and in newsgroups, message boards, and mailing lists.

18

AFTER THE AUCTION: CONCLUDING YOUR BUSINESS

You've waited the requisite 7 (or 3 or 5 or 10) days, and your auction has finally ended. What comes next?

The post-auction process involves more work, in most cases, than the listing process. You have to contact the seller, arrange payment, receive payment, pack the item, ship the item, and leave feedback. And that's if everything goes smoothly!

The post-auction process can also be a long one, depending on how the buyer pays. If the buyer pays by PayPal (or other credit card method) as soon as the auction ends, the post-auction process can be over that day or the next—as soon as you pack and ship the item. If, on the other hand, the buyer pays by check—and is a little slow in putting the check in the mail—the post-auction process can last two or three weeks.

That means, of course, that you need to remember this potential time lag when you're planning your auction activity. For example, if you're planning to go on vacation in two weeks, now is not the best time to list an item for auction. You need to allocate a full month, from beginning to end, when you're planning your auction listings. If your buyers help you complete the process faster, that's great. But there will always be that one last buyer who hasn't sent the check yet—and there goes your schedule!

The Post-Auction Process

What happens during the post-auction process is actually rather cut and dried. Put simply, you contact the winning bidder with a final price; he or she sends payment to you; you pocket the payment; you package and ship the item; the buyer receives the item; and you both leave feedback for each other.

In checklist form, here's what you have to look forward to:

Checklist—After the Auction

- ☐ Receive end-of-auction e-mail from eBay
- ☐ Send e-mail to the high bidder (containing final price and payment information)—alternately, rely on eBay's Checkout procedure for this entire process
- ☐ Receive payment from buyer—and wait for payment to clear, if necessary
- ☐ Package the item
- ☐ Ship the item to the high bidder
- ☐ Leave feedback for the buyer

Communicating with the Winning Bidder

Minutes after the conclusion of your auction, eBay will notify you by e-mail that your auction has ended. This e-mail message, like the one shown in Figure 18.1, will include the user ID and e-mail address of the item's high bidder.

FIGURE 18.1

A typical eBay e-mail notifying you of the end of your auction.

Congratulations trapperjohn2000!   eb**Y**

Dear trapperjohn2000,
john4044 has agreed to purchase the following eBay item on Oct-20-02 16:15:55 PDT:

LD: James Bond 007 CASINO ROYALE (widescreen) - Item # 1570608683

The buyer has been asked to pay for this item via accepted payment methods. If you want, you may create and send an invoice to the buyer.

Payment details:
		Your payment instructions to buyer:
Item price:	$21.60	I accept payment by personal check (will delay
Quantity:	1	shipment), money order, cashier's check, and
Subtotal:	**$21.60**	MasterCard & Visa via PayPal.
Shipping, handling:	$3.00	
Shipping insurance per item:	(not offered)	
Sales tax:	(None)	

It is now your responsibility to contact that high bidder to arrange payment and shipping. What you need to do, as soon as possible, is to e-mail the high bidder with the following information:

- Your name and address so the buyer will know where to send the payment
- Your e-mail address so the buyer can contact you with any questions or problems
- The total amount the buyer owes you—which will be the final auction price plus a reasonable shipping and handling fee
- Your preferred method of payment or payment options (check, cashier's check, money order, credit card, and so on)

Some sellers even go to the extreme of e-mailing the buyer a preformatted form (either as part of the e-mail message or attached in a Word document) that the buyer can print, fill out, and include with the payment. (That's a nice touch; I like it.)

If you haven't heard back from the buyer in a day or two, send another e-mail. If, after three days, you still haven't been able to contact the buyer, you can consider that person a *deadbeat bidder*. See Chapter 20, "Dealing with Deadbeat Bidders," to learn how to deal with this situation.

" Mike Sez "

The personal nature of e-mail communications is why I prefer *not* to use eBay's Checkout. With Checkout, all e-mails are sent by eBay, and are decidedly non-personal. (You can customize them a little, but not much.) I think it's better to make one-to-one contact with the buyer, which you do by not using Checkout—and by sending your own personal e-mail messages.

As you first learned in Chapter 17, "Managing the Auction Process," you can use third-party software programs and services to handle all this post-auction messaging and processing for you. Learn more about specific options in Chapter 28, "Using Auction Software and Services."

Accepting Payment

Now it's time to get paid. As recommended in Chapter 12, "Deciding on Your Payment Methods," you've presumably determined how you want to get paid, and indicated so in your item listing. You need to repeat your preferred payment methods in your post-auction e-mail to the high bidder, and then wait for that user to make the payment.

caution

Remember, if you receive a payment via personal check, wait at least 10 working days for that payment to clear before you ship the item.

Whatever you do, do *not* ship the item before you've received payment! Wait until you've received a cashier's check or money order in the mail, or been notified by PayPal that a credit card payment has been made, and *then* prepare to ship the item.

When you receive payment, it's good business practice to e-mail the buyer and let him or her know the payment has been received. If you know when you'll be shipping the item, include that information in the e-mail, as well.

And if the buyer never sends payment? Turn to Chapter 20 for my detailed advice.

Packing and Shipping

One of the most crucial parts of the post-auction process is packing the item you've just sold. This process is so important, and so complicated, that I've devoted an entire chapter to it. So when you're ready to pack, turn to Chapter 19, "Shipping It Out—Cheaply and Safely," for more information.

Finishing Things Up and Leaving Feedback

As you ship the sold item, there are two more things you need to do:

- First, send an e-mail to the buyer, letting him or her know that the item is on its way. (You should note in your message when and by which method the item was shipped—and if you have a tracking or confirmation number, pass it along.)
- Second, you need to leave feedback about the buyer. Whether it was a good transaction or a bad transaction, you need to let your fellow eBay members know how things turned out.

To leave feedback for the buyer, follow these instructions:

1. Go to the listing page for the item you just sold and click the Leave Feedback to Bidder link.

2. When the Leave Feedback About an eBay User page appears, indicate whether you're leaving Positive, Negative, or Neutral feedback, and then enter your comments (80 characters, maximum) in the Your Comment box.

3. Make sure you really want to leave the comments you've written, and then click the Leave Comment button. Your feedback will be registered and added into the buyer's other feedback comments.

See Chapter 24, "Understanding and Using Feedback," for more information about the type of feedback to leave in different situations.

Handling Buyer Complaints and Problems

Not all auctions go smoothly. Maybe the item arrived damaged. Maybe it didn't arrive at all. Maybe it wasn't exactly what the buyer thought he was getting. Maybe the buyer is a loud, complaining, major-league son of a rutabaga.

In any case, if you have a complaining customer, you need to do something about it. Here are some of your options:

- Ignore them. If you specified "all sales are final" in your item listing, you don't technically have to do anything else at this point. Of course, complaining customers tend to leave negative feedback, and might even complain to eBay about you.

- If the item never arrived, put a trace on the shipment, if you can.

- If the item was insured, you can initiate a claim for the lost or damaged item. (See Chapter 19 for more information on filing insurance claims.)

- Negotiate a lower price for a damaged or disappointing item, and refund the difference to the buyer.

- Offer to refund the purchase price if the item is returned to you.

- Offer a full refund on the item, no questions asked, no further action necessary. (With this option, the buyer doesn't have to bother with shipping it back to you; this is the way Nordstrom would take care of it.)

> **❝ Mike Sez ❞**
>
> There are really no hard and fast rules for handling post-auction problems. You have to play it by ear and resolve each complaint to the best of your ability. Most eBay users are easy to deal with and just want to be treated fairly. Others won't be satisfied no matter what you offer them. You have to use your own best judgment on how to handle each individual situation.

What If You *Didn't* Sell Your Item?

Not every item up for auction on eBay sells. (eBay's "close rate" is right around 50%—which means that half the items listed at any given time don't sell.) If you reach the end of the auction and you haven't received any bids—or you haven't received high-enough bids in a reserve auction—you need to drop back ten and punt, and figure out what to do next.

Perhaps the easiest thing to do if your item didn't sell is to try again—by relisting your item. eBay makes this easy for you, by including a Relist This Item link right on the original item listing page. (It's in the Seller Services section, at the top of the listing.) Click this link to create a new item listing, based on the old item listing.

When you relist an item that didn't sell the first time, eBay still charges you a listing fee for the second listing. However, eBay will refund this second listing fee if your item sells the second time around. (But not if it doesn't.) You will, of course, have to pay the normal end-of-auction fee if the item sells the second time around.

> **" Mike Sez "**
>
> If you choose to relist your item, realize that there was something about the first listing that kept the item from selling. Maybe the starting price was too high; maybe the headline stunk; maybe you didn't include a picture; maybe the description was too brief. (And maybe you just have an item that nobody wants to buy!) You need to figure out what was wrong with the first listing and change it on the relist—otherwise, you're probably doomed to another unsuccessful auction.

What If the Buyer Doesn't Pay?

To an eBay seller, the worst thing in the world is a high bidder who disappears from the face of the earth. When you never receive payment for an auction item, you're dealing with a *deadbeat bidder*—and you're pretty much hosed. Still, you can report the bum to eBay, ask for a refund of your final value fee, and maybe offer the item in question to the second-highest bidder.

To learn more about how to handle a non-paying buyer situation, turn to Chapter 20, "Dealing with Deadbeat Bidders."

THE ABSOLUTE MINIMUM

Here are the key points to remember from this chapter:

- When the auction ends, eBay will contact you (and the high bidder) with end-of-auction information.

- You should then contact the high bidder with your final price and payment information.

- After you receive payment, pack and ship the item—and leave feedback for the high bidder.

- If an item doesn't sell, relist it—and if it sells the second time around, eBay will refund the second listing fee.

- If the high bidder is somehow dissatisfied, try to work out a mutually agreeable solution.

19

SHIPPING IT OUT— CHEAPLY AND SAFELY

The auction's over, you've received payment from the high bidder, and now it's time to pack your item and ship it off. If you don't have much experience in shipping items cross-country, this might seem a bit daunting at first. Don't worry, though; if you've ever wrapped a Christmas present or mailed a letter, you have all the skills you need to ship just about anything anywhere in the world.

Packing 101

Before you ship, you have to pack—which doesn't sound too terribly difficult. However, if you pick the wrong container, don't cushion the contents properly, don't seal it securely, or mislabel the whole thing, you could risk damaging the contents during shipping—or, even worse, sending it to the wrong recipient. Even if you think you know how to pack and ship, you still probably want to read the following sections. You never know; you might pick up a few useful tips!

" Mike Sez "

I like to keep all my packing materials in a single, easy-to-access place—kind of like a ready-to-use packing station. For me, an otherwise unused kitchen counter does the job; other users clear out a portion of their garage or home office for the same purpose.

Essential Packing Supplies

Before you do any packing, you need to have some basic supplies on hand. I'm not just talking boxes here; I'm talking about the stuff you stuff inside the boxes, and seal them up with.

Any halfway busy eBay seller needs to have these basic packing supplies on hand, so that you're not constantly running off to the office supply store every time one of your auctions closes. These items should always be available and easily accessed.

Okay, so what supplies do you need to have at hand? Take a look at this checklist:

Checklist—Packing Supplies

- ☐ Packing tape, clear
- ☐ Bubble wrap
- ☐ Styrofoam peanuts

  or

- ☐ Old newspapers
- ☐ Scissors
- ☐ Box cutter or similar kind of knife
- ☐ Postal scale
- ☐ Black magic marker
- ☐ Large shipping labels
- ☐ Return address labels
- ☐ Other necessary labels—Fragile, This End Up, and so on
- ☐ Labels or forms provided by your shipping service of choice

Now for some explanations. I recommend clear tape over the normal brown because you can use it not just to seal the box but also to tape over the address label and make it somewhat waterproof. (That said, brown tape can be used to tape over labels and logos when you reuse an old box.) I also prefer peanuts to newspapers because peanuts don't leave ink stains, and because of the weight factor; using newspapers as filler can substantially increase your package weight, and thus your shipping costs. (Of course, newspapers are free and peanuts aren't—but peanuts are cheaper than the added shipping costs you'll incur with newspapers.)

The other materials are somewhat self-explanatory—although you might ask why you need a knife when you're packing. I find myself using the knife primarily to slice off old shipping labels from boxes I reuse for my eBay shipping. Although some old labels tear off rather easily, most don't; to remove them, you have to cut (shallowly) around the label and then lift off the outermost layer of the cardboard box.

Where to Find Boxes and Packing Materials

So where do you find all these packing materials and shipping containers? Lots of places.

First, some boxes are free. If you're shipping via the U.S. Postal Service, you can get free Priority Mail and Express Mail boxes, envelopes, and tubes. (Figure 19.1 shows some of the free boxes available for Priority Mail shipping.) Some post offices carry these free containers, or you can order in bulk (but still for free) from the USPS Web site at shop.usps.com.

FIGURE 19.1

Free shipping containers for USPS Priority Mail.

Most post office locations also sell various types of boxes, padded mailers, mailing tubes, and other packing materials, although their prices tend to be a little on the high side. (They must figure you're a captive customer at that point.) You can find better prices and a much bigger selection at any major office supply superstore (Office Depot, Office Max, Staples, and so on) or at specialty box and shipping stores.

Another good source of shipping supplies is eBay itself—or, more accurately, retailers who sell on the eBay service. There are several eBay Store sellers who specialize in packing supplies for other eBay sellers; go to `www.stores.ebay.com` and do a search for "shipping supplies" or "boxes."

Many eBay sellers also do a good job recycling old boxes. That's right, you can reuse boxes that were shipped to you, either from other eBay users or from online or direct mail retailers. (I'm a big fan of Amazon.com's boxes; they recycle quite nicely!)

You'd be amazed how many times a box can be reused. As long as the box is still structurally sound—and sturdy enough for whatever you're shipping—it can be pressed back into service. Just make sure you remove or cross out any old shipping labels and confirm the box is in good shape, with no weak spots or cracks—and reinforce the box with new tape, as necessary.

Finally, don't forget your local merchants. These stores receive a lot of merchandise on a daily basis, and all those goods are packed in *something*. All those shipping boxes come into the store, and end up in the trash or recycling bin.

note

Other carriers might or might not offer their own free shipping containers. FedEx, for example, offers certain sizes of envelopes and boxes for your (free) use. It's best to ask first—before you go buying an expensive new box.

tip

Many of these eBay Stores operate their own Web sites, as well; in particular, check out BubbleFAST (www.bubblefast.com), eSupplyStore.com (www.esupplystore.com), and ShippingSupply.com (www.shippingsupply.com).

What a retailer calls trash you might call reusable packing materials. Short of dumpster diving (which many eBay sellers are masters of), try making a deal with a local retailer to help dispose of those excess boxes and Styrofoam peanuts. You'll get free packing supplies, and the retailer gets a little less stuff to throw away.

Picking the Right Shipping Container

After you have all your shipping supplies assembled, all you need to do is put your item in the appropriate shipping container and seal it up. Easy, right? Not really—and the consequences of choosing the wrong container can be both disastrous and unnecessarily expensive.

First, you have to decide whether to use a box or an envelope. If you have a very large item to ship, the choice is easy. But what if you have something smaller and flatter, such as a laser disc or a coin? Your choice should be determined by the fragility of your item. If the item can bend or break, choose a box; if not, an envelope is probably a safe choice.

Whichever you choose, pick a container that's large enough to hold your item without the need to force it in or bend it in an inappropriate fashion. Also, make sure that the box has enough extra room to insert cushioning material.

On the other hand, the container shouldn't be so big as to leave room for the item to bounce around. Also, you pay for size and for weight; you don't want to pay to ship anything bigger or heavier than it needs to be.

If you're shipping in an envelope, consider using a bubble-pack envelope or reinforcing the envelope with pieces of cardboard. This is especially vital if your item shouldn't be bent or folded.

If you're shipping in a box, make sure it's made of heavy, corrugated cardboard and has its flaps intact. Thinner boxes—such as shoe boxes or gift boxes—simply aren't strong enough for shipping. When packing a box, never exceed the maximum gross weight for the box, which is usually printed on the bottom flap.

Although there are a bunch of different-sized boxes available, sometimes you need something somewhere in between this size and that size box. When you face this situation, you have two choices.

First, you can take a larger box and cut it down. That means cutting through each corner of the box to make it shorter, and then cutting off the ends of the flaps accordingly. Sometimes it's difficult to fold unscored flaps, so you may want to make your own scores by slicing a knife (shallowly) where you want to bend the box closed.

Second, you can combine two smaller boxes. If your box is 16 inches long and your item is 20 inches, just take two boxes and insert the open end of one inside the open end of the other. You'll need to use sufficient packing tape to keep the boxes from sliding apart, but you'll have created a box custom-sized for the item you're shipping.

caution

Use the combination box technique judiciously, as it can significantly increase the weight of the package—and thus your shipping costs.

How to Pack

Here's what you don't do: Drop your item in an empty box and then seal it up. A loose item in a big box will bounce around and get damaged, guaranteed. (Imagine your box being tossed around by a bunch of gorillas in a parking lot, and you get an accurate picture of what most packages endure in the shipping process.) No, you need to carefully pack your item to minimize any potential damage from dropping and rough handling—and from a variety of weather conditions, including rain, snow, and heat.

How do you pack your box? Professional shippers use Styrofoam peanuts, and lots of them; amateurs tend to use crumpled-up newspapers and other materials found around the house. Here's where you can learn something from the pros—peanuts are *much* lighter than newspaper. Weight is a factor in how much you'll pay for shipping, so anything you can do to lighten the weight of your package is important. Because peanuts cost... well, *peanuts*, they've become my preferred cushioning material. (And I used to be a crumpled-up newspaper kind of guy, until the latest increase in Priority Mail rates.)

As you might expect, packing needs vary for different types of items; you can use these packing tips when it's time to ship your next item:

- If you have the item's original box or packaging, use it! Nothing ships better than the original shipping container.

- If you're shipping a common item—DVDs, videotapes, books, and so on— look for item-specific shipping containers. For example, most office supply stores stock boxes and padded mailers specifically designed for CDs and DVDs. These containers typically do what they're advertised to do.

- Always cushion your package contents, using some combination of shredded or crumpled newspapers, bubble wrap, or Styrofoam peanuts. (For example, when I ship a CD or DVD, I wrap it in bubble wrap and cushion it with peanuts.)

- Whatever cushioning material you use, don't skimp on it. Pack your items tightly to avoid shifting of contents during transit, and make sure the cushioning material covers all sides of the item.

- Position the item toward the center of the box, away from the bottom, sides, and top. (This means placing peanuts *under* the item as well as on top of it.)

> **tip**
>
> You can also use plain (non-buttered!) air-popped popcorn for cushioning; it's inexpensive and environmentally friendly—and tastes good when you're watching a movie!

- If you're shipping several items in the same box, wrap each one separately (in separate smaller boxes, if you can) and provide enough cushioning to prevent movement and to keep the items from rubbing against each other.

- Not only should items be separated from each other in the box, but they should also be separated from the corners and sides of the box to prevent damage if the box is bumped or dropped.

- The previous point argues for another technique—double-boxing items that are especially fragile, such as glass or ceramic items. That means packing the item tightly in a smaller, form-fitting box, and then placing that box inside a slightly larger, shock-absorbing box—with at least 3 inches of cushioning material between the boxes.

- If your item has any protruding parts, cover them with extra padding or cardboard.

- Be careful with the bubble wrap. Although it's great to wrap around objects with flat sides, it can actually damage more fragile figurines or items with lots of little pieces and parts sticking out. If the bubble wrap is too tight, it can snap off any appendages during rough handling.

- Stuff glassware and other fragile hollow items, such as vases, with newspaper or other packing material. This provides an extra level of cushioning in case of rough handling.

- When shipping jars and other items with lids, either separate the lid from the base with several layers of bubble wrap or tissue paper or (better still) pack the lid in a separate small box.

- When shipping framed photographs or artwork, take the glass out of the frame and wrap it separately. Do not let artwork come in direct contact with paper or cardboard.

- Wrap paper items (photographs, books, magazines, and so on) in some sort of plastic bag or wrap, to protect against wetness in shipment.

- When shipping electronic items (including toys and consumer electronics devices), remove the batteries before you ship. Wrap and place the batteries next to the items in the shipping container.

" Mike Sez "

When you're packing an item, watch the weight. I make it a point to have a postal scale at my packing station, and to weigh the item—shipping container and all—during the packing process. When I'm using Priority Mail, the difference between shipping a one-pound package and a one-pound, one-ounce package is as much as $1.90, depending on where it's going. Finding some way to cut that extra ounce of packing material can save almost two bucks in shipping costs—which is why I want to know the weight before I seal the package.

■ When shipping computer parts—circuit boards, video cards, memory chips, and so on—pad the item well and pack it in an Electro Static Discharge (ESD) bag to prevent damaging static buildup. And *don't* use peanuts for filler—all that Styrofoam can carry a damaging static charge.

After you think you're done packing, gently shake the box. If nothing moves, it's ready to be sealed. If you can hear or feel things rattling around inside, however, it's time to add more cushioning material. (If you can shake it, they can break it!)

Packing for International Customers

Packing for international customers shouldn't be any different than for domestic customers—as long as you do it right. Foreign shipments are likely to get even rougher treatment than usual, so make sure the package is packed as securely as possible—with more than enough cushioning to survive the trip to Japan or Europe or wherever it happens to be going.

What *is* different about shipping internationally is the paperwork—and the shipping costs. I cover all this in Chapter 31, "Going International," so turn there if you have a non-U.S. buyer to deal with.

How to Seal the Package

After your box is packed, it's time to seal it. A strong seal is essential, so always use tape that is designed for shipping. Make sure you securely seal the center seams at both the top and the bottom of the box. Cover all other seams with tape, and be sure not to leave any open areas that could snag on machinery.

What kind of sealing materials should you use?

■ **Do** use tape that is designed for shipping, such as pressure-sensitive tape, nylon-reinforced kraft paper tape, glass-reinforced pressure-sensitive tape, or water-activated paper tape. Whichever tape you use, the wider and heavier, the better. Reinforced is always better than non-reinforced.

■ **Don't** use wrapping paper, string, masking tape, or cellophane tape.

One last thing: If you plan to insure your package, leave an untaped area on the cardboard where your postal clerk can stamp "Insured." (Ink doesn't adhere well to tape.)

Labeling 101

You've packed the box. You've sealed the box. Now it's time for the label.

Buying the Right Kinds of Labels

For most purposes, you can't beat the standard 4-inch×6-inch blank white label. Anything smaller is tough to work with, and anything larger just leaves a lot of wasted space. Stick with 4-inch×6-inch and you'll be happy. You can purchase these labels at any office supply store, or even get free versions (for Priority Mail shipping) at your local post office.

If you want to splurge, you can even purchase labels with your name and return address preprinted at the top. This is a good idea if you do a lot of shipping (a dozen or more items a week); otherwise, it's probably not cost-efficient.

You can also purchase or create your own return address labels, to use in conjunction with your main shipping labels. It's easy enough to print out a full page of smallish labels in Microsoft Word; most printing firms (such as Kinko's) can also do up a roll of address labels for a nominal charge.

If you use computer-generated labels (discussed a little later), you can program your label-making program to include your return address when it prints the label. This is a good (and lower-cost) alternative to using preprinted labels.

note

If you don't use a preprinted label, you'll want to hand-print your return address on the shipping container, or use some sort of return address label.

How to Create an Idiot-Proof Label

The best-packed box won't go anywhere if you get the label wrong. For fast and efficient delivery, keep these points in mind when addressing your package:

- Write, type, or print the complete address neatly.
- Always use complete address information, such as the suffixes Dr., Ave., St., and Blvd.
- Include the recipient's apartment or suite number, if applicable.
- Always use correct directions, such as N, S, E, W, SW, and so on.
- Use the correct zip code—and, when possible, use the four-digit add-on, ZIP+4. (Example: 46032-1434.) Make sure you hyphenate the ZIP+4.
- Always use the proper two-letter state abbreviations.
- When addressing to a P.O. Box or rural route destination, include the recipient's telephone number on the label.
- When shipping outside the U.S., include a contact name, telephone number, and postal code on the label—and don't forget to include the country name!

- If you're using any special services of the U.S. Postal Service (Priority Mail, First Class Mail, insurance, and so on), note this above the destination address and below and to the right of the return address.

- Always include your return address information.

- Place the delivery label on the top (not the side) of the box. To avoid confusion, place only one address label on the box. If using a packing slip, place it on the same surface of the box as the address label.

- Do not place the label over a seam or closure or on top of sealing tape.

- To avoid ink smudges and rain smears, place a strip of clear packing tape over the address label.

- If you're reusing a box for shipping, remove or cross out all old address labels or markings on a used box.

tip

Don't know the zip code for the address you're shipping to? Then, look it up at the U.S. Postal Service's Zip Code Finder at `www.usps.com/zip4/`.

If you're unsure what label to use, go with Avery; just about every software program out there supports Avery labels.

Some auction management programs and services also have label printing functions. Check with the manufacturer to see if your program or service offers this function.

And here's one last tip. Make a duplicate of your shipping label and stick it *inside* the box, before you seal it. This way if the original shipping label gets torn off or destroyed, anyone opening the box can read the duplicate label and figure out where the box is supposed to go.

Using Your Computer to Print Shipping Labels

If your handwriting is like mine (borderline illegible), you can appreciate the value of using your computer to print your shipping labels.

There are several dedicated label-printing programs on the market. These programs work with just about any standard-issue major-manufacturer blank labels.

The most popular label-making programs include:

- Avery Wizard and DesignPro (`www.avery.com`)

- NiceLabel Express, Pr, and Suite (`www.nicelabel.com/nicelabel/`)

- PrimaSoft Label Printer (`www.primasoft.com/lb.htm`)

- Visual Labels (`www.rkssoftware.com/visuallabels/overview.html`)

Of course, you don't have to buy a separate software program to print your labels. Microsoft Word, the world's most-used word processing program, has a built-in label printing function that's easy to learn and easy to use. All you have to do is pull down the Tools menu, select Letters and Mailings, and then choose Envelopes and Labels. When the Envelopes and Labels dialog box appears, select the Labels tab and fill in the blanks. It's as easy as that.

> **note**
>
> These instructions are for Word 2002/XP; other versions use a similar but slightly different command sequence.

Shipping 101

How often do you frequent your local post office? When was the last time you visited a UPS shipping center? Do you even know where your local FedEx branch is located?

If these questions make you nervous, you're not alone. For many users, the scariest part of the entire auction process is shipping the item. Not packing, not labeling, but actually taking the box to the shipping center and sending it on its way.

That's because when it comes to shipping, there are so many choices involved. Which carrier do you use? Which specific service offered by a carrier should you choose—the fastest one or the cheapest one? And what about all those extras, such as insurance and delivery confirmation? With all those choices, how do you avoid making the wrong decisions?

If shipping is somewhat foreign to you, don't worry about it. It isn't quite as difficult as it seems, and it'll become old hat after just a few trips to the shipping center.

Examining the Major Shipping Services

You have a number of choices when it comes to shipping your package. You can use the various services offered by the U.S. Postal Service (regular mail, Priority Mail, Express Mail, Media Mail, and so on) or any of the services offered by competing carriers, such as UPS or Federal Express. You can deal directly with any shipping service or use a local shipping store to handle the shipping (and even the packing)—but at a cost.

> **"Mike Sez"**
>
> Which shipping services do I use? For small items, I default to USPS Priority Mail; it's inexpensive and relatively fast, plus I get free packing materials from my local post office. For really big items (over 10 pounds or so), I go with UPS. On those rare instances where a buyer insists on immediate shipment (and is willing to pay for it), I go with FedEx. But I find that, 9 times out of 10, Priority Mail does the job for me—despite their rapidly increasing rates.

Which service should you use? That's a good question, but not always an easy one to answer. Ultimately, you have to strike a compromise between cost, convenience, and speed.

Using the U.S. Postal Service

The United States Postal Service (USPS) offers several different shipping options:

tip

Many sellers like Priority Mail for its free shipping boxes, envelopes, and labels, all of which help to reduce a seller's handling costs.

- **Priority Mail.** This is the preferred shipping method for many experienced auction sellers, if only for its relative convenience. Although Priority Mail used to be predictably low-cost (with flat fees based on weight, not distance), a recent series of price increases have left the service less competitive than before. (You also have to factor distance into the pricing equation, for packages over one pound.) I hesitate to quote prices, as the Postal Service will undoubtedly raise rates before this book gets into your hands, but as of Fall 2002 a small item shipped in one of their flat-rate envelopes costs just $3.85 to go anywhere in the U.S.; a two-pound package costs anywhere from $3.95 to $5.75, depending on distance. Service is typically in the one-to-three day range, and the postal service has lots of free Priority Mail boxes you can use.

- **Express Mail.** This is the USPS' fastest service, offering guaranteed next-day delivery 365 days a year, including weekends and holidays. Merchandise is automatically insured up to $100. Express Mail is considerably more expensive than Priority Mail.

- **First Class Mail.** This is an option if your item fits into a standard-sized envelope. It also provides the benefit of shipping directly from your mailbox, without necessitating a trip to the post office—assuming you can figure out the correct postage. Delivery is similar to Priority Mail, typically three days or less.

- **Parcel Post.** This used to be known as the "slow" USPS service for larger packages, but it's gotten faster of late—and it's priced much lower than Priority Mail. Still, it might take seven to nine days to ship something Parcel Post from coast to coast, as opposed to Priority Mail's two (or three) days.

- **Media Mail.** This is what USPS used to call "book rate" and can be used to ship books, DVDs, videotapes, compact discs, and other printed and prerecorded "media." The rates are much cheaper than Priority Mail, although delivery is typically in the Parcel Post range—seven to nine days. Still, this is a good, low-cost way to ship many popular items; the cost for shipping a CD across country is less than two bucks, compared to $3.85 for Priority Mail.

You can find out more about USPS shipping at the USPS Web site, located at www.usps.gov. This site includes a postage calculator (postcalc.usps.gov) for all levels of service.

Using UPS

UPS is a good option for shipping larger or heavier packages but can be a little costly for smaller items. UPS offers a variety of shipping options, including standard UPS Ground, Next Day Air, Next Day Air Saver, and 2nd Day Air.

You can find out more about UPS shipping—and access a rate calculator—at the UPS Web site, located at www.ups.com.

Using FedEx

FedEx is probably the most costly shipping service, but it's also the fastest. Its most popular shipping options are Priority Overnight, Standard Overnight, and 2Day.

You can find out more about FedEx shipping at its Web site, located at www.fedex.com. You can access its rate finder directly at www.fedex.com/us/rates/.

> **caution**
>
> Media Mail is reserved for publications without advertising—so you can't use it to ship magazines, newspapers, or comic books.
>
> Although every shipping service generates its share of horror stories, I tend to hear more bad comments (most often broken items due to rough handling) about UPS than I hear about competing services. Use UPS—and all shipping services—at your own risk.

> **note**
>
> Because FedEx tends to target the business market (which can afford its higher rates), it isn't widely used for auction shipments.

Using Other Shipping Companies

USPS, UPS, and FedEx are the three most popular shipping services in the US; they're not the only services available, however. Among the other services available are

- Airborne Express (www.airborne.com)
- DHL Worldwide Express (www.dhl.com), great for international shipments
- Purolator Courier (www.purolator.com)

Using a Professional Packing and Shipping Service

All this talk about services and rates get your head spinning? You can always let somebody else worry about the details. Many local shipping stores (such as Mail Boxes Etc.—located on the Web at www.mbe.com) provide packing and shipping services—and do everything from sell boxes to pack your items to serve as a "middleman" between you and UPS or FedEx. You'll pay for their services—some can be quite costly—but you don't have to get your hands dirty or concern yourself with any of those niggling details.

Calculating Shipping Costs

As you've no doubt gathered, there are some significant differences in shipping costs from one shipping service to another. The cost differential is typically based on a combination of weight and distance; the heavier an item is and the further it has to go (and the faster you need to get it to where it's going), the more it costs.

For this reason, it's a good idea to "shop" the major shipping services for the best shipping rates for the types of items you normally sell on eBay. As an example, Table 19.1 compares (as of Fall 2002) the costs of shipping three items from New York to Los Angeles—a one-pound envelope, a two-pound box, and a five-pound box.

> **tip**
>
> To find a shipping store in your area, check out AuctionSHIP (www.auctionship.com), a national network of retail stores that provide packing and shipping services. They even offer discounted rates for online auction customers.
>
> To compare shipping costs for a variety of services on a single Web page, check out iShip (www.iship.com). This site not only lets you compare shipping costs, but also provides tracking services for all major carriers.

TABLE 19.1   Comparison: Shipping from New York to Los Angeles

Service	Delivery Time	1-lb. Envelope	2-lb. Box	5-lb. Box
USPS Media Mail	7–9 days	$1.42	$1.84	$3.10
USPS Parcel Post	7–9 days	$3.75	$4.49	$9.43
USPS Priority Mail	1–3 days	$3.85	$5.75	$12.15
UPS Ground	2–5 days	$6.78	$7.70	$9.37
FedEx 2Day	2 days	$9.75	$11.50	$16.75
UPS 2nd Day Air	2 days	$11.64	$15.09	$21.57
USPS Express Mail	1–2 days	$13.65	$17.85	$27.30
FedEx Standard Overnight	1 day	$15.25	$25.50	$33.25
UPS Next Day Air Saver	1 day	$18.33	$30.73	$39.34
FedEx Priority Overnight	Next morning	$17.25	$29.00	$38.25

Of course, cost isn't the only factor you want to consider. You also want to compare how long it takes the package to arrive, what kind of track record the shipping service has, and how convenient it is for you to use. If you have to drive 20 miles to get to a UPS office, and you have a post office just down the street, that might offset a slightly higher cost for Priority Mail.

How to Reduce Shipping Weight—And Shipping Costs

Now that you know how important weight is in the shipping equation, here are a few tips for bringing down the weight of the items you ship:

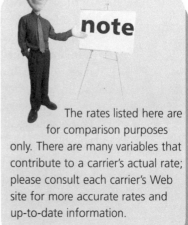

note

The rates listed here are for comparison purposes only. There are many variables that contribute to a carrier's actual rate; please consult each carrier's Web site for more accurate rates and up-to-date information.

- Use peanuts instead of paper for cushioning; peanuts are *much* lighter—and don't leave ink stains on the merchandise.

- Even better, use air instead of peanuts—in the form of those air-filled bags that Amazon.com uses to cushion their packages.

- Use less heavy-duty boxes, if you can. (This is generally an option only when you're shipping light objects.) You'd be surprised at the difference in weight between similarly sized boxes, based on the thickness of the cardboard.

■ Don't use oversized boxes. If the box is too large, either trim down the unused portion of the flaps or move to a smaller box.

Finally, make sure you include the weight of the box and the cushioning material when you weigh your item for shipment. A big box with lots of crumpled paper can easily add a half-pound or more to your item's weight—excess weight you'll have to pay for.

Shipping Large or Heavy Items

Some items are just too big to ship via conventional means. Suppose you just sold an old pinball machine, or a roll-top desk, or a waterbed. How do you deal with items that big?

Assuming that the item is too big even for UPS, you have to turn to traditional trucking services. Some of these services will pack or crate the item for you (for a fee); others require you to do all the crating. In addition, some of these firms require you to deliver the item to their shipping terminal, and for the buyer to pick it up from their dock. (Other firms offer door-to-door service—again, sometimes for a higher fee.) In any case, it helps to make a few calls and ask for specifics before you decide on a shipper.

When you have an oversized item to ship, here are some of the trucking services that other eBay sellers have used. Check with each firm individually as to its fees and shipping policies.

■ AAA Cooper Transportation (www.aaacooper.com)

■ Forward Air (www.forwardair.com)

■ Vintage Transport Services (www.vintagetransport.com)

■ Yellow Freight (www.yellowfreight.com)

note

Package size is determined from two separate measurements. You'll need to measure the length of the package and add it to the girth. (Girth is the height and width added together and then multiplied by two—in other words, the distance *around* the package.)

caution

Most of the standard shipping services I mentioned earlier in this chapter, such as the U.S. Postal Service, won't handle packages that weigh more than 150 pounds, or have a combined length and girth of more than 130 inches.

How to Price Shipping/Handling for Your Item Listings

Let's think back to the start of the auction process. You probably remember that I recommended you include your shipping/handling charges up front, so that bidders know what to expect.

But how do you figure shipping costs before you know where the item is going?

The solution is easy if you're shipping something that weighs (packaging included) less than a pound. For these lightweight items, you can use USPS Priority Mail, which ships one-pound packages anywhere in the U.S. for a single price ($3.85 at the time I write this). Because you can also use free boxes (provided by the postal service), you know your cost to package and ship a one-pound item will be $3.85. Easy.

If you're shipping books, CDs, or videos, you also have it easy—if you choose to ship via USPS Media Mail. Media Mail rates are so cheap that you can do some creative rounding of numbers and say that any item weighing two pounds or less can ship anywhere in the for $2.00. The actual Media Mail rate might be $1.42 or $1.84 or whatever, but $2.00 makes a convenient number to state up front; the gap between actual and projected shipping can go towards the purchase of an appropriate box or envelope.

When you're shipping other items that weigh more than a pound, the calculation gets much more complex. The fact is, if you're selling an item that weighs, let's say, four pounds, the actual shipping costs (via Priority Mail) can range from $5.30 to $10.35, depending on where you are and where the buyer is. There's no way to quote an exact cost until the auction is over and you get the buyer's Zip code.

There are three ways you can deal with this situation in your auction listings.

First, you can simply state that buyers will pay actual shipping cost based on location, and not include a flat shipping/handling charge. If you take this approach, you have to request the buyer's Zip code at the end of the auction, refer to various rate charts to figure the shipping cost, and then relay that cost to your buyer. It's a bit of work, but it gets the job done.

Next, you can calculate an *average* shipping cost for your item, figuring a cost halfway between the minimum and the maximum possible costs. Using our four-pound example, the minimum cost for Priority Mail shipping is $5.30 and the maximum is $10.35, so you would charge the buyer the average of these two numbers, or $7.83. (Maybe you round up to $8.00.) The theory here is that you lose money on some shipments and make it back on others, so over the long term it's a wash. Of course, nearby buyers might complain that they're paying too much (which they are, because they're in fact subsidizing sellers who live further away).

Finally, you can include the link to your shipping carrier's rate calculator in your item listing. You'll also have to include your Zip code and the weight of the item, but then you let the buyer do the shipping cost calculation.

Aside from the pure shipping costs, you have to consider *handling* costs. You need to be sure that you're compensated for any special materials you have to purchase to package the item. That doesn't mean you charge one buyer for an entire roll of tape, but maybe you add a few pennies to your shipping charge for these sorts of packaging consumables. And if you have to purchase a special box or envelope to ship an item, you should definitely include that cost in your shipping charge. (This argues for planning your shipping before placing your item listing—which is always a good idea.)

> **" Mike Sez "**
>
> Even when I'm shipping Priority Mail (and can use their free boxes), I tend to round up the shipping cost to cover my fixed shipping costs. So, for example, if I'm shipping a one-pound package via Priority Mail, I don't charge the buyer $3.85; I charge $4.00. That extra 15 cents goes to cover the cost of tape and labels and markers and whatnot.

Using Electronic Postage

A few years back there was a lot of buzz about electronic postage. This e-postage would make it easy for you to print out your own metered postage from your computer and printer (no extra hardware necessary), and thus eliminate a lot of trips to the post office. (If you put your own postage on your packages, your mailman can pick up your packages along with your regular mail at your place of business or residence.)

Thanks to the dot-com implosion, the e-postage buzz has died down somewhat and several companies have gone out of business. Electronic postage is still a viable option, however, and still offered by a handful of companies, the largest of which is Stamps.com (www.stamps.com).

If you sign up with Stamps.com or a similar firm, the process is fairly simple. You install the e-postage software on your computer, and prepay for a specified amount of postage. You enter the appropriate information (package size and weight, destination zip code, and so on) into the e-postage program, which uses that information to calculate exact postage and print that postage to an envelope or "stamp," via your printer.

If you're a high-volume eBay seller who primarily uses the U.S. Postal Service (for any form of shipping—First Class, Parcel Post, Priority Mail, or whatever), e-postage might be worth looking into. For the rest of us, it's probably not worth the hassle or the up-front costs.

How to Track Your Shipment

If you think the package might be lost in transit (it's taking too long to arrive), you can always avail yourself of the tracking services provided by UPS, FedEx, and other major carriers. These services typically provide tracking numbers for all packages shipped. In most cases, you can track your package by entering the package's tracking number into the carrier's Web site.

The one major shipping service that doesn't offer tracking (by default) is the U.S. Postal Service. What you can get from the postal service (at a cost of from $0.45 to $0.55) is delivery confirmation. USPS confirmation, however, does not confirm that an actual person received the package; it only confirms that the mail carrier delivered it. (Stuck it in the mailbox, that is.)

If you want a signature confirmation on a USPS shipment, you need to send your item with the certified mail option. Certified mail requires the recipient to sign on delivery, and costs $2.30. This is a preferred option if you're shipping something extremely valuable.

tip

You can buy USPS delivery confirmation forms in bulk from ShipperTools.com (www.shippertools.com). ShipperTools.com uses the official USPS delivery confirmation system, and lets you print an unlimited number of confirmation forms for just $6.95 a month.

When to Recommend Insurance

If you're shipping a moderately expensive item (over $50, let's say), it might be worth the expense to insure it. You can always give the buyer the option of buying insurance—or just do it yourself and include the costs in your normal shipping/handling fee.

caution

Just because you have insurance doesn't mean you can collect. Some carriers are particularly picky about paying claims—especially if the package wasn't perfectly packed to begin with.

As to cost, the U.S. Postal Service charges $1.30 to insure items up to $50, or $2.20 for items between $50 and $100. UPS includes $100 worth of insurance in its basic rates; additional insurance can be purchased for additional cost.

What to Do When Things Go Wrong

If the package never arrives—or arrives damaged—you have some work to do. If you insured the package, you have to file a claim with the carrier. Information for claim filing appears on most of the shipping services' Web sites, but you might have to visit your carrier's local office to obtain the proper claim forms.

Note, however, that the procedure for filing a claim can be long and involved. Take the example of the U.S. Postal Service. The process starts on the buyer's end, who must take the package (merchandise, box, peanuts, and all) to their local post office to fill in half of a claim form (PS 1000). After this form is processed, the post office sends you (the seller) the half-filled out form, via the mail. You then fill out the rest of the form and take it (along with your original insurance receipt) to *your* local post office for processing. When enough time goes by the USPS will (or won't, if you filled in something wrong) send a check for the insured amount directly to the buyer.

Other shipping services work differently, and some even send the insurance check to you instead of to the buyer. However it works, you need to communicate with the buyer while you're waiting for the claim to be paid, so that both of you are in the loop about what's going on. If you receive the insurance check, you'll then need to refund the buyer's money; if the buyer receives the check, he should notify you when he's been paid.

> **caution**
>
> If you didn't insure your package—or if the carrier didn't offer automatic insurance—then you have a situation. eBay protocol has it that the seller is responsible for any losses in shipment, so you might end up refunding the buyer's money out of your own pocket.

> **tip**
>
> You can speed this process up by obtaining the claim form yourself, filling in your part, and then sending the claim form and the original insurance receipt to the buyer—and let him deal with the post office through the rest of the process.

Tips for Less-Painful Shipping

To wrap things up, here are some additional tips you can use to take some of the hassle out of shipping your eBay items:

- When you're using the U.S. Postal Service for shipping, try to time your visits to avoid long lines. That means avoiding lunch hour and the last half hour or so before closing; avoiding Mondays; and avoiding peak shipping periods around major holidays, such as Christmas and Valentine's Day. Early morning and mid-afternoon are typically low-volume times.

- Don't feel obligated to ship every single day of the week. Save up your shipments and go to the post office just one or two days a week.

■ When you have a lot of packages to ship, don't go to the post office by your-self. Take a helper—and, if large shipments are common, invest in a small hand truck to help you cart all those boxes to the counter.

■ If you're a heavy shipper, consider setting up an account with a single ship-per and arranging daily pickups from your home. Pickup service will cost you a little more, but can be more than worth it in time savings. (Most carriers will also pick up single items if you arrange so in advance—but at a much higher fee.)

■ You may need to factor weather conditions into which type of shipping you choose. If it's summertime and you're shipping something that might melt in extreme heat (like an old vinyl LP), pick the fastest shipping method possible.

THE ABSOLUTE MINIMUM

Here are the key points to remember from this chapter:

■ Pack your item so that it doesn't rattle when you shake it.

■ Pack your item so that the package is as light as possible.

■ Calculate shipping costs based on the weight of the item being shipped *and* the packaging—including the box and cushioning material.

■ Get free boxes for Priority Mail shipping from the post office, or from the USPS Web site.

■ Don't be afraid to reuse boxes you receive from other sources—as long as they're still in serviceable shape and you remove all previous labels.

■ Make sure your label is neatly printed and includes a full address and Zip code.

■ Place a layer of clear tape over the delivery label so that it doesn't get smeared in transit.

■ For most packages, the U.S. Postal Service is a good shipping option, either via Priority Mail, Media Mail, or Parcel Post.

20

DEALING WITH DEADBEAT BIDDERS

A *deadbeat bidder* is someone who wins an auction but never follows through with the transaction. Not only should you leave negative feedback about these deadbeats, but you should also request a credit from eBay for your final value fee.

What do you do when you have a deadbeat bidder in one of your auctions? Fortunately, you still have the merchandise, which you can relist and (hopefully) sell again. You are out some eBay fees, however—although you can probably get them refunded when you report the deadbeat to eBay.

When eBay receives what it calls a Non-Paying Bidder Alert, the service automatically sends a warning to the user in question. If the alleged deadbeat receives three such warnings, he or she will be indefinitely suspended from the eBay service.

So there!

How to Handle Bum Bidders

If you are unfortunate enough to get stuck with a deadbeat bidder, there is a set procedure to follow, as you can see in the following checklist:

Checklist—Dealing with Deadbeat Bidders

☐ File a Non-Paying Bidder Alert

☐ Request a final value fee credit

☐ Leave negative feedback to the deadbeat bidder

☐ Offer the item in question to the second-highest bidder

or

☐ Relist the item

Contacting an Unresponsive Bidder

It's on your shoulders to go to whatever lengths possible to contact the high bidder in your eBay auctions. This should start with the standard post-auction e-mail, of course. If the buyer hasn't responded within three days, resend your original e-mail with an "URGENT" added to the subject line. You should also amend the message to give the buyer a deadline (two days is good) for his response.

If another two days go by without a response, send a new message informing the buyer that if you don't receive a response within two days, you'll be forced to cancel his high bid and report him to eBay as a deadbeat bidder.

If a full week goes by and you still haven't heard from the buyer, you can assume the worst. Which means it's time to let eBay know about the bum.

Filing a Non-Paying Bidder Alert

The way you notify eBay about a deadbeat bidder is to file a Non-Paying Bidder Alert form. You have to file this form (and wait the requisite amount of time) before you can request a final value fee credit on the auction in question.

A Non-Paying Bidder Alert must be filed between 7 and 45 days after your auction ends. You file the Alert by going to the Site Map page and clicking the Request Final Value Fee Credit link—or going directly to `pages.ebay.com/help/community/npb.html`. This page tells you all about how to deal with bad bidders; follow the instructions here to file the Non-Paying Bidder Alert.

If, by some quirk of fate, you end up working things out with the buyer after you've filed a Non-Paying Bidder Alert, you should file a Non-Paying Bidder Warning Removal form. You can find this form on the same page you use to file a Non-Paying Bidder Alert.

By the way, if you're a bidder and have a Non-Paying Bidder Alert filed against you (unfairly, of course), you can appeal the Alert. Go to the page you used to file the Non-Paying Bidder Alert and click the Non-Bidding Bidder Appeal Form link. Warnings will remain on your eBay record until they're successfully appealed.

Asking eBay to Refund Your Fees

After a Non-Paying Bidder Alert is filed, eBay sends a message to the bidder requesting that the two of you work things out. (It's not a very strong message, in my humble opinion.) You then have to wait 10 days before you can request a refund of your final value fee. You have to make the request no later than 60 days after the end of your auction, and your claim has to meet one of the following criteria:

- The high bidder did not respond to your e-mails or backed out and did not buy the item.
- The high bidder's check bounced or a stop payment was placed on it.
- The high bidder returned the item and you issued a refund.
- The high bidder backed out, but you sold the item to another bidder at a lower price.
- One or more of the bidders in a Dutch auction backed out of the sale.

If your situation fits, you're entitled to a full refund of eBay's final value fee—but you must request it. To request a refund, go to eBay's Site Map page and click the Final Value Fee Request link (in the Seller Services section). Follow the instructions there to receive your credit; eBay generally issues a credit to your account within 48 hours.

note

If the item in question was sold in a Dutch auction, this process gets a little trickier. You can only file one Non-Paying Bidder Alert form per auction—which means you have to include all the deadbeat bidders in that auction in a single form; you can't file additional alerts after the initial form has been filed.

caution

eBay's policy is not to refund insertion fees—although if you have a really special circumstance, there's no harm in asking.

Leaving Negative Feedback

Naturally, you want to alert other eBay members to the weasel among them. You do this by leaving negative feedback, along with a description of just what went wrong (no contact, no payment, whatever).

To leave negative feedback, go to the item listing page, click the Leave Feedback to Bidder link, and when the Leave Feedback About an eBay User page appears, check Negative and enter your comments. Click the Leave Comment button when done.

Giving Other Bidders a Second Chance

When a bidder backs out of an auction, you're stuck with the merchandise that you thought you had sold. Assuming you still want to sell the item, what do you do?

eBay offers the opportunity for you to make what it calls a Second Chance Offer to other bidders in your failed auction. This lets you try to sell your item to someone else who was definitely interested in what you had to sell.

You can make a Second Chance Offer to any of the under-bidders in your original auction. The offer can be made immediately on the end of the auction, and up to 60 days afterward.

To make a Second Chance Offer, return to your original item listing page and click the Make a Second Chance Offer link (in the Seller Services section). When the Second Chance Offer page appears, follow the onscreen instructions to fill out the form and make the offer.

note

When a bidder accepts your Second Chance Offer, eBay charges you a final value fee. You are not charged a listing fee. Buyers accepting Second Chance Offers are eligible for eBay's normal fraud protection services.

Relisting Your Item

If you don't have any takers on your Second Chance Offer, you can always try to sell the item again by relisting the item. See Chapter 18, "After the Auction: Concluding Your Business," for more details.

tip

Second Chance Offers can also be used, in a successful auction, to offer duplicate items to non-winning bidders.

THE ABSOLUTE MINIMUM

Here are the key points to remember from this chapter:

- If seven days go by with no contact from the high bidder in your auction, you probably have a deadbeat on your hands.

- After you've made all reasonable effort to contact the buyer, file a Non-Paying Bidder Alert with eBay.

- Wait another ten days, and then request a final value fee credit from eBay.

- You can try to sell the item in question by making a Second Chance Offer to other bidders, or by relisting the item in a new auction.

SECRETS OF SUCCESSFUL SELLERS

You have things to sell. You want to make sure you actually sell them and that you get the highest price possible. But you're also competing with millions of other items up for auction at the same time. How do you stand out from the crowd, attract a bunch of bidders, and goose up the high bids?

If you're looking for extra-special selling secrets, this chapter is for you. Discover the secrets and strategies that will help you be a successful online auction seller!

Two Different Strategies for Success

You can adopt two major strategies when putting an item up for auction:

- **The high road strategy.** Supporters of the high road strategy go after bidders who don't mind paying a little more for something good. Yours won't be the cheapest item on auction, but it will be the best—in terms of value to the ultimate buyer. Whether it's the rarity of your item, its superior condition, or your superior service, you have to make it worth the bidders' while to pay a little bit more. Better stuff commands higher prices.

- **The low road strategy.** Supporters of the low road strategy sell on price. They give buyers a lot for their money, in terms of quantity—but not necessarily quality. A low price grabs the bidders' attention, even if the merchandise is a little ordinary. Lower prices move more merchandise.

Both strategies have their strengths and weaknesses, and which one you use depends on the type of item you have for sale, your competition, and your own way of doing things.

The High Road—High Price, High Quality, High Value

Use the high road strategy when you have something truly unique to sell. Maybe it's an ultra-rare Hummel figurine, a mint-condition stamp, or a complete run of a certain comic book or magazine. Whatever—position your item as one-of-a-kind and high quality, and set your initial price accordingly.

When you create your high road item listing, make it classy. Include a lot of details, and play up its rare and unique nature. Put "rare" in the title, and include at least one good-quality picture of your item. Consider making your item a featured auction. Try to attract the elite buyers with everything you do.

When you price your high road item, price it high enough to weed out the riff-raff. Price it high enough that serious buyers take you seriously. Price it high enough that you don't get a lot of initial bids.

When you list your high road item, make sure you back up the quality with superior support. Tell your bidders that you provide insurance with your shipping and that you offer a 30-day money-back guarantee. Solicit their e-mail questions—and then answer them promptly. And follow through on your promises; make sure the end-of-auction communication is prompt, courteous, and complete. Ship the item in a new (that is, not re-used) box as quickly as possible.

When taking the high road, present at least the illusion of quality—and perception will become reality. The result will be higher bids from higher-class online auction citizens.

The Low Road—Low Price and a Lot of Excitement

Use the low road strategy when you want to generate a lot of attention fast—or when you have an item that is more common than it is rare. You want to grab bidders' attention with a low price and hope the resulting bidding frenzy will increase the price to a more acceptable level.

When you set your low road price, think cheap. Think really cheap. Think so ridiculously cheap that bidders would be crazy not to go for it. You want to get the bidding going fast, so your initial price should be significantly lower than what you expect the item to sell for. Ignore the normal 10% rule for setting the starting bid; go for a $0.99 starter, or something equally attention-getting.

When you create your low road item listing, be a salesman. Scream the deal at your potential bidders, and use every trick at your disposal to grab their attention. Use HTML to create an ad with bright colors, large fonts, and sizzling graphics. Put a lot of salesy buzzwords in your title, such as "new" and "free" and "deal." Consider throwing in other items to create an irresistible value pack—"three for the price of one" sort of stuff. Do everything in your power to attract the price shopper and the value hunter.

When taking the low road, you want to generate excitement—which will generate activity, which will generate bids.

Forty Sure-Fire Tips for Closing More Auctions— And Increasing Your Revenues

Whichever strategy you employ, you can do other things to increase your chances of selling your item at the highest possible price. Here are forty tips that can help anyone be a more profitable seller at any online auction.

Tip #1: Research Your Price

Don't sell without doing your homework first; make sure you know the true value of an item before you put it up for auction. Before you price your item, search for similar items in eBay's closed auctions. What was the starting bid price? What was the final selling price? You should also research the price of similar items offline; sometimes you can get a feel for relative value if you compare your item to a newer version of the same. Be informed, and you won't set the price too high or too low; you'll set it just right.

Tip #2: Make Your Listing Stand Out

Do everything in your power to make your item listings stand out from all the other listings currently online. Work on both the title and the description, and consider employing HTML (or using a listing-creation program or service) to create a more dynamic ad.

Tip #3: Create a Template for Your Item Listings

If you don't use a listing-creation service, you can make it easier to create HTML-enabled listings by working with a standard template. Create your listing template in any HTML or text editor, leaving blanks for the variable information, and save the result in a standard text file. You can then paste this HTML template into your item description, fill in the blanks for this particular item, and have a real head start in creating great-looking listings.

note

See Chapter 16, "Creating a Great-Looking Listing," for more ideas about creating eye-catching item listings.

See Chapter 14, "Writing a Listing That Sells," for more ideas for effective listing descriptions.

Tip #4: Get All the Buzzwords in the Title

Make sure you have the right words and phrases in the title of your item listing. If your audience looks for "compact discs," say **compact disc**; if they look for "CDs," say **CD**. If they look for both, use both. Use all possible words (up to your auction's character limit) to hit all possible keywords your potential bidders might be searching for—even if some of the words are redundant.

Tip #5: A Picture Says a Thousand Words

Nothing increases your chances of selling an item like including a picture of it in your listing. Take a photo of your item, scan it in, upload it, and include it with your listing—even if it's just a plain text (non-HTML) listing. (And when you take your picture, make sure it's a good one—there's no point in posting a picture if the item is too small and out of focus.)

Tip #6: Be Descriptive

Include as much descriptive text about your item as you can. The better you describe your item, the fewer mid-auction e-mails you'll get asking about it and the greater the chance that your ultimate buyer won't get any unpleasant surprises.

In addition, you never know when that single "unimportant" detail is just the thing a specific bidder is looking for—so don't overlook any detail, no matter how small.

Tip #7: Include Shipping and Payment Details

Don't forget to include all the details about shipping and handling (how much and who pays), payment methods, and the like. (That means estimating shipping/handling up front, if you can.) Don't leave anything open to interpretation.

Tip #8: Be Honest

Be honest in your description of the item. If the item has a few flaws, mention them. If there's damage or the item is otherwise imperfect, make note of it. Misleading a buyer will only cause you grief.

Tip #9: Promote Yourself with Your About Me Page

eBay's About Me page is the perfect way to provide more background information about you as a seller, and to drive potential bidders to your other live auctions. Make sure you create an About Me page—and use it to help "sell" yourself and your other items.

Tip #10: Make the Buyer Pay

Stipulate in your listing that the buyer pays all shipping and handling costs (and you might even want to detail these costs ahead of time in your listing). Also, make sure the buyer pays for any "extras" that might be added after the sale. If the buyer wants insurance, the buyer pays for it. If the buyer wants to use an escrow service, the buyer pays for it. If the buyer wants expedited shipping, the buyer pays for it. See the trend?

Tip #11: Go Long...

When it comes time to choose the length for your auction, go for the 7- or 10-day option. The longer your item is up for auction, the more potential bidders who will see it—and the more potential bidders, the better your chances of selling it for a higher price. Don't cheat yourself out of potential sales by choosing a shorter auction.

Tip #12:...Or Create a Short-Term Frenzy

On the other hand, if you have something really hot, create a bidding frenzy by choosing a very short auction length. If you do this, play it up in your item's title: **3 Days Only!** works pretty well.

Tip #13: There's No Reason to Reserve

I don't know of a single bidder who likes reserve price auctions. Why use something that scares some bidders away? (Remember, many beginning users don't understand reserve price auctions, and thus don't bid in them.) Set a realistic minimum, and get on with it.

Tip #14: Single Items Are Best...

If you're looking for the highest total dollar, don't group items together. Multiple-item lots seldom bring as much money as individual items sold individually.

Tip #15:...Although You Can Unload Some Dogs in a Pack

On the other hand, if you have a lot of things to sell, selling in lots can reduce your personal overhead, as well as help you unload some less attractive items that you probably couldn't sell individually. (Plus, you only get hit for a single insertion fee!)

Tip #16: Don't Compete Against Yourself

If five people are looking to buy footstools today, don't give them five choices all from one person (you). If you have five footstools to sell, don't sell them all at once. Sell one this week, one next week, and one the week after that. Spread it out to create an illusion of scarcity, and you'll generate more total revenue.

Tip #17: Start and End in Prime Time

When you start your auction is important—because that affects when your auction *ends*. If you start a seven-day auction at 6:00 p.m. on a Saturday, it will end exactly seven days later, at 6:00 p.m. the following Saturday.

Why is when your auction ends important? Because some of the most intense bidding takes place in the final few minutes of your auction, from snipers trying to steal the high bid at the last possible moment. To take advantage of last-minute bidders, your auction needs to end when the most possible bidders are online.

If you end your auction at 3:00 in the morning, everyone will be asleep and you'll lose out on any last-minute bids. Instead, try to end your auction during early evening hours, when the most number of users are online.

Remember, though, that you're dealing with a three-hour time-zone gap between the East and the West coasts. So, if you time your auction to end at 7:00 p.m. EST, you're ending at 4:00 p.m. PST—when most potential bidders are still at work. Conversely, if you choose to end at 9:00 p.m. PST, you just hit midnight in New York—and many potential bidders are already fast asleep.

The best times to end—and thus to *start*—your auction are between 9:00 p.m. and 11:00 p.m. EST, or between 6:00 p.m. and 8:00 p.m. PST. (Figure the in-between time zones yourself!) That way you'll catch the most potential bidders online for the final minutes of your auction—and possibly generate a bidding frenzy that will garner a higher price for your merchandise!

Note, however, that the best time to end an auction can be influenced by the type of item you're selling. For example, if you're selling an item that appeals to grade-school or high-school kids, try ending your auction in the late afternoon, after the kids get home from school and before they head off for dinner. Items with appeal to housewives do well with a late morning or early afternoon end time. And business items sell best when they end during normal business hours.

eBay operates on Pacific (West Coast) time. If you're in another time zone, be sure to do the math to determine the proper time for your area.

Tip #18: End on a Sunday

When you end your auction on a Sunday, you get one full Saturday and *two* Sundays (the starting Sunday and the ending one) for a 7-day item listing. Sunday is a great day to end auctions because almost everybody's home—no one's out partying, or stuck at work or in school. End your auction on a Sunday evening, and you're likely to get more bids—and higher prices.

There are exceptions, however.

As with the time you end your auction, your ending day might also be influenced by the type of item you're selling. If you're selling an item of interest to college students, for example, you might be better ending on a night during the week, as a lot of students travel home for the weekend; you'll catch them in the dorms on a Wednesday or Thursday night. Items targeted at churchgoers might also be better ending during the week, so you don't catch bidders when they're at Sunday evening church services.

Tip #19: Don't End on a Friday or Saturday Night

If Sunday is normally the best night of the week to end your auction, what's the worst night?

Friday and Saturday are probably the worst nights to end most auctions, because a lot of eBay users are out partying on these non-school nights. End an auction for any item (especially youth-oriented items) on a Friday or Saturday night, and you eliminate a large number of potential buyers.

You should also try not to end your auction right in the middle of a hit television series—some potential bidders might find it difficult to tear themselves away from the old boob tube. That means avoiding "Must See TV" Thursdays, and any blockbuster sporting events or award shows.

Tip #20: Slow Down in the Summer

For whatever reason, eBay traffic slows way down in the summertime. (Lots of potential buyers are on vacation, and even more are outside enjoying the sunshine.) If you want to maximize your bids, you'll get a higher price once fall and winter come along.

Tip #21: Promote Your Auctions

Let people outside eBay know about your auction. Mention your auction in relevant newsgroups and mailing lists; feature it on your personal Web site and send e-mails about it to all your friends. Include your item listing's URL in everything you do so that anyone interested can click the link to view your auction. Do anything you can think of to draw traffic to your listing—and thus increase your chances of selling it.

Tip #22: Track Your Auctions

Don't let your auction activity get away from you. Use My eBay or a third-party auction management program/service to look at all your auctions on a daily basis, or use auction management software to track your auctions automatically.

Tip #23: Use My eBay

The best way to track all your auction activity—selling *and* bidding—is via My eBay. My eBay can also track your favorite auction categories, as well as your feedback ratings and account status—and lets you access the pages you use most often, without having to click through useless parts of the site. Personalize your My eBay page the way you like and then bookmark it; it's a great home page for the heavy auction trader.

note

Learn more about My eBay in Chapter 22, "Creating a Home Base with My eBay."

Tip #24: Avoid Premature Cancellation

Know that many bidders wait until the very last minute to place a bid. (It's called sniping, and it really works.) If you cancel an auction early, you'll miss out on the bulk of the potential bids. So don't cancel!

Tip #25: Avoid Deadbeats

You don't have to sell to just anybody. You can stipulate that you won't sell to bidders with negative feedback or with feedback ratings below a certain level. If you receive bids from these potential deadbeats, cancel them. If the deadbeats continue to bid (after being warned off via e-mail by you), block their bids. You want to sell to someone who will actually consummate the transaction and send you payment; bidders with negative feedback are more likely to leave you high and dry.

Tip #26: Include All Your Shipping Costs

When figuring your shipping and handling costs, make sure you factor in all your costs—not just the shipping itself, but also the cost of the packaging, the labels, and the packing tape. Don't gouge your buyer (this isn't meant to be a profit center), but don't cheat yourself, either. If actual shipping costs are $3.50, think about charging the buyer $4 to cover your additional costs.

Tip #27: Don't Forget to Weigh the Box

When you ship your item, you don't just ship the item—you also ship the box and all cushioning materials. These items have weight, and must be included when you're weighing your item for shipment. (Those free Priority Mail boxes are especially heavy—and can easily increase your cost of shipping.)

Tip #28: Use a Middleman for Expensive Items

If you're selling a high-priced item, consider offering the buyer the option of using an escrow service. It's a good deal for you; the buyer pays for the service (in the neighborhood of 5 percent, typically), it provides a level of peace of mind for the buyer, and it lets you accept credit card payments that you might otherwise not accept.

Tip #29: Document Everything

In case something goes south, it helps to have good records of all aspects of your transaction. Print copies of the confirmation e-mail, plus all e-mail between you and the buyer. Make sure you write down the buyer's user ID, e-mail address, and physical address. If the transaction is ever disputed, you'll have all the backup you need to plead your case.

Tip #30: Communicate Quickly—And Clearly

When your auction ends, get in touch with the high bidder *immediately*. Don't wait until the next day; send your post-auction e-mail within minutes of the auction close. Remember, the faster you notify the high bidder, the faster you'll get paid.

When you send that e-mail to the high bidder, make sure that the message is clear and grammatically correct, and that you include all relevant information. Don't leave anything hanging—send a letter that reads something like this:

Congratulations!

You are the winning bidder on auction item number *123456*, *"Frizzbot Diddly Things."* Please send *$00.00* (*$00.00* + *$0.00* shipping/handling) to

Your Name

Your Address

Your City, State, and Zip

Please include your address and a copy of this e-mail with your payment. Money order or cashier's check gets immediate shipment via *Preferred Shipping Method*; payment by check holds shipment for 10 working days.

Please respond to this e-mail (and include your address, please) to confirm your winning bid.

Thanks again,

Your Name

E-mail the buyer again when you receive payment and once more when you're ready to ship the item. The more everyone knows, the fewer surprises there are.

Also, remember that not everyone reads his or her e-mail daily, so don't expect an immediate response. Still, if you don't receive a response, send another e-mail. If you're at all concerned at any point, get the buyer's phone number or physical address from the auction site and call or write him. A good phone conversation can clear up a wealth of misunderstandings.

Tip #31: Be Nice

Remember that you're dealing with another human being, someone who has feelings that can be hurt. A little bit of common courtesy goes a long way. Say please and thank you, be understanding and tolerant, and treat your trading partner in the same way you'd like to be treated. Follow the golden rule; do unto other auction traders as you would have them do unto you.

Tip #32: Ship Promptly

Ship promptly after you've received payment (and after the check has cleared). Nobody likes to wait too long for something they've paid for—and you don't want to gain a reputation as a slow shipper.

Tip #33: If Nobody Buys, Relist—With a Different Listing

If you didn't sell your item the first time, try it again. eBay lets you relist unsold items at no additional listing charge; even if you have to pay again, you still want to sell the item, right? But remember that if it didn't sell the first time, there was probably a reason why. Was your asking price too high? Was your description too vague? Was the title too boring? Should you have included a picture or used HTML to spice up the listing? Whatever you change, change something to increase your chances of selling your item the second time around.

Tip #34: If You Get Stiffed, Ask for a Refund

When your high bidder does a vanishing act, file a Non-Paying Bidder Alert and request a refund of the auction's final value fee. There's no sense paying eBay for something you didn't get paid for!

Tip #35: Don't Forget About Number Two

If you run up against a nonpaying bidder, you can try to sell the now-unsold item to the next highest bidder, if he or she is still interested. It never hurts to ask, in any case; just use eBay's Second Chance Offer feature and see if they bite.

Tip #36: The Customer Is Always Right...

Although many sellers take a hardball attitude and refuse any discussion of refunds, I recommend a more customer-friendly approach. When I have a dissatisfied buyer, I offer a full refund. Yeah, some buyers might try to take advantage of you, but most are honest. So if you have a buyer with a complaint, you can generally assume it's a legitimate beef. You'll get better feedback—and sleep easier at night—if you have the customer return the item and refund the purchase price. It's the right thing to do!

> **caution**
>
> If you do offer a refund, don't send the money until you've received and examined the item in dispute. Some smarmy buyers might try to dupe you by sending back a different item than the one you shipped!

Tip #37: ...or All Sales Are Final

If you choose *not* to offer a "satisfaction guaranteed" policy, make sure you state that "all sales are final" in your item listing. (Alternately, you can say that your item is "sold as-is" or that there are "no returns.")

Tip #38: Accept Credit Cards

One of the easiest ways to increase the number of bids in your auction is to accept payment via credit card. Unless you're a real business with a merchant bank account, this means signing up for PayPal or some other online payment service. (PayPal's the easiest to use; you can activate PayPal payments from eBay's Sell Your Item page.)

Tip #39: Wait for the Check to Clear

The reality is that many buyers prefer to pay by check. That's okay, as long as you wait a good 10 business days for the check to clear. Don't be stupid and ship an item before the check proves good—you're bound to get burned!

Tip #40: If It's a Business, You Pay Taxes

This book isn't meant to offer tax advice (and you'd be foolish to consult me for such!), but larger eBay sellers need to be aware of the tax issue. In general, if you're an individual who classifies as a casual eBay seller, you probably don't have to worry about collecting sales taxes or reporting taxable income. However, if you're a business or an individual at the power seller level, the Internal Revenue Service will want their share. The best advice here is that no matter what level your eBay sales, you should consult your accountant or a similar tax expert—and never, never try to fool Uncle Sam.

THE ABSOLUTE MINIMUM

Here are the key points to remember from this chapter:

- Experienced online sellers follow two major strategies: the high road and the low road.

- With the high road strategy, you position your item as rare and unique, and you price it relatively high—but provide superior information and service.

- With the low road strategy, you price your item low enough to generate a flurry of initial bidding activity—and do everything you can to fuel the flames and attract even more potential bidders.

- Whichever strategy you employ, you should do everything possible to provide the right kind of information and post-auction services to make your item attractive to the millions of users out there on eBay—all of them potential buyers!

PART IV

USING EBAY'S ADVANCED FEATURES

22

CREATING A HOME BASE WITH MY EBAY

If you're a buyer or a seller, how do you keep track of all the auctions you're currently participating in?

One approach is to navigate to eBay's Search page, select either the By Seller or By Bidder tab, enter your user ID, and click the Search button. You can select whether you just want to check your active auctions or whether you want to look at closed auctions as well. You can even choose to sort your auctions in a variety of ways (by start time, end time, current bid price, and the like).

To be honest, this process is a real pain. Do you really want to go to the Search page and re-enter your personal search parameters every time you want to check all your auctions? There has to be a better way to do this.

Fortunately, there is. It's called *My eBay*, and eBay calls it its "best-kept secret."

Accessing and Using My eBay

My eBay is not only a way to track your auction activity, but also a way to personalize your eBay experience. It's a page—actually, a set of pages—that you customize to your own personal preferences to track your own bidding and selling activity in your own way. I highly recommend you avail yourself of this useful feature.

You access My eBay by clicking the My eBay link above the Navigation Bar.

There are actually seven pages (or tabs) in your My eBay, accessed from links at the top of the page:

- Bidding/Watching
- Selling
- Favorites
- Accounts
- Feedback
- Preferences
- All

Each of these pages can be personalized; we'll look at each page separately.

Bidding/Watching Page

You use the Bidding/Watching page, shown in Figure 22.1, to keep track of all items you're either bidding on or watching—or have won or lost. The page contains four lists of use to bidders:

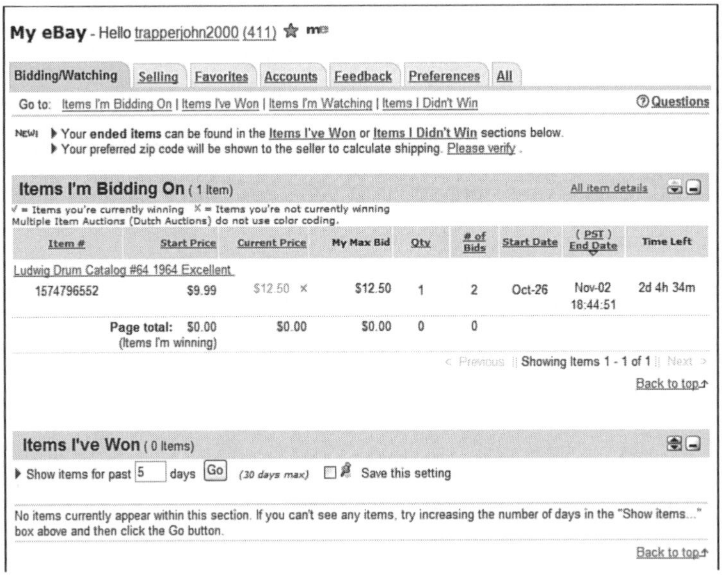

FIGURE 22.1

The My eBay Bidding/Watching page.

Items I Didn't Win (0 Items)

▸ Show items for past [5] days [Go] *(30 days max)* ☐ 🔖 Save this setting

No items currently appear within this section. If you can't see any items, try increasing the number of days in the "Show items..." box above and then click the Go button.

Back to top⤴

Items I'm Watching (3 Items; 30 Items max)

Select (all)	Item #	Item Title	Current Price	# of Bids	Time Left △	Bid on this item
☐	916086253	Fibes Snare Drum SFT Strainer & Butt	$20.00	1	0d 20h 48m	🔍 Bid Now!
☐	729037443	RCA Victor 16-pg 50-60's Stereo Brochure NR!	$5.00	1	6d 1h 43m	🔍 Bid Now!
☐	730157779	MARSHALL ROGERS ORIGINAL ART JLE BATMAN	--	--	9d 2h 49m	🔍 Bid Now!

[Delete] selected items

Back to top⤴

Buying-Related Links

Bidding information
'New to eBay' tutorial
Buyer's Guide
Tips for buyers
Bidding basics
Bidding Frequently Asked Questions
Retracting a bid
What to do after the auction ends

Services
Item authentication
All about escrow
eBay Payments
Apply for an eBay Visa with Cash Rewards

Help Boards
Bidding | Feedback | eBay Payments | Search

Trust & Safety
Safe trading tips
Feedback Forum - how does feedback work
Filing a fraud complaint
Reporting trading violations
Dispute resolution
Buyer Purchase Protection

Finding what you want
Advanced Search

eBay Stores
Shop eBay Stores | Learn more

- Items I'm Bidding On
- Items I've Won
- Items I Didn't Win
- Items I'm Watching

At the bottom of the page is a set of links to buying-related services on the eBay site.

Selling Page

You use the Selling page, shown in Figure 22.2, to keep track of all the items you're currently selling or have recently sold. The page contains three lists of use to sellers:

> **tip**
>
> The Bidding/Watching page is the best way to view all your bidding activity at a glance. All auctions that you're currently winning are in green; all auctions that you're currently losing are in red. (Dutch auctions don't display in color, whatever your bid is.)

FIGURE 22.2

The My eBay
Selling page.

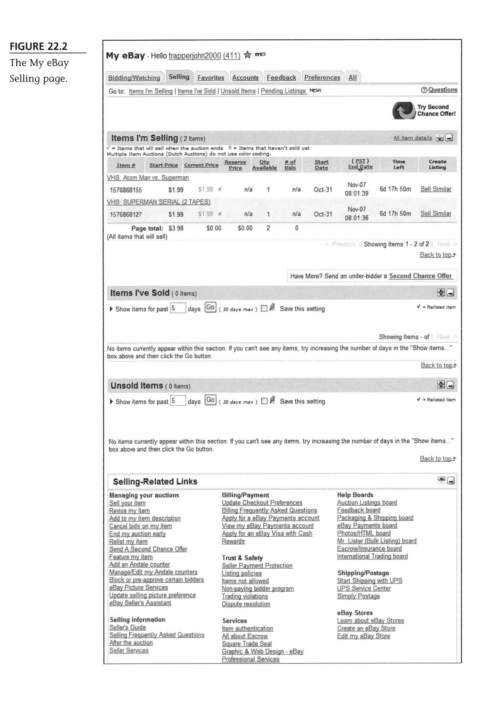

- Items I'm Selling
- Items I've Sold
- Unsold Items

At the bottom of the page is a set of links to selling-related services on the eBay site.

Favorites Page

The Favorites page, shown in Figure 22.3, is where you can access your most-used categories, searches, and sellers. There are three lists on this page:

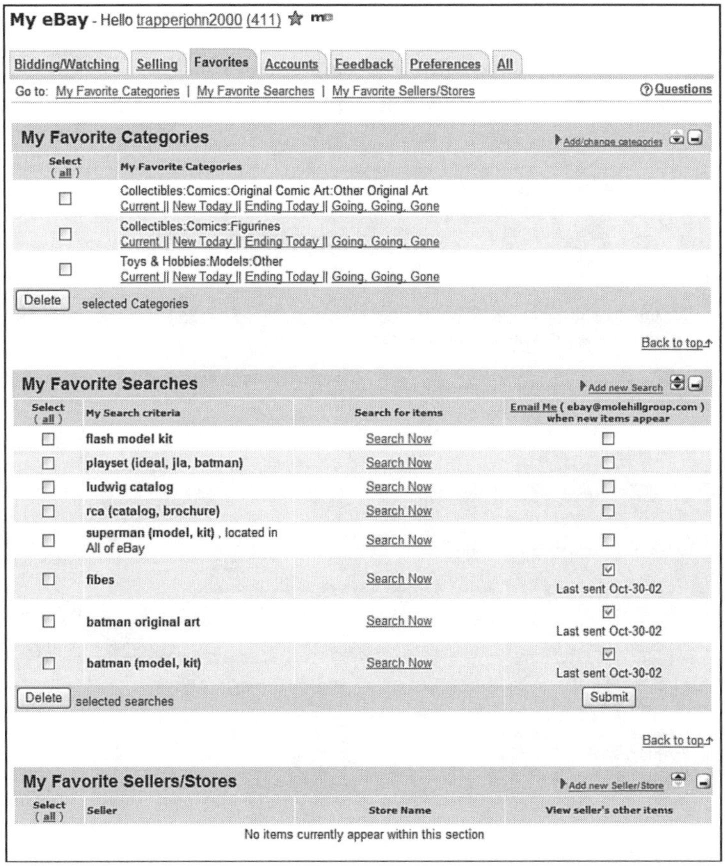

tip

The Selling page is a great way to see, in a single glance, the status of everything you're currently selling on eBay. All items that currently have a high bid higher than your minimum or reserve price are listed in green. All items that haven't yet reached the minimum bid level are listed in red.

FIGURE 22.3

The My eBay
Favorites page.

FIGURE 22.3

The My eBay Favorites page.

My eBay - Hello trapperjohn2000 (411) ⭐ m🔲

| Bidding/Watching | Selling | **Favorites** | Accounts | Feedback | Preferences | All |

Go to: My Favorite Categories | My Favorite Searches | My Favorite Sellers/Stores   ⑦ Questions

My Favorite Categories   ▶ Add/change categories 🔲🔲

Select (all)	My Favorite Categories
☐	Collectibles:Comics:Original Comic Art:Other Original Art Current || New Today || Ending Today || Going, Going, Gone
☐	Collectibles:Comics:Figurines Current || New Today || Ending Today || Going, Going, Gone
☐	Toys & Hobbies:Models:Other Current || New Today || Ending Today || Going, Going, Gone

| Delete | selected Categories

Back to top ↑

My Favorite Searches   ▶ Add new Search 🔲🔲

Select (all)	My Search criteria	Search for items	Email Me (ebay@molehillgroup.com) when new items appear
☐	flash model kit	Search Now	☐
☐	playset (ideal, jla, batman)	Search Now	☐
☐	ludwig catalog	Search Now	☐
☐	rca (catalog, brochure)	Search Now	☐
☐	superman (model, kit) , located in All of eBay	Search Now	☐
☐	fibes	Search Now	☑ Last sent Oct-30-02
☐	batman original art	Search Now	☑ Last sent Oct-30-02
☐	batman (model, kit)	Search Now	☑ Last sent Oct-30-02

| Delete | selected searches | Submit |

Back to top ↑

My Favorite Sellers/Stores   ▶ Add new Seller/Store 🔲🔲

Select (all)	Seller	Store Name	View seller's other items

No items currently appear within this section

- My Favorite Categories
- My Favorite Searches
- My Favorite Sellers/Stores

You can add items to your favorites by clicking the Add links to the right of each list— Add/Change Categories, Add New Search, and Add New Seller/Store. From there, follow the onscreen instructions to add the items you want to appear on the My eBay Favorites page in the future.

Accounts Page

The Accounts page, shown in Figure 22.4, is where you can manage your eBay seller's account. You can view your account status and balance, update your account to accept eBay Payments, pay your monthly bill, and update your account information.

> **tip**
>
> The Accounts page is particularly useful because it contains direct links to some of eBay's normally well-hidden customer service features, including fees and credits, payment terms, credit card setup, credit requests, and refunds. It's easier to click these services here than to hunt them down on eBay's Site Map page.

FIGURE 22.4

The My eBay Accounts page.

My eBay - Hello trapperjohn2000 (411) ☆ m⊡

Bidding/ Watching | Selling | Favorites | **Accounts** | Feedback | Preferences | All

Go to: My eBay Seller Account | eBay Payments account | Account-Related Links   ⑦ Questions

My eBay Seller Account

Account balance: -US $27.51 * As of Oct-31-02 08:01:39 PST

View account status   View account since my last invoice
View my last invoice   View ENTIRE account (*may take a while*)
View/update automatic payment option

* Accounts are not created until the first credit or debit is posted, so no data will appear until your first account activity.

                                                                    Back to top↑

eBay Payments ⓑ Account

eBay Online Payments by eBay Payments (Visa/MC/Disc)

Accept fast, online payments from winning bidders!

(*Apply Now!*) Click "Apply Now!" for more information or to apply for eBay Payments.

                                                                    Back to top↑

Account-Related Links

How to pay eBay: Information about Fees & Payments:
Make a one time payment   Payment terms
                                        Fees & credits
Use a checking account for automatic billing   Credit request
Use a credit card for automatic billing   Refunds

Personal Information:
Update my personal information

Feedback Page

The Feedback page, shown in Figure 22.5, serves as your personal gateway into eBay's feedback system. From this page you can leave feedback on your closed auctions, view your feedback summary, and view your most recent feedback comments.

FIGURE 22.5

The My eBay Feedback page.

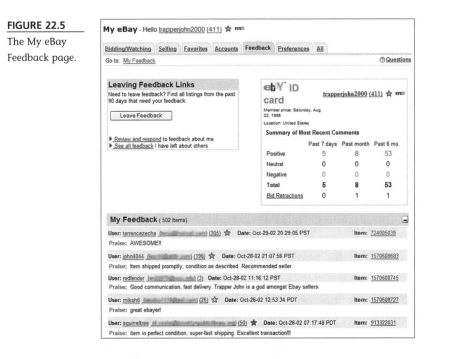

Preferences Page

The Preferences page, shown in Figure 22.6, lets you configure three different types of preferences for your eBay activities:

- Personal Information
- My eBay Preferences
- Sign In Activities

As you'll learn later in this chapter, you can use the My eBay Preferences part of this page to personalize the way you view your My eBay pages.

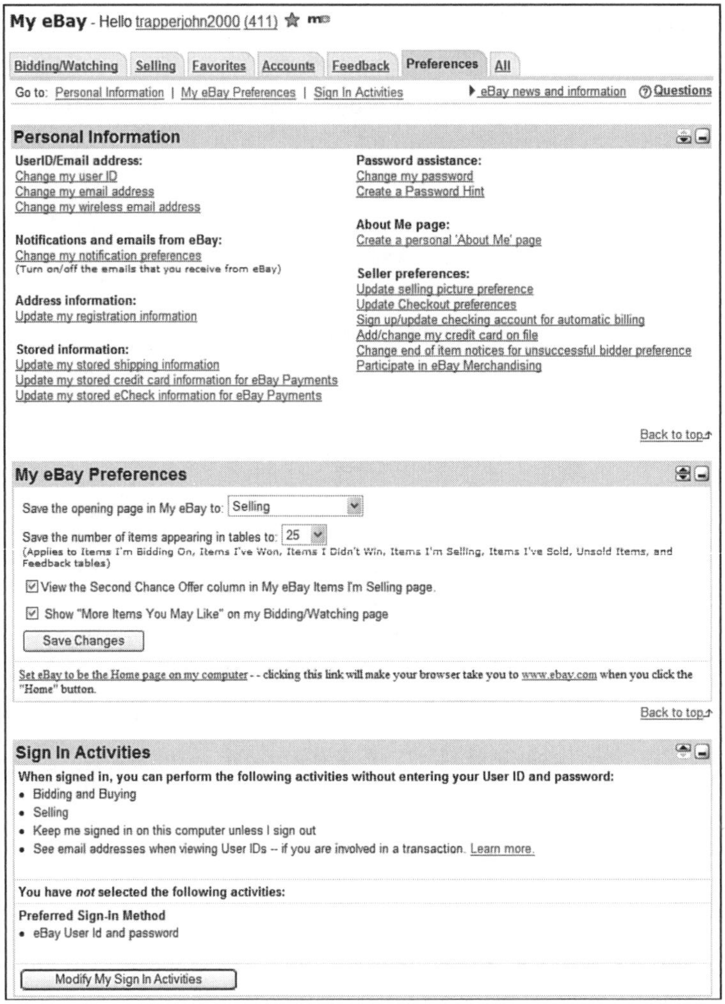

FIGURE 22.6

The My eBay
Preferences
page.

All Page

Want to view *all* your auction information on a single page? Then go to the My eBay All page, which combines the first five My eBay pages into a single, very long, page.

Personalizing My eBay

Each of the seven My eBay pages can be personalized in terms of what sections are displayed and in what order, how your item lists are sorted, and how many items are displayed in each list.

Hide or Display Lists

Any list on a My eBay page can be hidden by clicking the minimize button at the far right of the section heading. When a section is hidden, the minimize button changes to a maximize button; click the maximize button to redisplay the list.

Change What Goes Where

You can also change the order of the lists on any My eBay page. Just use the up and down arrow buttons at the far right of the section heading to move the section up or down on the page.

Change the List Order

Next, you get to pick how you want the item listings in any given section sorted. You can choose to sort your listings by any of the underlined columns in the list. For example, in the Items I'm Watching list (refer to Figure 22.1), you could sort by Item #, Item Title, Current Price, # of Bids, or Time Left.

To sort by a particular column, just click the column header. Click the header again to reverse the order of the sort.

Change How Many Listings to Display

For many lists on the My eBay pages, you can select how many days worth of listings you want to display. The default value is 2 days; you can display up to 30 days' worth of items if you want.

Change Universal Settings

There are a handful of parameters you can change across all your My eBay pages. Just navigate to the Preferences page and scroll down to the My eBay Preferences section. Here you can set the following options:

- The opening page that displays when you click the My eBay link
- The number of items displayed in each My eBay list
- Whether or not the Second Chance Offer column is displayed on the Selling page
- Whether or not "More Items You May Like" are displayed on the Bidding/Watching page

> **"Mike Sez"**
>
> My eBay is such a useful tool I make it my primary gateway to the entire eBay site. (I never use eBay's home page—I use My eBay, instead!) What I like to do is work with the All page (because everything you want is there, somewhere) and hide those sections I don't want to see. Then I go through and resort each of the lists the way I want them sorted, change the days to display to something longer than two, and save these settings as the new page default. *Voila*—a totally personalized My eBay page!

Make your changes here and then click the Save Changes button.

In addition, any changes you make to the sort criteria or number of items listed in any My eBay list can be saved as default settings for all your future My eBay sessions. Just check the Save This Setting box (shown in Figure 22.7) before you click the Go button, and the changes you make will be saved for all future sessions.

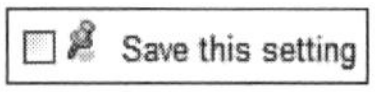

FIGURE 22.7

Saving your sort and display settings as the new default.

☐ 🔏 Save this setting

The Absolute Minimum

Here are the key points to remember from this chapter:

- ■ My eBay lets you track all your eBay activities and information in one place.

- ■ My eBay includes separate pages for tracking items you're bidding on or watching, items you're selling, your favorite searches and categories, your eBay account, your feedback, and your preferences.

- ■ You can customize My eBay for your own personal preferences—including how you like your lists sorted, and how many days' worth of items you want to display.

23

CREATING YOUR OWN PERSONAL ABOUT ME PAGE

The My eBay page is a personalized Web page just for you—nobody else can view it. But haven't you ever thought about a page you could show to other users, to those sellers and potential bidders you might be working with, that tells them all about yourself and items you have for sale?

Such a page is now a reality—and it's called About Me.

Introducing the About Me Page

eBay's About Me page is a personal Web page just for you. It's easy to create (no HTML coding necessary), and lets you tell other eBay users a little bit about yourself. It also lets you show other users your current auctions, most recent feedback, and interesting items you've found online.

Although eBay uses a trio of templates to construct users' About Me pages, there is sufficient personalization available to make your About Me page different from your neighbors. Figure 23.1 shows *my* About Me page, which you can access directly at members.ebay.com/aboutme/trapperjohn2000/.

FIGURE 23.1

About *Me*, your author!

This page is maintained by trapperjohn2000 (411) ☆

Michael Miller: Best-Selling Author and eBay Professional

About Michael Miller

Michael Miller is an author, consultant, musician, and the President of The Molehill Group, an Indianapolis-based writing and consulting firm. He has been an eBay member since Saturday, Aug 22, 1998.

Among the four dozen books he has authored over the past fifteen years are the award-winning **The Complete Idiot's Guide to Online Auctions**, as well as numerous books about computer, business, and music topics. His new book, **Absolute Beginner's Guide to eBay**, is due out in early 2003.

As a frequent eBay seller, Miller prides himself on his useful communication, fast shipping, and first-rate packaging. His buyers frequently comment on the quality of his auction transactions.

Collections

At present, Michael Miller collects superhero-related model kits, as well as Batman-related original comic book and animation art. He is also an avid DVD and CD collector. His auctions frequently feature DVDs, laserdiscs, CDs, videotapes, books, and DC superhero comic books and collections. Watch this page for the latest bargains!

Favorite Links
Michael Miller: The Molehill Group
The Complete Idiot's Guide to Online Auctions
Complete Bibliography

Listings

Current Items for Sale

Item	Start	End	Price	Title	High Bidder
1576868127	Oct-31-02	Nov-07-02 08:01:36	$1.99	VHS: SUPERMAN SERIAL (2 TAPES)	No Bids Yet
1576868155	Oct-31-02	Nov-07-02 08:01:39	$1.99	VHS: Atom Man vs. Superman	No Bids Yet

Feedback

User: terrencezecha (305) ☆ **Date:** Oct-29-02 20:29:05 PST
Praise: AWESOME!!

User: john4044 (196) ☆ **Date:** Oct-28-02 21:07:56 PST
Praise: Item shipped promptly, condition as described. Recommended seller.

User: redfender (3) **Date:** Oct-28-02 11:16:12 PST
Praise: Good communication, fast delivery. Trapper John is a god amongst Ebay sellers.

User: mikoh6 (26) ☆ **Date:** Oct-26-02 12:53:34 PDT
Praise: great ebayer!

User: squirreltree (50) ★ **Date:** Oct-26-02 07:17:48 PDT
Praise: item in perfect condition, super-fast shipping. Excellent transaction!!!

User: dude888 (19) ☆ **Date:** Oct-24-02 12:15:02 PDT
Praise: Quick shipping... Got the item today! Thanks!!

You can view any user's About Me page by clicking the Me icon next to their user name on any item listing page. (If there's no icon displayed, that user doesn't have an About Me page.) You can search for other users' About Me pages by clicking the Search link on the Navigation Bar and then clicking Find Members to display the Find Members page; scroll down to the bottom of the page to search for About Me pages by user ID.

Creating Your Own About Me Page

As I said, you don't have to be a Web programmer to create your own About Me page. All you have to do is click a few options and fill in some blanks, and you're ready to go.

Follow these steps:

1. From the Navigation Bar, click Services and then click About Me.

2. When the About Me Login page appears, click the Create and Edit Your Page button.

3. When the About Me Styles page appears (shown in Figure 23.2), select either a two-column, newspaper (three-column), or centered (single-column) layout.

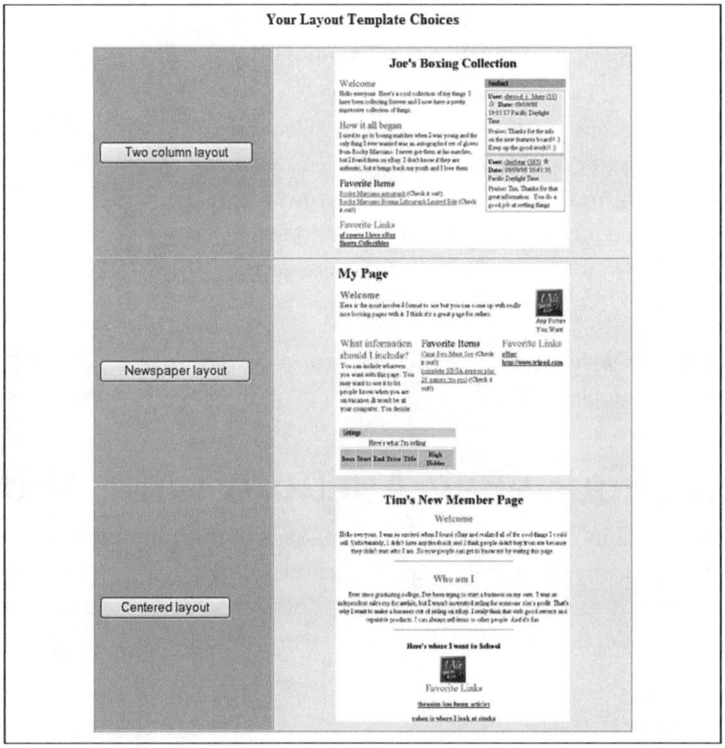

FIGURE 23.2

Choose a layout for your About Me page.

4. When the Select Template Elements page appears, it's time to fill in the blanks. In particular, you need to enter a title for your page; a short welcome message (with optional heading); one or more other paragraphs (also with optional head); and a link to a picture (also optional). You can also opt to display your most recent feedback comments; the items you currently have for sale; links for up to three of your favorite Web pages; and up to three items currently listed on eBay. (For the feedback and items for sale options, you can also select how many items to display on the page.) Click the Preview Your Page button when you're done.

5. You now see a preview of your About Me page. If you like what you see, click the Save My Page button. If you want to change a few items, click the Edit Some More button to return to the previous page. If you'd rather fine-tune the page with your own HTML, click the Edit Using HTML button.

6. If you clicked the Save My Page button, you now see the Confirm Your Selection page, otherwise known as the Ready to Save Your Page? page. If you want to edit some more, click the Keep Editing for Now button. If you're sure you're done, click the Save My Page button.

You'll now be taken directly to your brand new About Me page.

> **" Mike Sez "**
>
> If you have a separate personal Web page outside of eBay, list it in the favorite links section. That's a better use of space than the favorite eBay items section, which is almost immediately out of date when the auctions end and is better ignored. Also, you can include multiple descriptive paragraphs by entering a **<p>** paragraph break tag in either the Welcome Message or Another Paragraph text.

> **tip**
>
> You can edit your About Me page at any time by repeating steps one and two, which will take you to your preview page. Click the Edit Some More button to make changes to your page.

Publicizing Your eBay Auctions with About Me

The great thing about the About Me page is that it's a page with a non-changing URL that always lists your current auctions. When you want to direct other users to your eBay auctions, it's easier to direct them to your About Me page than it is to enter the individual URLs for all your item listing pages.

The address for your About Me page is shown in the address box of your Web browser. The address is typically in the form of `members.ebay.com/aboutme/userid/`; just replace `userid` with your own user ID and you should have the URL. (As mentioned previously, my eBay ID is trapperjohn2000, so my About Me address is `members.ebay.com/aboutme/trapperjohn2000/`.)

You can then insert this URL into your personal Web page, your e-mail signature, or any other item you can think of. It's a great way to publicize your ongoing eBay activity!

"Mike Sez"

The About Me page is also a good way for other eBay users to get to know you—especially those who are bidding in your auctions, or hosting auctions in which you're bidding. Make sure you include text that positions you as a reputable eBay citizen—and not some goofball flake who's likely to cause trouble.

THE ABSOLUTE MINIMUM

Here are the key points to remember from this chapter:

- The About Me page is your personal page on the eBay site.
- You can typically create your own About Me page in less than five minutes—with no HTML coding necessary.
- Your About Me page can include descriptive text, a photo, links to your favorite sites, a list of your current auctions, and a list of your most recent feedback comments.
- You can use your About Me page to publicize your eBay activities outside of the eBay site.

24

UNDERSTANDING AND USING FEEDBACK

eBay regards its feedback function as the best protection against fraudulent transactions. I certainly recommend that, whether a transaction went swell or went south, you leave feedback about your partner in every transaction. I know that I check the feedback rating of every seller I choose to deal with; it really is a good way to judge the quality of the other party in your eBay transactions.

What Do All Those Stars and Numbers Mean?

Next to every buyer and seller's name on eBay is a number and (more often than not) a colored star. (Figure 24.1 shows my personal star and feedback number.) These numbers and stars represent that user's feedback rating. The larger the number, the better the feedback (and the more transactions that user has participated in).

FIGURE 24.1

Check the feedback rating next to a member's name.

Seller (Rating)	**trapperjohn2000 (411)** ☆ me

How are feedback ratings calculated?

First, every new user starts with 0 points. (A clean slate!) For every positive feedback received, eBay adds 1 point to your feedback rating. For every negative feedback received, eBay subtracts 1 point. Neutral comments add 0 points to your rating.

Let's say you're a new user, starting with a 0 rating. On the first two items you buy, the sellers like the fact that you paid quickly and give you positive feedback. On the third transaction, however, you forgot to mail the check for a few weeks, and the seller left you negative feedback. After these three transactions, your feedback rating would be 1. (That's 0 + 1 + 1 – 1 = 1.)

note

Sunglasses (instead of a star) next to a user name indicates that this is a new user— or an old user who has recently changed his or her ID.

If you build up a lot of positive feedback, you qualify for a star next to your name. Different colored stars represent different levels of positive feedback, as noted in Table 24.1.

TABLE 24.1 eBay Feedback Ratings

Color/Type	Points
Yellow star	10–49
Blue star	50–99
Turquoise star	100–499
Purple star	500–999
Red star	1,000–4,999
Green star	5,000–9,999

Color/Type	Points
Yellow shooting star	10,000–24,999
Turquoise shooting star	25,000–49,999
Purple shooting star	50,000–99,999
Red shooting star	100,000 or more

Obviously, heavy users can build up positive feedback faster than occasional users. If you're dealing with a shooting-star user (of any color), you know you're dealing with a trustworthy eBay pro.

Reading Feedback Comments

You can also read the individual comments left by other users by going to the user's Feedback Profile page. To access this page, just click the number next to a user's name. (Figure 24.2 shows a typical Feedback Profile.)

FIGURE 24.2

A typical feedback profile; hey, people like this guy!

Overall profile makeup
502 positives. 411 are from unique users and count toward the final rating.

0 neutrals.

0 negatives. 0 are from unique users and count toward the final rating.

ebY ID card   trapperjohn2000 (411) ☆ me

Member since: Saturday, Aug 22, 1998
Location: United States

Summary of Most Recent Comments

	Past 7 days	Past month	Past 6 mo.
Positive	5	8	53
Neutral	0	0	0
Negative	0	0	0
Total	5	8	53
Bid Retractions	0	1	1

View trapperjohn2000 's Auctions | ID History | Feedback About Others

trapperjohn2000 's feedback   Feedback Help | FAQ

Feedback 1 - 25 of 502

[1] 2 3 4 5 6 7 8 9 10 11 12 13 14 15 16 17 18 19 20 21 (next page)

leave feedback for trapperjohn2000   If you are trapperjohn2000 : Respond to comments   trapperjohn2000 was the **Seller** = S   trapperjohn2000 was the **Buyer** = B

Left by	Date	Item#	S/B
terrencezecha (305) ☆	Oct-29-02 20:29:05 PST	724005039	S
Praise : AWESOME!!			
john4044 (196) ☆	Oct-28-02 21:07:56 PST	1570608683	S
Praise : Item shipped promptly, condition as described. Recommended seller.			
redfender (3)	Oct-28-02 11:16:12 PST	1570608745	S
Praise : Good communication, fast delivery. Trapper John is a god amongst Ebay sellers.			
mikoh6 (26) ☆	Oct-26-02 12:53:34 PDT	1570608727	S
Praise : great ebayer!			
squirreltree (50) ★	Oct-26-02 07:17:48 PDT	913322031	S
Praise : item in perfect condition, super-fast shipping. Excellent transaction!!!			
dude888 (19) ☆	Oct-24-02 12:15:02 PDT	1389662183	S
Praise : Quick shipping... Got the item today! Thanks!!			
jjs077@netzero.net (209) ☆	Oct-24-02 05:35:32 PDT	1570608712	S
Praise : FAST delivery GREAT merchandise Highly reccommend			
dipick (619) ☆	Oct-21-02 17:48:43 PST	913387834	B
Praise : Fast payer. Excellent communications. Excellent transaction. Thanks!			

The Feedback Profile page includes the ID Card box (at the top) that summarizes feedback left in the past seven days, month, and six months. The individual feedback comments are shown below, and you can jump back to the auctions in question if you want.

View Feedback About You

There are at least three ways to view all feedback left about you.

- Go to your My eBay page and select the Feedback tab (page).
- Click the feedback rating next to your name in any auction.
- Go to the Feedback Forum (discussed next) and click the Review and Respond to Feedback Comments Left to You link.

Using the Feedback Forum

eBay's Feedback Forum is the central clearinghouse for all things feedback-related. You access the Feedback Forum by clicking the Services link in the Navigation Bar and then clicking the Feedback Forum link—or by going directly to pages.ebay.com/services/forum/feedback.html.

From the Feedback Forum you can

- Learn more about feedback
- Review and respond to feedback comments about you
- View feedback about other eBay users
- Leave feedback about other users—and see all the auctions where you *need* to leave feedback
- Review and follow up on feedback you've left for other users
- View feedback a member left about other users
- Access eBay's Star Recognition program, where you can earn prizes based on your feedback rating

How to Leave Feedback

You can leave feedback from the Feedback Forum or from any item listing page. (Click either the Leave Feedback to Seller or Leave Feedback to Bidder link.)

You can then choose to leave Positive, Negative, or Neutral feedback, along with a brief comment (80 characters maximum).

Make sure your feedback is accurate before you click the Leave Comment button; you can't change your comments after they've been registered.

Figuring Out What Kind of Feedback to Leave

You should leave feedback at the end of every auction—whether it was a positive or a negative experience for you. Don't miss your chance to inform other eBay users about the quality of the person you just got done dealing with.

Table 24.2 offers some guidelines on when you should leave positive or negative feedback—and the types of comments you might use to embellish your feedback.

TABLE 24.2   Recommended eBay Feedback

Transaction	Feedback	Comments
Transaction transpires in a timely fashion.	Positive	"Great transaction. Fast payment/shipment. Recommended."
Transaction goes through, but buyer/seller is slow or you have to pester the other user.	Positive	"Item received as described" or "Payment received," accompanied by "a little slow, but otherwise a good seller/buyer."
Transaction is very slow (over a month to completion).	Neutral	"Very slow payment/shipment;" if you're buying, followed by "item received as described."
Other user backs out of transaction, with a good excuse.	Neutral	"Buyer/seller didn't follow through on sale but had a reasonable excuse."
Other user backs out of transaction without a good excuse, disappears off the face of the earth before paying/shipping, or bounces a check.	Negative	"Buyer/seller didn't complete transaction; avoid!"
Transaction goes through, but item isn't what you expected or was damaged in transit; seller refunds your money.	Positive	"Inaccurate description of item; seller refunded money."
Transaction goes through, but item isn't what you expected; seller won't refund your money.	Negative	"Item not as described, and seller ignored my complaint; avoid!"

As you can see, there's a proper feedback and response for every situation. Just make sure you think twice before leaving *any* feedback (particularly negative feedback). After you submit your feedback, you can't retract it.

Dealing with Negative Feedback

Many eBay users are zealous about their feedback ratings. Although it's a good thing to want to build up a high rating, some users get quite obsessive about it.

For that reason, you want to be very sure of yourself before you leave negative feedback about a user. Some overly zealous users might retaliate by leaving negative feedback about you—even if it wasn't warranted.

Unfortunately, there's not much you can do if you receive negative feedback; feedback comments cannot be retracted. (That's one of eBay's faults, if you ask me.) What you can do is offer a response to the feedback, which you do by going to the Feedback Forum and clicking the Review and Respond to Feedback Comments Left to You link. When the feedback comments list appears, click the Respond link next to a particular comment and then enter your response. Your new comment is listed below the original feedback comment on the Feedback Profile page.

THE ABSOLUTE MINIMUM

Here are the key points to remember from this chapter:

- You can use feedback ratings and comments to judge the trustworthiness of other eBay users.

- For quick reference, different levels of feedback ratings are indicated by a different color and type of star.

- You can view other users' feedback by clicking on the feedback rating number next to their user names.

- At the end of every auction you should take the time to leave feedback about the other user—although you should be cautious about leaving negative feedback.

25

PARTICIPATING IN THE eBAY COMMUNITY

If you're a heavy eBay user, you probably already know that eBay is more than a marketplace—it's a community. And with close to 50 million users, it's a *big* community.

The eBay community can be a godsend for both new and experienced buyers and sellers. Having trouble with a deadbeat bidder? Ask other members for advice. Not sure how to ship an odd-sized package? No need to reinvent the wheel; chances are some other member has shipped something similar, and can tell you what to do. Got a gripe with eBay itself? You're not alone—as you'll soon find out if you voice your complaint on one of the many online forums devoted to online auctions in general and eBay in particular.

Using eBay's Community Forums

When you want to talk with other eBay users, the first place to look is on the eBay site itself. eBay hosts a variety of message boards where you can ask questions, offer comments, or just hang out and socialize with other eBay members. Some of these message boards are even frequented by eBay personnel, so you can use them as a kind of real-life help system when you encounter difficulties.

eBay's discussion boards are found on the Discussion, Help, & Chat page located at `pages.ebay.com/community/chat/`. You can also access this page by clicking the Community link on the Navigation Bar, and then clicking Chat.

eBay offers a variety of message boards, which are like giant electronic bulletin boards where you can read and respond to short messages about specific topics. There are several types of message boards on eBay, including:

- Community help chat and discussion boards, where you can ask questions (and offer advice) about specific auction features and processes. There are boards here for auction listings, bidding, Checkout, and other eBay-specific topics. These boards are frequented by eBay support staff, so you're likely to get your questions answered here.

- Category-specific chat and discussion boards, where you can interact with others who share your hobbies and activities. There are boards here for animals, antiques, comics, photography, and more.

- General chat and discussion boards, which host topics that don't fit into narrow definitions (and encourage a certain amount of broad socializing). These boards and chat rooms have names like the Front Porch, the Homestead, the eBay Café (shown in Figure 25.1), the eBay Town Square, and so on.

- eBay Workshops, which are special event boards hosted by eBay staff.

caution

eBay calls some of its message boards "discussion boards" and others "chat rooms." That last phrase is just plain wrong; a real Internet chat room is a virtual gathering place where you participate in real-time text messaging with other users who are currently online. eBay offers nothing of the sort; all of its "chat rooms" are plain old message boards.

" Mike Sez "

If you want to find out about the status of the eBay Web site (when maintenance is scheduled, when a technical outage might be repaired, and so on), go to a board that isn't listed on this page—the System Status Announcement board, located at `www2.ebay.com/aw/announce.shtml`. In addition, you can view more formal eBay announcements at the eBay News and Information page. Click Community and then News, or go directly to `pages.ebay.com/community/news/`.

FIGURE 25.1

The eBay Café message board.

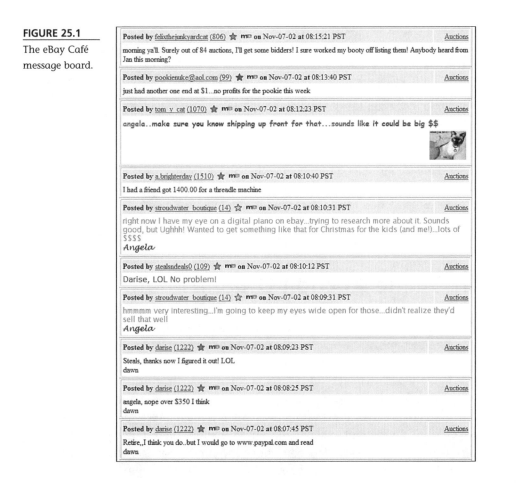

If you're a new user, the New to eBay Board is a good place to start. If you have specific questions, use the appropriate community help board.

Communicating via Third-Party Forums

You don't have to log on to eBay to talk about eBay. Some of the most popular message boards exist outside the eBay service, hosted by third-party Web sites and organizations. These third-party message boards are particularly useful on those (increasingly rare) occasions when the eBay site itself is plagued by technical problems and otherwise inaccessible; when you can't get to eBay, you can get to these message boards to gripe about it!

The most popular of these third-party message boards include:

■ Andale's Online Traders Web Alliance (OTWA) Community
(community.otwa.com)

- AuctionBytes Forums
  (www.auctionbytes.com/forum/phpBB/)
- AuctionWatch Community (www.auctionwatch.com/mesg/)
- Online Auction Users Association (OAUA)
  Discussion Board
  (www.auctionusers.org/forums/)

Most of these forums offer a number of different boards, organized around specific topics. For example, AuctionBytes offers an Online Fraud Forum, an Online Marketing Forum, and individual forums for book, porcelain, record, and toy collectors.

" Mike Sez "

Another good source of online auction community and information is the TAGnotes e-mail mailing list, hosted by the Auction Guild at Yahoo! Groups. Go to groups.yahoo.com/group/TheAuctionGuildnotes/ to subscribe.

Joining an Online Auction Organization

Many of the sites that offer eBay-oriented message boards also offer other products and services, and serve as auxiliary communities to the main eBay communities. In particular, AuctionBytes (www.auctionbytes.com) and AuctionWatch (www.auctionwatch.com) are good sites to check out; they both provide news and articles of interest to eBay buyers and sellers, in addition to their message boards.

Even more worthwhile is the Online Auction Users Association (OAUA), located at www.auctionusers.org. The OAUA is an association formed to provide a collective voice for small buyers and sellers in the online auction community by identifying shared issues, providing training, education, and support services, and lobbying to promote laws and regulations that benefit the online auction users.

I can't tell you to join the OAUA, but I can tell you it's a fine organization with your needs in mind. The OAUA gives individual auction users a voice in the industry, lobbies for your benefit, and provides a wealth of information, education, and discussion. Best of all, membership is free—so there's no excuse *not* to join!

THE ABSOLUTE MINIMUM

Here are the key points to remember from this chapter:

- To communicate with and ask advice of other eBay users, check out the message boards and chat rooms on the eBay site.

- To find out the status of system upgrades and outages, check out the System Status Announcement board (www2.ebay.com/aw/announce.shtml).

- You can find other eBay-oriented message boards at various third-party sites, such as AuctionBytes and AuctionWatch.

- Another good source of online auction community can be found at the Online Auction Users Association—which also provides information, education, and discussion.

26

BUYING AND SELLING RIGHT NOW: EBAY STORES AND HALF.COM

eBay offers more than just online auctions. (As if that weren't enough….) eBay offers two additional marketplaces where buyers and sellers can interact outside the auction environment. The first of these marketplaces is a kind of online mall for those retailers selling through the eBay service, called eBay Stores; the second is a fixed-price shopping environment called Half.com.

Buying and Selling at eBay Stores

eBay Stores (www.stores.ebay.com) is the place to find those retailers, large and small, who market their goods via eBay auctions. If you're a heavy seller thinking of making the move into real honest-to-goodness retailing, eBay Stores is a relatively painless way to start.

Shopping at eBay Stores

As you can see in Figure 26.1, eBay Stores merchants are organized by the same categories as the eBay auction site—Antiques, Art, Books, and so on. You can also search for a specific store or a store selling a certain type of item, or view an alphabetical list of all stores.

note

You can also access eBay stores from the regular eBay site. Just click the Browse link in the Navigation Bar, and then select Stores.

FIGURE 26.1

The home page for eBay Stores.

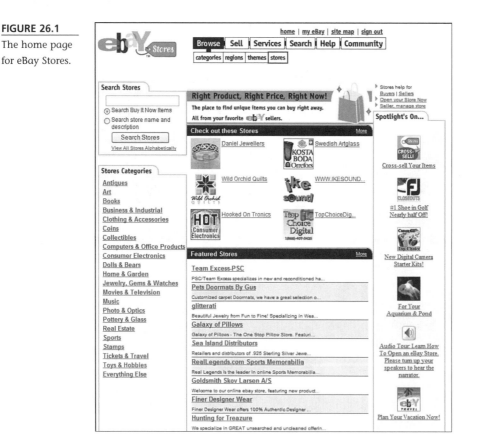

The items offered by eBay Stores merchants are a combination of items currently for auction on eBay and additional fixed-price inventory. When you access a particular eBay Store retailer, you have access to this entire collection of merchandise; if you tried searching on eBay proper, you wouldn't find the non-auction items the retailer might have for sale.

Buying an item from an eBay Store retailer is a little like buying from any other online merchant, and a little like winning an item in an eBay auction. On the one hand, you're buying from an actual merchant at a fixed price, and you can always pay by credit card. On the other hand, you have all the niceties you have on eBay, including the ability to check the merchant's feedback rating.

If you want to buy a specific type of item, you can either browse for it (clicking through the categories on the eBay Stores main page) or search for it (using the Search Stores feature at the top of the main page). After you locate an item, you're taken to the "virtual storefront" of the eBay Store that is selling the item. When you're in a specific store, you can purchase the item you were looking at or shop for additional items. Your checkout is handled from within the store.

Setting Up Your Own eBay Store

Just about any retailer can open its own eBay Store. To open an eBay store, you must meet the following criteria:

- Be a registered eBay seller, with credit card on file
- Have a feedback rating of 20 or more, or be ID verified
- Accept credit cards for all fixed-price sales

Given that accepting credit cards can mean using PayPal, you can see that you don't actually have to be a big traditional retailer to open an eBay Store. Any individual meeting the requirements can also open an eBay Store, thus making eBay Stores a great way for entrepreneurial types to get started in retailing.

Why would you want to open your own eBay Store? Well, it certainly isn't for casual sellers; you do have to set up your own Web page, and keep the store filled with merchandise. But if you're a high-volume seller who specializes in a single category (or even a handful of categories), there are benefits to opening your own store. These include being able to sell more merchandise (through your store) than you can otherwise list in auctions; being able to display a special eBay Stores icon next to all of your auction lists; and being able to generate repeat business from future sales to current purchasers.

To open an eBay store, all you have to do is click the Open Your Store Now link in the upper-right corner of the eBay Stores main page and follow the instructions there. You'll need to create your store, customize your pages (otherwise known as your virtual storefront), and list the items you want to sell.

Naturally, it costs money to open an eBay Store. (eBay isn't in this for the betterment of mankind, after all.) You pay a monthly fee to be an eBay Store merchant, and there are three subscription levels to choose from, as shown in Table 26.1.

> **" Mike Sez "**
>
> eBay Stores are great for small merchants who don't otherwise have a Web presence. They're overkill for the casual seller, however—and probably not worth the effort for larger retailers.

TABLE 26.1   eBay Stores Subscription Levels

Subscription	Price	Description
Basic	$9.95/month	Store listed in every category directory where you have items listed; position based on number of items listed
Featured	$49.95/month	All features of Basic, plus store rotated through a special featured section on the eBay Stores home page; store receives priority placement in Related Stores section of search and listings pages; store featured within the top-level category pages where you have items listed; you can cross-sell products on view item pages; and you receive monthly sales and performance reports
Anchor	$499.95/month	All features of Featured, plus premium placement in Related Stores section of search and listings pages; and your store logo will rotate through category directory pages (1 million impressions)

You also have to pay eBay for each item you list and each item you sell—just as in a normal auction. The difference is you're not listing for a (relatively short) auction; you're listing for longer-term inventory.

Table 26.2 details the insertion fees that eBay charges for eBay Stores listings. Note that eBay allows listings of up to 120 days in length—although the longer listings carry an insertion fee surcharge.

TABLE 26.2   eBay Stores Insertion Fees

Listing Length	Insertion Fee (Plus Surcharge)
30 days	$0.05
60 days	$0.05 + $0.05
90 days	$0.05 + $0.10
120 days	$0.05 + $0.15

For every item you sell in your eBay Store, eBay charges a final value fee. Table 26.3 lists the final value fee charges.

TABLE 26.3   eBay Stores Final Value Fees

Closing Value	Fee
$0.01–$24.99	5.25%
$25.00–$999.99	5.25% on first $25 *plus* $2.75% on remaining balance
$1,000 and up	5.25% on first $25 *plus* $2.75% on the part between $25 and $1,000 *plus* 1.5% on remaining balance

eBay Stores also offers a full assortment of listing upgrades, just like the ones you can use in regular eBay auctions. These enhancements—gallery, bold, highlight, and so on—are priced according to the length of your listing. You can also offer multiples of the same item in Dutch auction format.

Buying and Selling at Half.com

Half.com (half.ebay.com) is like eBay without the auctions. That is, individuals and small retailers offer merchandise for sale to other individuals, but without the hassle of bidding on an online auction. All the merchandise offered at Half.com is offered at a fixed price, for immediate purchase. (Although it isn't all half-price—so don't get taken in by the name!)

Shopping at Half.com

As you can see in Figure 26.2, shopping at Half.com is a lot like shopping at any mall-type site that offers merchandise from a variety of merchants. You can shop by category (and the categories are different from the normal eBay categories, by the way) or search across categories for specific types of items. The best way to browse is to use the category tabs at the top of the page (which look suspiciously like the tabs on the rival Amazon.com site) or the category links at the side of the page. To search, just enter your query into the Search box at the top of the page, select a category in which to search, and then click the Go button.

FIGURE 26.2

Shopping for fixed-price merchandise at Half.com.

When you find an item you want to buy, click the Buy link to place the item in your shopping cart. When you're done shopping, click the Cart link at the top of any Half.com page to access your shopping cart; click Proceed to Checkout to complete your purchase.

Even though Half.com uses a single shopping cart for all your purchases, you're actually buying merchandise from other Half.com members, not from Half.com (or eBay) itself. Half.com consolidates the ordering process (and offers credit card payments), but the items are still sold and shipped by other members.

Selling Your Merchandise at Half.com

As a seller, listing items on Half.com is very similar to listing on the main eBay auction site. The big difference is that you don't pay a listing fee on Half.com—although you're still charged a final value fee. The other difference is that your listing isn't for a set period of time; your item stays listed until it's sold.

The listing process is also a little different, in that you don't have to bother with creating an actual listing. In most instances, details about your item are already in the Half.com database, so you only have to supply the title or UPC code, and Half.com fills in the rest of the details. (That's to ensure that buyers will see uniform, catalog-like listings when they're shopping.)

Selling an item is also a little different, in that Half.com handles most of the post-sale process. The buyer pays Half.com and then Half.com notifies you that the item has been sold. You ship the item and Half.com makes a direct deposit into your bank account (my recommendation) or sends you a paper check. Other than shipping the item, there is no direct interaction between you and the buyer. Half.com makes its money from the 15% commission it charges on all sales.

To list an item with Half.com, go to any Half.com page and click the Sell Your Stuff link. Start entering your items, and your items will soon be listed for sale.

" Mike Sez "

With all the millions of items for auction on eBay, why bother shopping at Half.com? Well, sometimes you can't find what you want on eBay—and you *can* find it on Half.com. (Plus, you might just prefer making fixed-price purchases.) I like to think of Half.com as my second-chance option—if I can't find an item on the eBay site proper, I search through Half.com.

Half.com is especially suited for selling books, CDs, DVDs, video-tapes, and video games. Use Half.com when you're not in a hurry to sell an item and don't want to mess with the normal auction listing and management process.

note

Payments from Half.com are made twice monthly.

THE ABSOLUTE MINIMUM

Here are the key points to remember from this chapter:

- When you can't find the item you want to buy for auction on eBay, check out the eBay Stores and Half.com sites.

- Purchases made at an eBay Store are made directly from the store.

- Purchases made at Half.com are paid for through Half.com, but shipped by individual sellers.

- Opening an eBay Store is a good way for individuals and small retailers to sell a variety of fixed-price merchandise through the eBay system.

- Half.com is a good way to sell fixed-price goods without hassling with the auction process.

27

BUYING AND SELLING WHEELS AND WALLS: EBAY MOTORS AND REAL ESTATE

Most people think of eBay as a marketplace for small, easily shippable items—collectibles, clothing, compact discs, and the like. It might come as a surprise that eBay is increasingly becoming a viable marketplace for much larger, more expensive items, such as cars and homes. Read on to learn more about these big-ticket components of the eBay site—eBay Motors and eBay Real Estate.

Buying and Selling Vehicles on eBay Motors

eBay Motors is a one-stop shop for anyone buying or selling used or collectible vehicles. And not just automobiles; eBay Motors offers categories for Cars, Luxury Cars, Minivans & Vans, SUVs, Trucks, Collector Cars, Motorcycles, and other vehicles—including ATVs, Aircraft, Boats & Watercraft, Buses and Motorcoaches, Commercial Trucks, RVs and Campers, Scooters & Minibikes, and Snowmobiles. eBay Motors also helps users buy and sell all manner of automotive, aircraft, and boating accessories.

You can access eBay Motors from the eBay home page, or by going directly to pages.ebay.com/ebaymotors/.

Shopping for Cars and Other Vehicles

The eBay Motors home page is shown in Figure 27.1. From here you can shop for vehicles in three different ways:

FIGURE 27.1
Shopping for cars and boats and planes at eBay Motors.

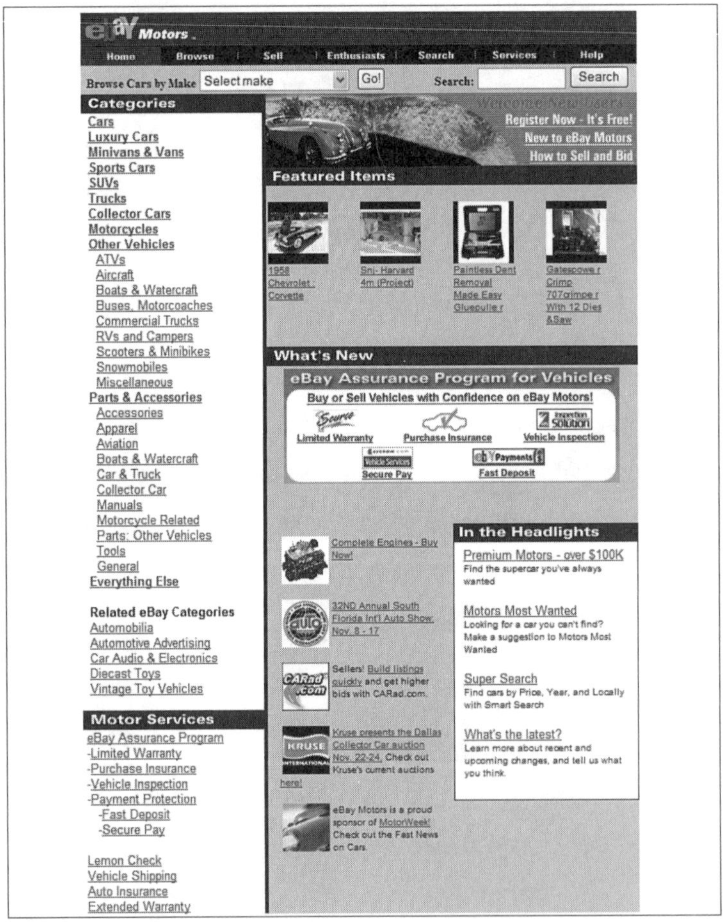

- Browse by category, using the Categories links on the left side of the page
- Shop by make of vehicle, using the Browse Cars by Make pull-down list at the top of the page
- Search by make, model, or other criteria, using the Search box at the top of the page

tip

You can use the VIN to look up the car's maintenance record on Carfax (www.carfax.com).

Figure 27.2 shows a typical vehicle listing. As you can see, an eBay Motors listing is a little different from a regular eBay auction listing. First, almost all vehicle listings include photographs, which you might expect. Second, underneath the photo is a standardized features listing, which describes the car's mileage, engine, number of doors, type of transmission, used/new status, status of the vehicle's title, exterior/interior colors, and the car's vehicle inspection number (VIN).

FIGURE 27.2

A typical eBay Motors vehicle listing.

1998 Toyota : Supra	Item # 1871587494
1998 Toyota Supra Twin Turbo Kandy Tangerine	Item located in: Passenger Vehicles : Toyota : Supra

Currently **US $31,100.00** (reserve not yet met)

bid

The seller lowered the reserve price. Learn More.

Time left **2 days, 8 hours +**

Started Oct-30-02 16:35:53 PST
ends Nov-09-02 16:35:53 PST

Seller (rating) a2298a (26) ☆
(View seller's feedback)
(View seller's other items)
(Ask seller a question)

High bid dxwolfscsa (23) ☆

# of bids **15** (bid history)
Location **Highland Park, NJ**
Country/Region **United States/New York**

Payment See item description for payment methods accepted

Shipping Buyer pays actual shipping charges. Will ship to United States and the following regions: Canada.

Revise item
Item Revised To review revisions made to this item by the
Before First Bid seller, click here .

✉(mail this auction to a friend)
Watch this item

· 41575 Miles · 6 - Cyl.
· 2 doors · Manual transmission
· Used · Clear title
· Other Color Exterior - Beige/Tan Interior · Existing Warranty
· VIN:

Options
· Air Conditioning · Power Locks · Cassette
· Leather Seats · Power Windows · Driver Airbag
· Anti Lock Brakes · Passenger Airbag · Power Seats
· Cruise Control · CD Player

Underneath all this is another standardized section for the vehicle's included options, such as air conditioning, leather seats, and so on. Underneath that section are three standardized text paragraphs, for Vehicle Description, Vehicle Condition, and Terms of Sale. The rest of the listing (including additional pictures) is similar to regular eBay listings.

Making a bid on a vehicle is similar to making a bid in a regular eBay auction. Just scroll to the bottom of the page, enter your Bid amount, and then click the Preview Bid button.

If you win an eBay Motors auction, you have to arrange payment (which might mean placing a down payment and then arranging an auto loan), as well as shipping or pickup. Assuming that you and the seller don't live in the same city, you'll probably want to avail yourself of eBay's vehicle delivery service, discussed in the following section.

Using eBay Motors Services

eBay Motors offers a variety of services (most provided by third parties) useful to both buyers and sellers. Links to these services are found in the Motor Services part of the eBay Motors home page (or by clicking the Services link at the top of any eBay Motors page), and include:

- **eBay Assurance Program.** This program offers a set of separate services for eBay buyers and sellers, including a limited warranty, purchase insurance, vehicle inspection, and secure payment (with fast deposit).

- **Limited Warranty.** eBay provides a free one-month/1,000-mile limited warranty (courtesy of 1SourceAutoWarranty.com) on eligible used cars under 10 years old and with less than 125,000 miles on the odometer.

- **Purchase Insurance.** eBay offers (via a third party) free protection against fraud or material misrepresentation, up to $20,000 (with a $500 deductible).

- **Vehicle Inspection.** eBay can arrange a third-party inspection of the vehicle you're buying.

- **Payment Protection.** Through Escrow.com, eBay offers secure payment and fast deposit for $22 per transaction.

- **Lemon Check.** eBay uses Carfax to verify (via the VIN) the repair, salvage, accident, and ownership history of the vehicle you're looking at.

tip

Because you're probably bidding on a vehicle sight unseen, arranging an independent inspection of the vehicle is a way to ensure you're getting what you think you're getting.

▪ **Vehicle Shipping.** To get your car from there to here, eBay can arrange with Dependable Auto Shippers (DAS) for door-to-door shipment and delivery of your vehicle, at additional charge. (Quotes are free.)

▪ **Auto Insurance.** Because you'll need insurance on your new vehicle, eBay has deals with both Progressive and Insweb for automobile insurance.

▪ **Extended Warranty.** If you want to purchase an extended warranty (beyond eBay's one-month warranty) on your car, eBay can hook you up with a policy from 1SourceAutoWarranty.com.

Selling Your Car Online

To sell a used vehicle on eBay Motors, you must create an item listing just as you do in a regular eBay auction. The big difference is the amount of detail you need to provide; eBay Motors requires you to enter a fair amount of vehicle-specific information, as shown in the following checklist:

Checklist—Before You Sell Your Vehicle

☐ Vehicle type

☐ Model year

☐ Mileage

☐ Exterior color

☐ Interior color

☐ Number of cylinders

☐ Transmission (automatic or manual)

☐ Number of doors

☐ Other important options and safety features

☐ Condition (new or used)

☐ Existing warranty?

☐ Type of vehicle title (clear, salvage, or other)

☐ Vehicle inspection?

In addition, you'll get more bids if you supply your car's vehicle identification number (VIN), as buyers will use the VIN to look up the car's ownership and repair history. You should also check off any options and safety features included with the vehicle, such as sunroof, CD player, antilock brakes, and so on.

Pricing the vehicle in your listing is identical to pricing a regular eBay auction, complete with starting price, optional reserve price, and optional Buy It Now price—except that the numbers are probably a bit bigger than what you're used to. You can add pictures to your listing (recommended) as well as choose to list your vehicle (for free) on the AutoTrader.com Web site.

Listing and final value fees work a little differently than they do in other auctions. You'll pay $40 to list most vehicles ($25 for motorcycles), as well as a flat $40 final value fee (also $25 for motorcycles). No percentages, just the two flat fees.

When the auction is over, you'll need to arrange delivery to the high bidder. The best option here, assuming the two of you aren't within driving distance, is to use a vehicle carrier service—such as the one offered by DAS, accessible from the eBay Motors home page.

Buying and Selling Houses on eBay Real Estate

If a car is the second-largest expenditure you'll make in your life, a home is the largest. Through its eBay Real Estate site, eBay now offers listings and auctions for all types of real estate, including Residential, Timeshares, Office/Commercial, and Land. (The Residential listings include existing, new, foreclosed, and vacation homes.)

Shopping for Houses and Other Real Estate

You access eBay Real Estate from the Categories list on the eBay home page) or by going directly to pages.ebay.com/realestate/. As you can see in Figure 27.3, you can browse by category or search by title or description—or, if you're interested in a house, click the Residential link. This takes you to the Residential Real Estate page, which offers a Home Finder search by state, city, number of bedrooms, price, and so on.

FIGURE 27.3

House hunting at eBay Real Estate.

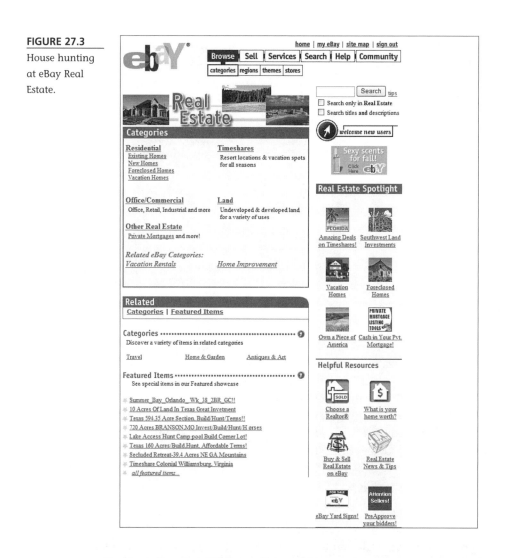

The typical eBay Real Estate listing, like the one shown in Figure 27.4, includes a variety of real estate-specific information, including square footage, number of bedrooms, and so on. Also included is the property's Zip code, a link to a map of the property's immediate neighborhood, and a link to a neighborhood profile.

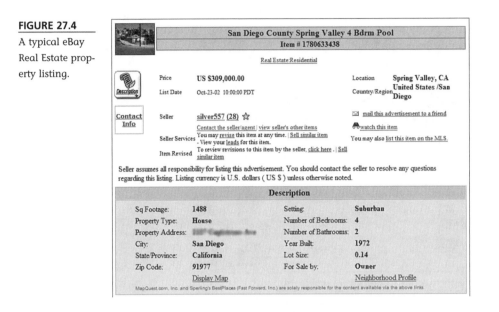

What's different about eBay Real Estate is that the listings are not legally binding
auctions. In fact, many of the listings don't involve auctions at all; sellers can
choose to use eBay Real Estate as a traditional listing service, which means you have
to contact the seller (or the seller's agent) to make a bid for the property. If there is
no Bid link in the listing, you'll see a Contact Information section instead. Enter
your name and contact information and click the Submit button, and your information will be forwarded to the seller/agent.

Listing Your House Online

Many homeowners are choosing the "for sale by owner" option when it comes time
to sell their property. If you're up to the extra work, you can eliminate realtor's fees
when you sell it yourself—and eBay Real Estate is the perfect place to list your home
for sale. (eBay Real Estate is also popular among the realtor crowd; it's a great way
to gain exposure for *any* home for sale.)

When you click the Sell link at the top of the eBay Real Estate page, you're offered a
choice of three different selling formats. You can choose to sell your property at a
traditional auction, sell at a fixed price, or simply use eBay to advertise your real
estate. From there, you enter the specifics of your property—number of bedrooms,
number of bathrooms, type of property, square footage, lot size, year built, and so
on. You can also choose to run a 3-, 5-, 7-, 10-, or 30-day auction, or a 30- or 90-day
non-auction listing.

eBay Real Estate charges both listing and final value fees. The charge for an 3-, 5-, 7-, or 10-day auction listing is $100; a 30-day auction listing costs $150. If you prefer to use a non-auction listing, you'll pay $150 for a 30-day listing, or $300 for a 90-day listing. The final value fee for a completed auction transaction is a flat $3; there are no final value fees on non-auction listings. (Fees for the Land and Timeshare categories are slightly lower.)

"Mike Sez"

Because eBay Real Estate auctions are legally non-binding, you're better off running your listing as a non-auction ad. (The price of a 30-day auction listing and a 30-day ad listing is the same—$150.) You pay no final value fee on ad listings.

THE ABSOLUTE MINIMUM

Here are the key points to remember from this chapter:

- eBay Motors lets you buy or sell any type of new or used vehicle, including cars, trucks, motor homes, boats, or aircraft.

- When you purchase a vehicle via eBay Motors, eBay provides a variety of useful services to help you complete your transaction—including limited warranty, purchase insurance, vehicle inspection, Carfax history reports, and vehicle delivery.

- eBay Real Estate functions more like a traditional real estate listing service, in that it allows property listings in addition to (non-binding) auctions.

PART V

BECOMING A POWER SELLER

28

USING AUCTION SOFTWARE AND SERVICES

Throughout this book I've mentioned several third-party software programs and services you can use to automate various parts of the online auction process. This chapter is where you get the complete list of products and services, along with some personal comments and recommendations about which are the best to use.

So, if you want to make bidding and selling in eBay auctions a little easier—particularly important if you're a high-volume power seller—this chapter is for you!

Listing and Auction Management

If you're running a lot of auctions at one time, you need some way to keep track of which auctions are still open, which have closed, which need e-mails sent to high bidders, which need to be shipped out, and so on. It also helps if you can somehow automate the listing process itself, and create great-looking HTML-based listings to boot.

Making life easier for eBay power sellers has become somewhat of a cottage industry. There are a large number of software programs and Web-based services that handle some or all of the eBay selling process—from ad creation to post-auction management.

The software and services listed here are the most popular of what's currently available. Although many perform similar functions, there are a lot of important differences, so pay attention. And know that most of these programs and Web sites cost real money to use—in some cases, the kind of serious bucks that only big-volume sellers can afford.

> **note**
>
> Most of the software programs listed in this chapter work only on the Windows operating system. If you're an Apple Macintosh user, you might want to check out eLister, Auction Monitor, and eNotifier, all from Black Magik Software (`www.blackmagik.com/gavelware.html`).

All My Auctions

All My Auctions (`www.rajeware.com/auction/`) is a basic auction management software program. It includes template-based listing creation, live auction management (including the ability to track competitors' auctions), end-of-auction e-mail notification, and report generation. The price is $39.95 with no monthly subscription fees.

Andale

Andale (`www.andale.com`) is a site that offers a variety of services for eBay sellers. Andale Research looks at past auctions to determine average selling price and success rate for specific types of items; cost is $2.95 per month. Andale Images is an image hosting and management service; price varies by amount of space used, starting at $3.00 per month for 3MB of storage. Andale Lister is a listing creation, posting, and inventory tracking service; price varies by number of listings created, starting at $2.00 per month for 10 listings. Andale Checkout is a post-auction management service; price varies by number of auctions using their checkout, starting at $2.00 per month for 10 listings. Andale Reports is a series of reports to help you analyze your auction business; price is $19.95 per month.

Andale also offers traffic counters, feedback listing, their own gallery listings and stores, and e-mail list management.

I used to like Andale when most of their services were free. I still like their services, but dislike their a la carte pricing for every little service they offer. To take advantage of all their services, you end up getting nickel and dimed to death. Just using Andale Lister and Andale Checkout will cost you a total of $0.20 per item; when you combine this with mandatory eBay fees, PayPal fees, fees for Andale Research, Images, and Reports, and who knows what else, you can easily wipe out any profit from your auctions. Perhaps the fees can be justified if you're selling high-cost items, but for low-cost items—books, CDs, and the like—it doesn't make much sense.

Auction Hawk

Auction Hawk (www.auctionhawk.com) is a Web-based listing-creation and image-hosting service. Price is dependent on how many auctions you list, starting at $6.99 per month for up to 25 listings. (Auction Hawk also offers post-auction and inventory management features at their upper tiers of pricing.)

Auction Lizard

Auction Lizard (www.auction-lizard.com) is an easy-to-use listing-creation software program. It creates great-looking HTML-based listings using forms and templates. Auction Lizard is shareware, with a $29.00 registration fee.

Auction Sentry

Auction Sentry (www.auction-sentry.com) is billed as a software program for both buyers and sellers, although its seller-oriented features are somewhat limited—basically, all it does is track your live auctions. (And it costs $9.95 for this.) It's a much better bidder's tool, as discussed in the "Sniping and Bidding Tools" section of this chapter.

Auction Wizard 2000

Auction Wizard 2000 (www.auctionwizard2000.com) is an auction management software program that includes an image editor, listing creator, report generator, FTP manager, and auction database. Auction Wizard 2000 costs $75 with no monthly subscription fees.

Auction-X

Auction-X (www.auction-x.com) offers Web-based auction management and listing creation tools, as well as image hosting, counters, shipping labels, invoices, and more. The cost for these services is a flat $4.95 per month.

AuctionDesigner

AuctionDesigner (www.auctiondesigner.com) is a listing-creation software program that generates and lists HTML-based auction listings. It's a little pricey for its limited functions; price is $49.95 (with no additional monthly fees).

AuctionHelper

AuctionHelper (www.auctionhelper.com) offers a variety of Web-based auction management tools for power sellers, including template-based listing creation, image hosting, and shipping label generation, feedback generation, and other post-auction management. Pricing is 1.5% of your final sales price, with a minimum fee of $0.15 and a maximum fee of $0.70 per transaction; the site also charges a minimum total fee of $10.00 per month.

AuctionTamer

AuctionTamer (www.auctiontamer.com) is an all-in-one auction management software program for both sellers and bidders. For sellers, it lets you create auction listings, schedule delayed auction listings, manage your live auctions, send post-auction e-mails, and print shipping labels. AuctionTamer has four levels of Seller Access Plans—$29.95 for 3 months, $49.95 for 6 months, $69.95 for a whole year, or a one-time fee of $249.95 for lifetime access. (AuctionTamer's Buyer Access Plan is extra.)

AuctionWatch

AuctionWatch (www.auctionwatch.com) is an all-purpose online auction services site, offering a variety of information, education, community, and tools for eBay sellers. The site offers image hosting, cross-site auction search, their own online stores for power sellers, and auction management services.

AuctionWatch offers two separate but integrated auction management solutions. Sales Manager is a Web-based service that offers listing creation, inventory management, auction tracking, and automated checkout. Sales Manager Pro is a separate bulk upload software program.

You can choose from several different monthly plans for both Sales Manager and Sales Manager Pro. For example, the Sales Manager Variable Rate Premium Plan costs $12.95 per month plus a $0.05 listing fee and 1% of the item's selling price. The Flat Rate Premium Plan costs $12.95 per month plus a $0.20 listing fee but with no final value fee. And the Pay As You Go Plan has no monthly fee, but charges $0.10 per listing and 1% of the final selling price.

For what it's worth, AuctionWatch Sales Manager is one of the more popular third-party auction management services, with more than 100,000 users. I find the service easy to use, but the fees (even on the Pay As You Go Plan) difficult to swallow—especially on lower-cost items.

Auctionworks

Auctionworks (www.auctionworks.com) offers a variety of "power tools" for power sellers. The site offers a variety of Web-based auction management services, including listing creation, bulk uploads, auction tracking, e-mail notifications, feedback listing, and more. Auctionworks charges 2% of the final selling price, with a $0.10 minimum and a $3.00 maximum.

> **caution**
>
> Remember to factor the costs of these programs and services into your overall auction costs. If a service charges $20/month and you only list 20 auctions, you've just added a buck to the cost of each of your auctions. Same thing if a service charges on a per-listing basis, or as a percentage of your selling fee. Believe me, these costs add up fast—especially if you're a relatively small seller!

Auctiva Auction Poster

Auctiva (www.auctiva.com) offers a variety of online auction information and services targeted at small businesses—not at individual users. Auctiva Basic is a free service offering basic auction tracking, and isn't too useful. Auctiva Pro offers listing creation and posting, image hosting, and post-auction management; it's priced starting at $14.95 per month.

ChannelAdvisor Pro

ChannelAdvisor Pro (www.channeladvisor.com/pro.htm) is a Web-based suite of auction management tools that lets you organize and track your inventory, create HTML-based auction listings, manage your auctions and post-auction activities, and even create and run your own Web-based store. The complete suite of services costs $29.95 per month (or $270 per year) with no per-transaction fees. As you can probably tell by the cost, ChannelAdvisor Pro is designed for true power sellers and small merchants—I don't recommend it for the casual or occasional seller.

CollectorOnline

CollectorOnline (www.collectoronline.com) is a Web site that offers a variety of information and services for serious collectors, including auction management services. These Web-based services include listing creation, bulk uploading, image management, and post-auction management and communication. Pricing starts at $19.95 per month.

eBay Seller's Assistant

eBay's official listing creation and auction management software is called eBay Seller's Assistant (pages.ebay.com/sellers_assistant/). It's available in both Basic and Pro versions.

Seller's Assistant Basic is best for casual users, offering HTML-based listing creation (using forms and templates), auction tracking, and basic post-auction management (including automatic e-mail notification and feedback generation). The software is available on a per-month subscription; you'll pay $4.99 each month, no matter how many listings you create.

Figure 28.1 shows the Seller's Assistant Basic listing creation screen; fill in the blanks, pick a template, and the software creates a decent-looking listing.

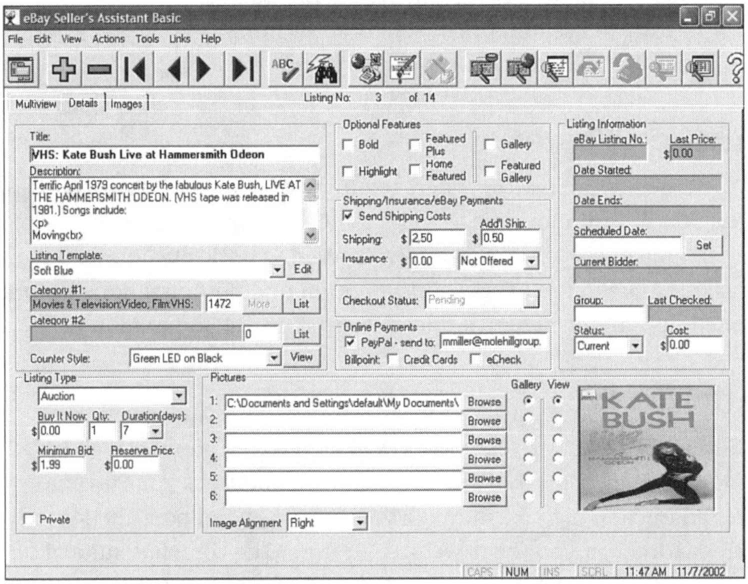

FIGURE 28.1

Using eBay Seller's Assistant Basic to create HTML-based auction listings.

Seller's Assistant Pro adds features of value to power sellers, including bulk listing and relisting, scheduled listings, inventory management, report generation, and the ability to create and print shipping labels. The subscription fee is $15.99 per month.

eBay Turbo Lister

eBay Turbo Lister (`pages.ebay.com/turbo_lister/`) is eBay's official software program for the bulk uploading of multiple auctions. Turbo Lister is an okay listing creator (Seller's Assistant is better), but excels at bulk uploading—especially if you're listing hundreds (or thousands!) of items at a time. It offers no ongoing auction tracking or post-auction management features. Then again, it's free, so you might want to give it a download and take it out for a spin.

Learn more about eBay Turbo Lister in Chapter 29, "Selling in Quantity."

inkFrog

inkFrog (`www.inkfrog.com`) is a cute name for some heavy-duty Web-based auction management services. inkFrog offers auction listing, tracking, and management, along with image hosting and listing creation and design. Various plans are offered, starting at $7.95 per month.

ManageAuctions

ManageAuctions (`www.manageauctions.com`) offers Web-based listing creation, auction tracking, e-mail notification, shipping label printing, feedback generation, and other post-auction management. Pricing is on an a la carte basis; listings cost $0.05 apiece and post-sale management is $0.05 per auction. There's a minimum monthly charge of $4.95, and a maximum of $24.95; image hosting is extra.

MyAuctionMate

MyAuctionMate (`www.myauctionmate.com`) is an auction management software program that offers listing creation, batch uploading, auction tracking and management, end-of-auction e-mail notifications, automatic feedback posting, report generation, and more. The program costs $43. (The company also offers its listing-creation module, MyAuctionDesigner, separately, for just $9.95.)

Trak Auctions

Trak Auctions (www.trakauction.com) offers Web-based auction management in two different editions. The Light Edition is best for casual users, whereas the Pro Edition is designed for small merchants and power users with their own online stores. The fees are the same for either version—$0.05 for each listing, with a maximum charge of $9.99 per month.

Virtual Auction Ad Pro

Virtual Auction Ad Pro (www.firstdesign.com/vadpro/) is a software program that lets you create great-looking HTML-based ad listings. It also offers templates for listing titles and descriptions, for those without strong copywriting skills. Cost is $14.99.

Zoovy

Zoovy (www.zoovy.com) is a collection of Web-based auction-management services designed for small businesses—not individual users. Packages start at $33.25 per month.

Sniping and Bidding Tools

Just as there are a lot of third-party tools available for eBay sellers, there are also a variety of software and services designed for serious eBay buyers. Most of these programs and Web sites help you track auctions you're interested in, and then perform automated last-minute bidding—otherwise known as sniping. (If you don't remember sniping, refer to Chapter 9, "Secrets of Successful Bidders.")

" Mike Sez "

When it comes to the software and services listed here, you can see that most of the big sites price the little sellers out of the market. Indeed, services like Andale and ChannelAdvisor are designed for power sellers and small merchants, not for casual sellers and individual users. For us average Joes, I recommend eBay Seller's Assistant Basic. I liked it back when it was distributed by Blackthorne Software, and I like it now that eBay has acquired it. But even this recommendation comes with a caveat—you have to be listing a half-dozen or more auctions a month to make the $4.95/month fee financially palatable. If you're only listing a few auctions a week, you might want to check out AuctionWatch or Trak Auctions, both of which charge on a per-auction basis.

I don't really have a favorite among these sniping programs and services. However, I do prefer the sniping sites over the software, as you don't have to bother with having your computer on and connected to the Internet for the sniping to take place. (It's important to note that the sniping sites typically charge a percentage of your winning bid—whereas the sniping programs only have a one-time purchase price.)

Auction Sentry

Auction Sentry (www.auction-sentry.com) is a software program for auction tracking, bidding, and sniping. You can use Auction Sentry just to watch auctions you're interested in, to alert you when someone else makes a bid on an item, to place instant bids, or to make scheduled snipes. The Auction Sentry program costs $9.95.

note

Auction Sentry also offers rudimentary auction tracking for sellers, as discussed in the "Listing and Auction Management" section.

Auction Sniper

Auction Sniper (www.auctionsniper.com) is a Web-based sniping service with more than 70,000 registered users. You're charged 1% of the final value fee, with a minimum charge of $0.25 and a maximum of $5.

AuctionStealer

AuctionStealer (www.auctionstealer.com) is a Web-based service that lets you track an unlimited number of auctions and perform unattended auction sniping. The site claims to have sniped more than 2.5 million auctions to date, and to have more than 85,000 active registered users. The service itself is free, although you're charged $1 for each successful snipe.

AuctionTamer

We discussed AuctionTamer (www.auctiontamer.com) back in the "Listing and Auction Management" section, because it's a tool for both bidders and sellers. For bidders, it lets you search and track auctions across multiple auction sites, save and repeat your most popular item searches, automatically snipe auctions, and leave feedback on items you've won. You pay $15 per year for AuctionTamer's Buyer Access Plan; seller features are extra.

BidNapper

BidNapper (www.bidnapper.com) is a Web-based subscription sniping service that costs $4.95 per month or $39.95 a year.

BidRobot

BidRobot (www.bidrobot.com) is a Web-based sniping service. Pricing plans include $3.95 for three weeks, $19.95 for six months, or $34.95 for twelve months.

BidSlammer

BidSlammer (www.bidslammer.com) is a Web-based sniping service. Cost is $0.10 per bid, and 1% of the winning bid price if you win—with a minimum charge of $0.25 and a maximum charge of $5.00.

BidSpyder

BidSpyder (www.bidspyder.com) is a free sniping program—although donations are encouraged.

Cricket Jr.

Cricket Jr. (www.cricketsniper.com) is a simple, easy-to-use eBay sniping program. It costs $19.95.

eSearch

eSearch (www.mazepath.com) isn't a sniping tool, it's a search tool. This software program lets you perform more targeted eBay searches, and then save those searches for future use. eSearch costs $24.00, with no additional fees.

eSnipe

eSnipe (www.esnipe.com) is a Web-based sniping tool that claims more than 100,000 users. The site charges approximately 1% of the final value fee for each successful snipe.

HammerSnipe

HammerSnipe (www.hammertap.com) is a Web-based sniping service that comes with its own customized browser, called HammerSnipe PowerTool. The PowerTool software is free, as is the basic ad-supported service.

> **note**
>
> Cricket Software offers several other interesting eBay utilities, including Cricket Power Chat (for eBay's message boards); Safe2Bid (feedback submission and retrieval); and Cricket Multi Browser (favorites and bookmarks for your Web browser).
>
> HammerTap offers additional tools you might be interested in, including Auction Informant (bid alerts for your eBay auctions); BayCheck and BayCheck Pro (eBay user tracking); BayMail and BayMail Pro (eBay e-mail management); BidderBlock (blocked bidder list management); DeepAnalysis (eBay auction research); and FeeFinder (shipping fee calculator). You can obtain all these utilities on a single CD-ROM (called the HammerSuite) for just $9.99—although registration for each individual program costs extra.

THE ABSOLUTE MINIMUM

Here are the key points to remember from this chapter:

- Many big Web sites offer news, education, community, and auction management services for online auction users—particularly for power sellers.

- If you're a power seller (listing dozens of auctions every week), check out sites like Andale, Auctionworks, and ChannelAdvisor.

- If you're a smaller seller (listing a half-dozen or fewer auctions a week), check out eBay's Seller's Assistant Basic software, or the AuctionWatch or Trak Auctions Web sites.

- If you're a serious eBay buyer, consider using a sniping service or software program to automate your last-second bids.

- Whichever programs or services you use, remember to factor the cost of the software/service into your overall auction costs.

29

SELLING IN QUANTITY

If you're a true power seller, you're listing dozens of items a week on eBay. Creating these listings one at a time, by hand, can be a real pain—and take up a *lot* of your time. When you're listing this many items at a time, you can make the process easier by using *bulk listing software*—software that lets you upload hundreds—or even thousands!—of auctions at the click of a single button.

Read on to learn more.

Introducing eBay Turbo Lister

eBay offers its own bulk listing software, called eBay Turbo Lister. To download the Turbo Lister software, go to pages.ebay.com/turbo_lister/. The program is free.

Turbo Lister lets you create your item listings offline, at your leisure. (It also offers HTML-based templates you can use to spruce up your item listings.) Then, when you're ready, it uploads all your listings at once, with the click of a button. Creating multiple auctions couldn't be easier.

Creating Individual Item Listings

The Turbo Lister software is quite easy to use. It uses a series of forms to request information about your listings, as well as a WYSIWYG editor for creating great-looking listings. Here's how it works:

1. From the main Turbo Lister screen, click the Create Item button.

2. When the Create a New Item page appears, select the country you're selling in and your preferred auction format. Click Next to proceed.

3. When the New Auction Item page appears, enter your item title, select a category, and choose other auction specifics. Click Next to proceed.

4. When the Design Your Listing page appears, as shown in Figure 29.1, select a visual theme; select a layout; enter your description text; and upload your listing photo(s). Click Next to proceed.

5. When the Format Specifics page appears, enter the remaining details of your item listings.

6. Click the Save button to save this listing.

This item is now added to your item inventory. You use this inventory to upload individual listings to eBay.

FIGURE 29.1

Use Turbo Lister's WYSI-WYG editor to design great-looking item listings.

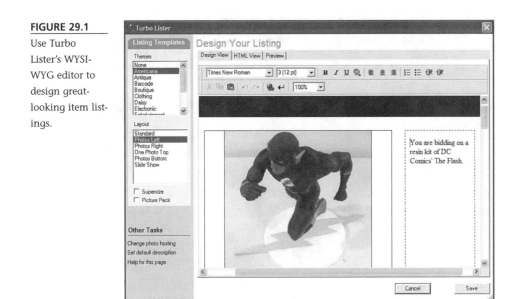

Managing Your Auction Inventory and Uploading Your Listings

To view the items you've added to your inventory, click the Item Inventory tab. This screen lists all the items you've created; from here you can edit, delete, or create duplicate items.

When you have an item that you want to list on eBay, select the item and click the Add to Upload button. You can see all the items in your upload queue by click the Listings Waiting to Upload tab. As you can see in Figure 29.2, this page shows all items waiting to be uploaded. While they're waiting, you can calculate listing fees and change the start time for any specific auction.

Uploading your pending auctions is as easy as clicking the Upload All to eBay button. Listings set to start immediately do so, and items with a future start time are sent to eBay's Pending Listings section. These auctions will go live at the time(s) you previously scheduled.

caution

If you choose to schedule your auctions to start at a later time, you'll pay eBay 10 cents a listing for this privilege.

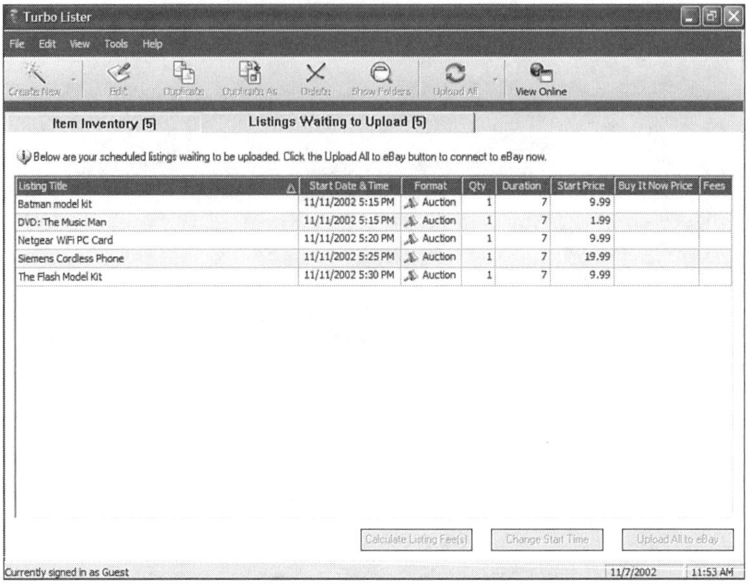

FIGURE 29.2

Items waiting to
be uploaded
with Turbo
Lister.

FIGURE 29.2
Items waiting to be uploaded with Turbo Lister.

Other Bulk Listing Software and Services

eBay Turbo Lister isn't the only bulk listing option available to you. Several third-party programs and Web sites offer similar bulk creation and listing features—although you'll pay for them. (These sites typically offer additional services beyond simple bulk listing, thus justifying their fees.)

I already discussed many of these services back in Chapter 28, "Using Auction Software and Services," so you can turn there for more information. As a quick reminder, the most popular of these third-party bulk-listing software and services include:

- Andale (www.andale.com)
- Auction Hawk (www.auctionhawk.com)
- AuctionWatch Sales Manager (www.auctionwatch.com)
- Auctionworks (www.auctionworks.com)
- Auctiva Pro (www.auctiva.com)
- ChannelAdvisor Pro (www.channeladvisor.com/pro.htm)

THE ABSOLUTE MINIMUM

Here are the key points to remember from this chapter:

- If you're listing hundreds—or thousands—of items a week, you need bulk uploading software.

- eBay's bulk uploading program is called Turbo Lister, and it's free.

- To use Turbo Lister, you first create an inventory of items and their associated listings, and then upload selected listings to the eBay site.

- Other sites offer bulk uploading for a fee—but also offer additional auction management services.

30

USING PAYPAL AND OTHER PAYMENT SERVICES

In the old days (about three years ago—an eternity in Internet time), there was no practical way for an individual user to accept credit card payments for online auctions or other transactions. That changed with the advent of the *online payment service*, which serves as the middle-man for such transactions; the buyer pays the service via credit card, and the service handles all the credit card paperwork and sends a check to the seller (or deposits funds in the seller's checking account). The charge for this service? A percent or two of the sale, paid for by the seller.

It's safe to say that these online payment services changed the face of online auctions. Now any auction seller can accept credit card payments, thanks to the online payment services. And that means more buyers can buy more things and pay faster—via the convenience of plastic. Almost overnight the standard method of payment shifted from personal check to credit card, and everyone is happy about that.

Of course, you can use an online payment service for more than just auction payments. Most payment services let any individual send money to any other individual (or company) anywhere across the country. Need to send money to your kid at college? Want to send cash to your nephew as a birthday present? Then an online payment service is the way to go.

Using PayPal for eBay Auctions

With more than 20 million users, PayPal is the largest and most prosperous of these online payment services. If you're an eBay seller, it's almost a given that you want to accept PayPal payments. In addition, more than 3 million businesses have signed up with PayPal, finding it cheaper or more convenient than trying to establish a traditional merchant credit card account with their local bank.

Because PayPal is now a part of eBay, it's the payment service of choice for the eBay service. Unless you object to the fees (and, like most fees, they can be objectionable), there's no reason *not* to accept PayPal payments for your eBay auctions.

PayPal's eBay-specific features can now be accessed directly from the eBay site. In addition, PayPal offers even more features—such as direct money transfers and online bill payment—that can only be accessed from the PayPal site, located at www.paypal.com.

PayPal accepts payments by American Express, Discover, MasterCard, and Visa. Although it's primarily a U.S.-based service, it also accepts payments to or from 37 other countries, including:

note

Using PayPal with your eBay auctions just got easier, as eBay recently completed its acquisition of the PayPal service. This means that PayPal payments can now be integrated into your auction listings—no need for you or your buyers to use the separate PayPal site.

Anguilla	France	Netherlands
Argentina	Germany	New Zealand
Australia	Greece	Norway
Austria	Hong Kong	Portugal
Belgium	Iceland	Singapore
Brazil	India	South Korea
Canada	Ireland	Spain
Chile	Israel	Sweden
China	Italy	Switzerland
Costa Rica	Jamaica	Taiwan
Denmark	Japan	United Kingdom
Dominican Republic	Luxembourg	
Finland	Mexico	

This makes PayPal the ideal way to receive payments in those international auctions you'll learn about in Chapter 31, "Going International."

Signing Up for PayPal

Before you can use PayPal as a seller, you must sign up for PayPal membership. You do this by going to the PayPal Web site (www.paypal.com) and clicking the Sign Up for Your Free PayPal Account link.

You can choose from three different types of PayPal accounts:

- A Personal account is great for eBay buyers, but not quite enough for sellers. You can send money for free, but can only receive non-credit card payments. (For no charge, though.)

- A Premier account is the best way to go for most eBay sellers. You can still send money for free, and you can now accept both credit card and non-credit card payments (for a fee).

- A Business account is necessary if you're receiving a high volume of payments. With this type of account you can do business under a corporate or group name, and use multiple logins.

All PayPal accounts are insured by the FDIC for up to $100,000.

There is no charge for becoming a PayPal member—although there are fees for actually using the service.(The exception being the Personal account, which charges no fees for anything—but doesn't let you accept credit card payments.)

Paying for PayPal

The fee you pay to PayPal is separate from any other fees you pay to eBay. The way PayPal works is that the buyer doesn't pay any fees; it's the seller who is assessed a fee based on the amount of money transferred.

PayPal's fee (as of November, 2002) is either 2.2% (the Merchant rate for sellers with $3,000 in sales over the past three months) or 2.9% (the Standard rate for lower-volume sellers) of the transaction amount, plus an additional $0.30 per transaction.

These fees are deducted from your account with every transaction.

> **caution**
>
> This last point is important. PayPal charges fees based on the total amount of money paid, *not* on the selling price of the item. That means if a $10 item has a $5 shipping/handling cost, the buyer pays PayPal a total of $15— and PayPal bases its fee on that $15 payment.

Choosing PayPal in Your New Auction Listing

The easiest way to accept PayPal payments in your eBay auctions is to choose the PayPal option when you're creating an item listing. This is as simple as checking the PayPal box and entering your PayPal ID on the Sell Your Item: Enter Payment & Shipping page.

When you choose this option, a PayPal payments section is added to your item listing, as shown in Figure 30.1. PayPal will also appear as a payment option in your eBay Checkout, on your post-auction item listing page, and in eBay's end-of-auction e-mail to the winning bidder.

FIGURE 30.1

The PayPal payment section added to an eBay auction listing.

Adding PayPal to an Existing Auction Listing

If, after you've launched an eBay auction, you decide you want to accept PayPal payments, it's easy to add the PayPal logo and payment info to your existing auction listings. Just go to the PayPal site and follow these steps:

1. Click the Sell tab to go to the Seller Tools page.

2. In the Sell On an Auction column, click Automatic Logos to display the Automatic Logo Insertion page.

3. Select your eBay user ID, and then click the Submit button.

Once a day (typically in the evening), PayPal searches for all open auctions in your name, and adds its logo to the bottom of the item listings. (Figure 30.2 shows one of the many PayPal logos you can add to your eBay item listings.)

FIGURE 30.2

PayPal payment added to an existing auction listing.

Paying via PayPal

As a buyer, it's easy to use PayPal to pay for any auctions you've won. All you need is to click your mouse a few times and have your credit card handy.

If you use the eBay Checkout, you can pay via PayPal by clicking the PayPal button. If you prefer not to use Checkout, you can still pay via PayPal by clicking the PayPal logo at the bottom of the item listing, or in the end-of-auction notification e-mail. In any case, you'll now be transferred to the PayPal site, where you can enter your credit card number and complete payment.

You can also pay for an eBay auction directly from the PayPal site. Just make sure you know the seller's eBay ID or e-mail address, the number and title of the auction, and the total amount you owe (including shipping and handling). From the PayPal main page, click the Send Money tab to display the Send Money page. Follow the instructions there to enter the seller's e-mail address and necessary auction information.

note

If you're not yet a PayPal member, you might be prompted to create a Personal account before you can initiate a payment. Personal membership is free.

Finally, PayPal offers the AuctionFinder service. When you use AuctionFinder, PayPal searches eBay for all auctions won by you that have not been paid for by PayPal. You can then pay for any of these auctions by clicking the Pay button next to the item listing. To use AuctionFinder, click the My Account tab and then the Overview tab, and then click the Auctions Won link to display the AuctionFinder page.

Collecting PayPal Payments

When a buyer makes a PayPal payment, those funds are immediately transferred to the seller's PayPal account, and an e-mail notification of the payment is sent to the seller. In most cases, this e-mail will include all the information the seller needs to link it to a specific auction and ship the item to the seller.

When you sign into the PayPal site, you're taken to the My Account tab, and the Overview tab within that. As you can see in Figure 30.3, this displays an overview of your recent PayPal activity, including payments made by buyers into your account. Click any item to view more detail about the activity.

FIGURE 30.3

Viewing an overview of your PayPal activity.

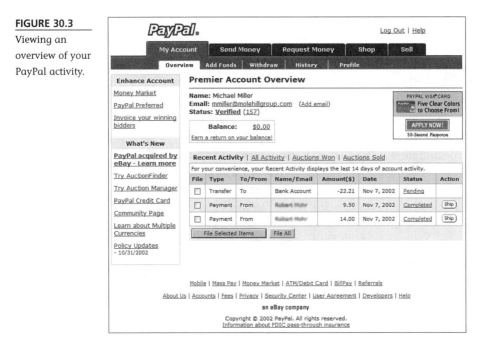

In most cases, the buyers' payments come into your account free and clear, ready to be withdrawn from your checking account. There are two primary exceptions to this, however:

■ eCheck payments, where a buyer pays PayPal from his or her personal checking account. Because PayPal has to wait until the "electronic check" clears to receive its funds, you can't be paid until then, either. PayPal will send you an e-mail when an electronic payment clears.

■ Buyers with unconfirmed addresses. Every PayPal member is encouraged to enter his or her street address. This address is then confirmed by PayPal. If you receive a payment from a buyer who has not entered an address (or whose address has not yet been confirmed), PayPal won't automatically authorize the transaction. Instead, you'll be asked whether you want to accept the payment, unconfirmed address and all. Only after you manually accept the payment will the funds be transferred to your PayPal account.

Using PayPal for Auction Management

You can also use PayPal to send end-of-auction notices to your high bidders, and to function as a checkout site for all your eBay auctions.

One of the neatest features offered by PayPal is their Winning Bidder Notification. When you enable this feature, PayPal will automatically notify all your winning bidders (via e-mail) within one hour of each auction's close. The e-mail directs users to click an included link to pay for the item via PayPal. You activate Winning Bidding Notification by selecting the Sell tab to go to the Selling Tools page, clicking Winning Bidder Notification, and then following the instructions on the Winning Bidder Notification Registration page.

You can also instruct PayPal to manually send a payment request to the high bidder in any individual auction. To send a payment request—an invoice, really—follow these steps:

1. Click the Request Money tab on the Navigation Bar to display the Request Money page.

2. Enter the buyer's e-mail address and the amount due.

3. Pull down the Type list and select Goods – Auction.

4. Enter an optional subject line and note, and then click the Continue button.

5. When the Request Money (Auction) page appears, enter the necessary information, including the auction item number, the URL of the item listing page, and the auction title.

6. Click the Continue button to review and then send the payment request.

Finally, you can use PayPal's Auction Manager, shown in Figure 30.4, to view the status of all your ended auctions within the past 30 days. You access Auction Manager by going to your Overview page and clicking the Auctions Sold link.

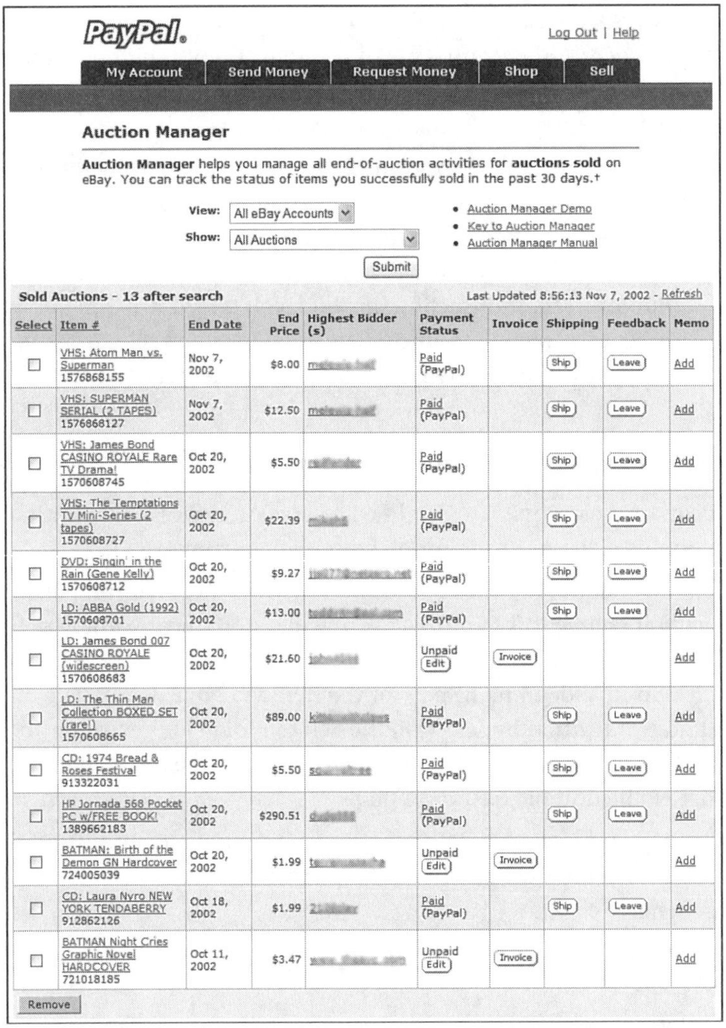

FIGURE 30.4

Use PayPal's
Auction
Manager to
manage your
ended auctions.

If an item has not yet been paid for, you can click that auction's Invoice button to send a payment request to the high bidder. You can also use the Ship button to create a UPS shipping label for the item, or the Leave button (in the Feedback column) to leave feedback for the buyer.

Withdrawing PayPal Funds

You can let your funds build up in your PayPal account, or you can choose (at any time) to withdraw all or part of your funds. You have the option of okaying an electronic withdrawal directly to your checking account (no charge; takes 3–4 business days) or requesting a check for the requested amount ($1.50 charge; takes 1–2 weeks). Just click the Withdraw tab (from the Overview tab) and click the appropriate text link.

" Mike Sez "

I prefer to empty my PayPal account at the end of each day, via an electronic transfer to my checking account. I find this the fastest, no-hassle way to receive PayPal funds due.

Using PayPal for Non-Auction Transactions

PayPal isn't just for online auctions. There are a variety of services on the PayPal site of use to individuals and businesses who might never log on to an online auction site.

Sending Money to Friends and Family

You can use PayPal to send money to anyone with an Internet connection and an e-mail address. You can use either your credit card or checking account to send the funds; the recipient gets an e-mail message that says "You've Got Cash." They then have to register for a (free) PayPal Personal account, and can then choose to have a check cut or the funds electronically deposited in their normal checking account.

To send funds via PayPal, follow these steps:

1. Click the Send Money tab on the Navigation Bar to display the Send Money page.

2. Enter the recipient's e-mail address and the amount you want to send.

3. Pull down the Type list and select the type of transaction. (If you're sending a gift, select Quasi-Cash.)

4. Enter an optional subject and note, and then click Continue.

5. When the Check Payment Details page appears, look at the Source of Funds section. If you're okay with the choice selected, fine. If not, click the More Funding Options link to select another source of funds.

note

You have to have at least a Personal account to send money via PayPal.

6. After you've confirmed all the other details of the transaction, click the Send Money button.

Paying Your Bills with PayPal

If you're into electronic banking, you'll like PayPal's BillPay feature. BillPay is a free service for paying your bills online. To use BillPay to pay a bill, click the BillPay link at the bottom of any PayPal page. When the BillPay page appears, follow the onscreen instructions to add a new payee and make a payment.

Using PayPal in Your Business

For small online businesses, PayPal is an easy way to accept credit card payments. The site offers a variety of services of use to online retailers.

To accept eBay payments on your Web site, you have to add a PayPal Shopping Cart—just like the professional shopping carts you see on Amazon.com and other big e-tail sites. To create a shopping cart and create your Add To Cart buttons, select the Sell tab to display the Seller Tools page, and then click the Shopping Cart link in the Sell on a Website column. Follow the instructions there to integrate PayPal services into your Web site.

If your business offers subscription-based services, you can use PayPal Subscriptions toaccept these recurring payments. Just go to the Seller Tools page and click the Subscriptions link to set up future payments.

Finally, you can also use PayPal to pay your creditors—and employees. PayPal Mass Payment lets you set up instant electronic payments in lieu of traditional (and labor-intensive) checks; you'll pay 2% of the check amount (with a $1.00 cap) to use this feature. Just click the Mass Pay link at the bottom of any PayPal page to display the Mass Payment Overview page; follow the instructions there to set up the Mass Payment feature.

tip

PayPal can also be used to collect political contributions. Click the Donations link on the Seller Tools to learn more.

Using the PayPal Debit Card and Money Market Accounts

PayPal offers its own ATM/debit card you can use to withdraw funds from your PayPal account. Click the ATM/Debit Card link at the bottom of any PayPal page to learn more.

In addition, PayPal would like to encourage you to leave your money in your PayPal account as long as possible by letting you sign up for a special PayPal Money Market Fund. Naturally, PayPal earns a cut of the proceeds; you're generally better off to withdraw your funds as soon as possible and deposit them in your own money market account. To learn more, click the Money Market link at the bottom of any PayPal page.

Using PayPal Shops

The last thing to know about PayPal is that it offers its own online marketplace, consisting of the more than 30,000 Web sites that accept PayPal payments. Click the Shop tab on the Navigation Bar to go to the PayPal Shops page, where you can browse through and search for specific types of merchants and merchandise.

Other Online Payment Services

Aside from PayPal, there are several other online payment services you can use for your online auctions and for general money transfers. Though not as popular as PayPal, they may offer unique features that appeal to your own personal circumstances.

BidPay

BidPay (www.bidpay.com) started out as a strong competitor to PayPal and Billpoint, but has faded into the background somewhat. It's currently owned by Western Union, a company with a lot of experience transferring funds by wire. You can use BidPay to send money orders to online auction sellers, or to other businesses or individuals.

Billpoint

Billpoint (www.billpoint.com) is the formerly independent service that was acquired by eBay. With PayPal now in the fold, Billpoint's out in the cold, and is being phased out. By the time you read these words, it will probably have ceased to exist.

C2it

C2it (www.c2it.com) is an online payment service owned by Citibank. You can use C2it to send money to anyone with a U.S. e-mail account (for a flat fee of $10), or to people in over one hundred other countries.

MoneyZap

MoneyZap (www.moneyzap.com) is another online payment service run by Western Union. Its primary focus is electronic payments to merchants; they recently discontinued the ability to send payment to other users via e-mail.

PayingFast

PayingFast (www.payingfast.com) lets you use your MasterCard or Visa to send money orders to individuals or businesses, or to pay for online auctions.

ProPay

ProPay (www.propay.com) lets individuals and small merchants accept credit card payments on their Web sites.

Yahoo! PayDirect

Yahoo! PayDirect (paydirect.yahoo.com) is an online payment service run by Yahoo!. You can use PayDirect to pay for items in Yahoo! Auctions, or to send money direct to anyone with an e-mail address.

> **"Mike Sez"**
>
> Most of these services do pretty much what PayPal does for pretty much the same costs. For that reason, I see no reason *not* to use PayPal, which is far and away the most popular of these services.

THE ABSOLUTE MINIMUM

Here are the key points to remember from this chapter:

- PayPal is an online payment service that lets any eBay seller accept credit card payments.
- When a buyer pays PayPal, those funds are transferred to the seller's PayPal account—where they're available for immediate withdrawal.
- Buyers never pay for using PayPal; sellers pay anywhere from 2.2% to 2.9% of the total payment, plus 30 cents per transaction.
- You can also use PayPal—and other online payment services—to send money to anyone with an e-mail account.

31

GOING INTERNATIONAL

If you're a seller doing any amount of volume on eBay, you will sooner or later be faced with an interesting situation—someone from outside the U.S. bidding on one of your items. Becoming an international seller sounds exotic and glamorous, but the honor comes with an increase in paperwork and effort on your part. Although you might be able to increase the number of potential bidders by offering your merchandise outside the U.S., you also increase your workload—and, more importantly, your risk.

Should you sell internationally? And if so, how do you handle payment and shipping and all those other niggling details? Read on to learn more about international sales via eBay—as well as hear my own opinion on the subject.

Pros and Cons of Selling Internationally

Let's start with the big question: Should you sell internationally? The answer to this isn't a simple one. It depends a lot on your tolerance for differences (in money, in language, in routine), and your ability to deal with unusual post-auction activity—especially in regards to payment and shipping.

The pros of opening up your auctions to non-U.S. bidders include:

- You might be able to attract additional bidders—and thus sell more items at (presumably) higher prices.
- You establish a reputation as a hard-working global trader.
- It's fun (sometimes) to interact with people from different countries and cultures.

The cons of selling outside the U.S. include:

- You might run into difficulties communicating with bidders from outside the United States.
- You might have to deal with payment in non-U.S. funds, on non-U.S. banks.
- You'll have to put extra effort into the packing of an item to be shipped over great distances.
- You probably won't be able to use your standard shipping services—which means investigating new shipping services and options.
- Shipping costs will be higher than what you're used to—and will need to be passed onto the buyer.
- You'll need to deal with the appropriate paperwork for shipping outside the U.S.— including those pesky customs forms.
- If there are any problems or disputes with the item shipped, you have an international-sized incident on your hands.

Just looking at this list, it may appear that the cons outweigh the pros. That might not always be the case, however—especially if you're a real people person.

" Mike Sez "

My personal opinions on international sales are sure to invite argument. The bottom line is that I don't ship internationally, period. I've done it in the past, and the hassle factor simply isn't worth it. Even if the transaction goes smoothly (and it often doesn't, all things considered), the big issue is that the procedures involved are just too different from what I have set up for my normal day-to-day auction activities. In other words, international auctions are unusual transactions that mess up my normal domestic auction production line. My apologies to buyers outside the U.S.—most of whom I've found to be wonderful people to deal with—but I can't afford to have my normal activity jeopardized by these high-maintenance shipments. (My only exceptions are small items shipping into Canada that can be handled without much additional paperwork or hassle.)

Many eBay sellers get great joy from interacting with people from different cultures, sometimes turning foreign buyers into lasting friends. I can vouch from my limited personal experience that most non-U.S. buyers I've dealt with are exceedingly polite and tolerant of the extra effort required to complete an international transaction.

If you decide to sell outside the U.S., you'll want to state this in your auctions, along with a line indicating that "Shipping/handling outside the U.S. is higher," or something to that effect. If, on the other hand, you decide *not* to sell internationally, state that in your ad also—with a "U.S. bidders only"-type notice.

Selling Outside the U.S.

If you decide to take the leap and open your auctions to an international audience, you need to be prepared for a new world of activities—no pun intended. Selling outside the U.S.—especially the shipping part of the process—is much different than selling to someone in New York or California. Although I can't prepare you for all the issues you might encounter, I will point out some of the bigger hassles to look out for.

Communicating with International Bidders

One of the joys—and challenges—of selling internationally is communicating with non-U.S. bidders. Although citizens of many countries speak English, not all do—or do so well. This means you're likely to receive e-mails in fractured English, or in some language that you might not be able to easily translate.

The solution to this problem isn't always easy. It's one thing to say you should send non-English-language e-mails back to the buyer, requesting communication in English. But if the buyer can't read or write English, how is he supposed to read your request? This problem is a tricky one.

I have found, however, that communication goes more smoothly if you keep your written communications short and simple. Use straightforward wording, and avoid slang terms and abbreviations.

In addition, you have to deal with the time difference between the U.S. and many other countries. If you're dealing with a buyer in the Far East, you're sleeping while he's sending e-mails, and vice versa. This introduces an unavoidable lag into the communication that can sometimes be problematic.

The only advice I can give you here is to be aware of the time differences, and plan accordingly. Don't expect an immediate response from someone on a different continent, and try to avoid the kind of back-and-forth communications that can go on for days and days.

Accepting Foreign Payments

One of the issues with selling outside the U.S. is dealing with foreign currency. First, you have to convert it to U.S. dollars. (How many lira to the dollar today?) Then you have to receive it in a form that is both secure and trusted. (Do you trust a personal check drawn on a small Spanish bank?) Then you have to find a way to deposit those funds—and convert them to U.S. dollars. (Does your bank handle foreign deposits?)

The currency issue is simplified somewhat when you specify bidding and payment in U.S. funds only. This puts the onus of currency conversion on the buyer, which is a plus.

The payment process can be further simplified when the buyer pays by credit card—or, even better, by PayPal. PayPal is now active in 38 countries (including the U.S.), and can handle all the payment, conversion, and deposit functions for you.

Payment via international money order is also a good option. Make sure you specify that you need funds in U.S. dollars, and most U.S. banks (as well as your local post office) should be able to cash one of these money orders with little or no hassle.

> **tip**
>
> eBay offers a real-time currency converter at pages.gc.ebay.com/ included/ staticCurrConversion.html.
>
> Given the increased chances of loss or damage when shipping great distances, you should purchase insurance for all items shipping outside North America.

Shipping Across Borders—And Oceans

The biggest difficulty in selling to non-U.S. buyers is shipping the item. Not only are longer distances involved (which necessitates more secure packaging—and longer shipping times), but you have to deal with different shipping options and all sorts of new paperwork.

Chances are your normal method of shipping won't work for your international shipments. For example, you can't use Priority Mail to ship outside the U.S.—not even to Canada or Mexico. This means you'll need to evaluate new shipping methods, and possibly new shipping services.

If you want to stick with the U.S. Postal Service, you can check out Global Express Mail (fast but expensive), Airmail (almost as fast, not quite as expensive), or Surface/Parcel Post (slow but less expensive). In addition, UPS offers its Worldwide Express service, FedEx offers its FedEx Express service internationally, and DHL is always a good option for shipping outside the U.S. Make sure you check out your options beforehand, and charge the buyer the actual costs incurred.

You'll also have to deal with a bit of paperwork while you're preparing your shipment. All packages shipping outside U.S. borders must clear customs to enter the destination country—and require the completion of specific customs forms to make the trip. Depending on the type of item you're shipping and the weight of your package, you'll need either Form 2976 (green) or Form 2976-A (white). Both of these forms should be available at your local post office.

tip

eBay offers several pages of advice for international trading at pages.ebay.com/ internationaltrading/.

When you're filling out these forms, describe the item in terms that ordinary people can understand. That means using simple, generic terms. A "greatest hits CD compilation" becomes "compact disc." A "SimCity extension pack" becomes "video game." And so on.

You should also be honest about what you're shipping. Some buyers will try to talk you into describing the item as a gift, so they can save on duties or tax on their end. That's lying, and you shouldn't do it.

In addition, there are certain items you can't ship to foreign countries—firearms, live animals and animal products, and so on. (There are also some technology items you can't ship, for security reasons.) You need to check the government's list of import and export restrictions to see what items you're prohibited from shipping outside U.S. borders.

eBay's International Marketplaces

To better participate in marketplaces outside the U.S., eBay has established separate sites for 16 foreign countries. Each of these sites list items in the country's native language, using the local currency. (You can see this in Figure 31.1, which shows the eBay France site.)

The list of eBay's international sites includes:

- Argentina (www.mercadolibre.com.ar)
- Australia (www.ebay.com.au)
- Austria (www.ebay.at)
- Belgium (www.ebay.be)
- Brazil (www.mercadolivre.com.br)
- Canada (www.ebay.ca)

- France (www.ebay.fr)
- Germany (www.ebay.de)
- Ireland (pages.ebay.com/ie/)
- Italy (www.ebay.it)
- Korea (www.auction.co.kr)
- Mexico (www.mercadolibre.com.mx)
- Netherlands (www.ebay.nl)
- New Zealand (pages.ebay.com/nz/)
- Singapore (www.ebay.com.sg)
- Spain (www.ebay.com/es/)
- Sweden (www.ebaysweden.com/)
- Switzerland (www.ebay.ch)
- Taiwan (www.tw.ebay.com)
- United Kingdom (www.ebay.co.uk)

tip

You can access all of eBay's international sites from the Global Sites section on the eBay home page.

Although these sites were designed for trading within a specific country, there's nothing keeping you from searching them for items to buy—which will put you on the opposite side of the international buyer/seller argument!

FIGURE 31.1

One of eBay's many international sites: eBay France.

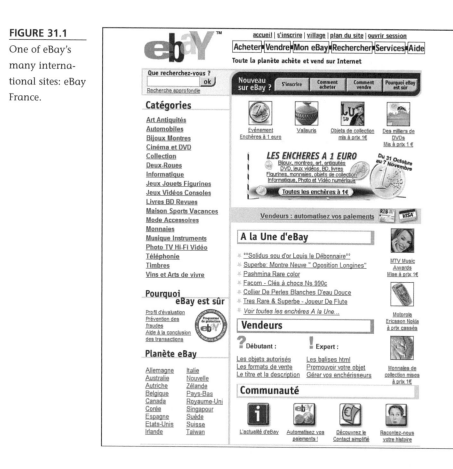

THE ABSOLUTE MINIMUM

Here are the key points to remember from this chapter:

- When dealing with non-U.S. buyers, be sure to specify payment in U.S. funds—ideally via PayPal or an international money order.

- Shipping outside the U.S. requires the completion of customs forms (available at your local post office) and the use of special international shipping services.

- eBay offers 16 country-specific online auction sites, for trading within each local region.

32

MAKING A LIVING FROM EBAY

Chances are you're just starting out on your online auction adventures—learning how to buy and sell and take advantage of everything eBay has to offer. As you gain more experience, however, you may decide that you're pretty good at the whole thing, and start to wonder what it might take to ramp up your eBay activities. You might even dream about one day making your living from selling goods online.

For tens of thousands of eBay users, making a living from online auctions isn't a dream—it's reality. It's definitely possible to sell enough items to generate a livable income from eBay auctions. It takes a lot of hard work and it's as complex as running any other business, but it can be done.

Let me tell you how.

Becoming an eBay PowerSeller

The first step to running your own eBay business is to become an eBay PowerSeller. PowerSellers generate enough business to warrant special attention from eBay, in the form of dedicated customer support, useful tools, and special offers.

To become a PowerSeller, you must do the following:

- Maintain a consistently high level of eBay sales (see Table 32.1)
- Maintain a minimum of four average monthly total item listings for three straight months
- Have been an active eBay seller for at least 90 days
- Achieve and maintain a minimum feedback rating of 100, 98% positive
- Deliver post-auction messages to successful bidders within three business days
- Be an eBay member in good standing, and uphold eBay's "community values"—including honesty, timeliness, and mutual respect

The most important point is the first, because it's the most quantifiable. There are five different levels of PowerSeller, each requiring a specific level of average gross monthly sales, calculated over the past three months of selling activity. Table 32.1 shows the requirements for the five PowerSeller levels, along with the perks that come with each level.

TABLE 32.1   PowerSeller Requirements and Rewards

Level	Requirement (average monthly sales)	Rewards
Bronze	$1,000	24/7 e-mail with fast response time
Silver	$3,000	24/7 e-mail with fast response time *plus* free phone support during normal business hours
Gold	$10,000	24/7 e-mail with fast response time *plus* 24/7 phone support *plus* a dedicated account manager
Platinum	$25,000	24/7 e-mail with fast response time *plus* 24/7 phone support *plus* a dedicated account manager
Titanium	$100,000	24/7 e-mail with fast response time *plus* 24/7 phone support *plus* a dedicated account manager

That's right, there are some eBay sellers who average $100,000 or more a month. That's more than a million dollars a year in revenues from eBay auctions—no slight accomplishment!

Membership in eBay's PowerSellers program is free. When you become a PowerSeller, a special logo will display next to your user ID in all your eBay auctions, and you'll automatically qualify for the rewards appropriate to your level.

Learn more about eBay's PowerSellers program at `pages.ebay.com/services/buyandsell/ powersellers.html`. From here you can submit a request to join up; if you qualify for PowerSeller status, eBay will send you an e-mail invitation to join the program.

note

eBay is also in the process of creating health insurance plans for certain levels of its PowerSellers program.

How to Turn Online Auctions into a Real Business

How easy is it to turn your online auction hobby into a profitable business? It's all a matter of volume—and good business planning and management.

Let's consider an example. Caitlin has found a source for iron-on transfers for t-shirts and sweatshirts. She can buy these transfers for $1.00 apiece, and (based on her experience and research) can sell them on eBay for an average price of $5.00. That's four dollars profit for every transfer she sells.

Caitlin has huddled over her copy of Quicken and determined that she needs to generate $30,000 in profit (*not* in revenues!) to make her eBay business worthwhile. Assuming that she works 50 weeks a year (everyone needs a vacation), that means she needs to average $600 in profit each week. At $4 profit per item, she has to sell an average of 150 iron-on transfers a week—each and every week.

Because only about half of all eBay auctions end with a sale, Caitlin knows that to sell those 150 items she has to launch 300 auctions each week. That's a lot of work, as you can imagine.

Can Caitlin make a go of it? It depends. Can she physically manage 300 auctions a week? Can she pack and ship 150 items a week? And, more importantly, can she realistically *sell* 150 items a week—is the market big enough to support that sort of sales volume?

If Caitlin answers yes to all those questions, there's still more planning to be done. To begin with, this example greatly simplified the costs involved. Caitlin will need to figure eBay's costs for all those auctions—the listing fees for 300 auctions, and the final value fees for 150 completions. If she accepts PayPal payments, she'll need to determine what percentage of her buyers will use PayPal, and what her fees for those transactions will amount to. Assuming she uses a third-party Web site to help her launch and manage those auctions, she'll also need to figure those fees into her cost structure.

All totaled, these auction listing and management costs can add up to 5%–10% of her revenues. That means increasing her cost per item from $1.00 to $1.50 or more—which reduces her profit per item to just $3.50. With this reduced profit margin, she'll need to sell even more items to hit her profit dollar targets—an extra 20 or so successful auctions each week.

All this needs to be factored in—before Caitlin launches a single auction. And at these volume levels she's definitely running a business, which means reporting the income to the IRS and paying taxes. There's also the matter of *sales taxes*, which she'll need to collect on all sales made to buyers in her home state.

The takeaway here is that making a living from eBay sales is just like running a business, especially in its financial complexities. Anyone contemplating this type of endeavor should do some serious business planning, which should include consulting an accountant or other financial planner.

If the numbers work out, you need to answer one more question: Is this something you'll enjoy doing every day of the week, every week of the year? Even if you can make money at it, managing hundreds of auctions a week can wear down even the best of us. Make sure you're up to it, and that you'll enjoy it, before you take the leap.

Maintaining Your Sales Inventory

If you need to be launching several hundred auctions a week, where do you find all those items to list? It's a simple fact that you can't become a power seller by listing onesies and twosies. Instead, you need to find an item you can buy in bulk, and then list multiples of that item week after week.

Although beginning eBayers can find items to sell by haunting flea markets and estate auctions, power sellers most likely won't find what they need in those venues. A better strategy is to approach local retailers or wholesalers and offer to buy 10 or 20 (or more) of a particular item. Buy whatever quantity earns you the best price break—as long as you think you can move them.

If you're a serious collector, you might have your eBay business right there. When your comics collection numbers in the tens of thousands, or you have thousands of rare coins filed away in your basement, you're ready for power selling—and power buying. Just remember to buy low and sell high, and you'll be in business.

Finally, consider the selling price of the items you want to sell. You have to sell a lot more of a $5.00 item than you do of a $50.00 item to make the same amount of profit—and the more items you sell, the more work you have to do. The most successful power sellers do it by selling higher-priced items, where the revenues—and the profits—add up a lot quicker.

Automating Your Auction Activities

Managing hundreds of simultaneous auctions is hard work. Most power sellers end up working more than a standard 8-hour day, and more than five days a week. (eBay reports that most of their PowerSellers work anywhere from 10 to 16 hours a day on their auctions!) The time it takes to find new items to sell, photograph them, write detailed item descriptions, post the auctions, send post-auction e-mails, and pack and ship all those items quickly adds up.

The more auctions you list, the more it behooves you to automate as much of the auction process as possible. For most power sellers, that means signing up with one of the big Web sites that offer bulk listing and post-auction management, such as Andale, AuctionWatch, or ChannelAdvisor Pro. Make sure you factor the site's fees into your cost structure, and let them help you manage all your auctions.

You should also try to automate your physical auction activity. That means creating some sort of auction "office" or workspace in your home. This workspace should include everything you need to create auction listings (including your digital camera and scanner) and to pack and ship your finished auction items. In addition, you'll need space to store all your excess auction inventory; this may be your basement or garage, or even a rented storage locker.

Automating your processes also means establishing some sort of auction-related schedule. Pick one or two days a week to launch all your auctions; pick one or two days to visit the post office. Stick to your schedule and you'll avoid running around like a chicken with your head cut off; after all, dead chickens aren't known for their business efficiency.

note

See Chapter 28, "Using Auction Software and Services," to learn more about the services offered by these sites.

On the subject of shipping, you should try to simplify your packing and shipping activities as much as possible. This means limiting the items you sell to just a few, so that you can standardize on packaging. It's much easier to stock just one or two different-sized boxes than a dozen or more different sizes. If you sell a limited variety of merchandise, you'll also be able to better estimate your shipping costs ahead of time.

Using Caitlin's iron-on transfer business as an example, this is a great item to sell. She's dealing with a standard-size product that's both flat and light—ideal for shipping in an oversized envelope, at a flat rate. This means she can not only purchase shipping envelopes in bulk, but she can also purchase postage ahead of time—and eliminate those regular trips to the post office.

Tracking Revenues and Costs

Every business should keep detailed records, and your online auction business is no exception. Whether you use an auction management service that offers report generation, a financial-management program like Quicken, or your own homemade spreadsheet or database, you need to track what you're doing.

In particular, you want to track unit cost and final selling price for every auction you list. You should also track all your ancillary costs—shipping, PayPal fees, eBay listing and final value fees, and so on. By tracking all your costs and revenues, you can generate an accurate profit and loss statement, and thus determine how much money (if any) you're generating from your online auction activities.

It also helps to track information about the buyers of your auction items—name, shipping address, e-mail address, and so on. The name and shipping address are necessary in case an item gets lost in transit; the e-mail address is necessary not only for auction-related communication but also for promotional purposes—which we'll discuss next.

Promoting Your Online Auctions

If you're running a hundred or more auctions a week, you want to draw attention to your auctions. That might mean splurging for some of eBay's listing enhancements (boldface, gallery, and so on), although these extras typically aren't worth the extra cost. Better to promote your auctions on your personal Web site, via message board postings, and in all your e-mails.

Probably the most important type of promotion, however, is word of mouth—based on your good reputation. You want to encourage repeat bidders and drive buyers into your online store (if you have one) for additional sales. That means treating your buyers fairly and with respect, and going the extra mile to ensure their satisfaction. It also means sending previous buyers e-mails when you have items up for auction that they might be interested in. (Which argues, of course, for keeping comprehensive records of all your eBay auctions.)

Supplementing Your Auctions with an Online Store

Successful businesses know how to maximize revenues from their existing customers. You can do this by creating an online store—possibly via eBay Stores—to offer additional merchandise to your auction bidders. If you're selling printer cartridges, direct your buyers to your online store selling paper and other printer supplies. If you're selling collectibles, direct your buyers to your online store selling non-auction collectibles. Or, in Caitlin's example, she can direct buyers of her iron-on transfers to her store selling t-shirts and sweatshirts—as well as additional transfers.

It's all a matter of maximizing revenue. Yes, it's additional work—but it can result in additional sales.

note

Learn more about creating online stores in Chapter 26, "Buying and Selling Right Now: eBay Stores and Half.com."

The Absolute Minimum

Here are the key points to remember from this chapter:

- If you're selling more than $1,000 per month, you're eligible for eBay's PowerSellers program.

- To turn your eBay hobby into a money-making profession, you need to start with some detailed business and financial planning.

- Most power sellers specialize in a specific type of item—and buy it in bulk.

- Successful eBay businesses keep detailed records and perform regular analyses of their auction activities.

- The more auctions you list, the more value you'll get from third-party auction management sites and services.

- When you start making a living from your eBay auctions, make sure you engage the services of a qualified accountant—to manage your tax liabilities, if nothing else.

Index

private auctions, 129
promoting, 208, 353
publicizing, 274-275
real estate listings, 118
receiving items, 86
relisting items, 216
reserve auctions, 252
reserve price auctions,
   127-128
   bidding, 50-52
   fees, 33
searches, 67, 105-106
sellers
   answering bidder ques-
      tions, 207
   auction feedback, 86
   auction strategies,
      248-258
   contacting unresponsive
      bidders, 242
   contacting winning bid-
      ders, 213
   deadbeat bidders, 216,
      244
   deleting bidders, 206
   eBay Checkout service, 83
   end-of-auction notifica-
      tions, 82
   Feedback rating system
      (eBay), 90, 105
   feedback ratings,
      214-215, 278-280
   finding items to sell,
      136-138
   handling complaints, 215
   PowerSellers, 348-353
   Verified eBay Users, 90
   viewing ID histories, 91
AuctionSHIP Web site, 232
AuctionStealer Web site, 317
**AuctionTamer Web site, 312,
317**
**AuctionWatch Web site, 286,
312-313, 324**
**Auctionworks Web site, 313,
324**
Auctiva Pro Web site, 324
Auctiva Web site, 313

**auto insurance service (eBay
Motors), 301**
auto-sniping programs, 102
automating auctions, 351-352

B

bad bids, retracting, 54
**Basic stores (eBay Stores),
292**
**Bid Cancellation page (eBay),
207**
bid amounts
   determining, 38-39
   increasing, 53
bid discovery, 96
**Bid History link (item list-
ings), 43**
bid shielding, 95
bid siphoning, 96
**bidder interest counter (item
listings), 44**
bidder searches, 66
bidders
   blocking, 131
   deadbeat bidders, 216
      auction strategies, 255
      leaving negative feedback,
         244
      Non-Paying Bidder Alert
         forms, 242
      Non-Paying Bidder Alerts,
         241
      Non-Paying Bidder Appeal
         forms, 243
      Non-Paying Bidder Bidder
         Warning Removal forms,
         243
      refunding eBay fees, 243
      Second Chance Offers,
         244
   deleting, 206
   international auctions, 341
   questions, answering, 207
   sniping, 100-102
   unresponsive bidders, 242

Verified eBay Users, 90
winning bidders, contacting,
   213
bidding, 11, 34, 37
   bad bids, retracting, 54
   bid amounts
      determining, 38-39
      increasing, 53
   bidding tools, 316-318
   Buy It Now! option, 52
   car bids, 300
   confirming bids, 47
   deleting bids, 131
   dutch auctions, 47-50
   last-minute bids, 55
   low bids, 139-140
   minimum bids, 11
   outbidding, 54
   payment, arranging, 84-85
   placing bids, 44-47
   proxy bidding, 38-40
   researching bids, 38
   reserve price auctions, 50-52
   seller feedback ratings, 46
   shipping charges, 46, 83
   single bids, 141
   strategies
      buyer/seller communica-
         tion, 111
      credit card payments, 109
      deadbeat bids, 108
      discipline, 103
      early bids, 107
      eBay official clock, 108
      eBay proxy bidding soft-
         ware, 104
      eBay toolbar, 107
      expensive items, 110
      fine print, reading, 109
      fraud protection, 111
      inspecting items on
         arrival, 111
      insurance, 110
      item research, 103
      last-minute bargains, 107
      last-minute bids, 107
      logging auctions, 110
      money order payments,
         109
      My eBay, 108

How can we make this index more useful? Email us at indexes@quepublishing.com

Q – R

S

How can we make this index more useful? Email us at indexes@quepublishing.com